TANGIBLE AND INTANGIBLE HERITAGE IN THE AGE OF GLOBALISATION

Tangible and Intangible Heritage in the Age of Globalisation

Edited by Lilia Makhloufi

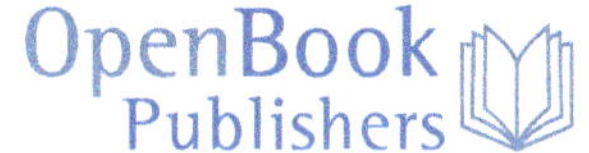

https://www.openbookpublishers.com

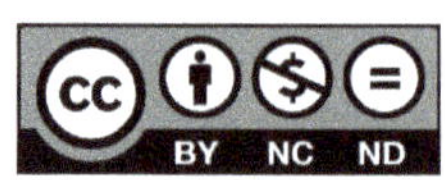

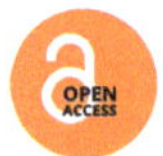

All external links were active at the time of publication unless otherwise stated and have been archived via the Internet Archive Wayback Machine at https://archive.org/web

Any digital material and resources associated with this volume will be available at https://doi.org/10.11647/OBP.0388#resources

ISBN Paperback: 978-1-80511-212-9
ISBN Hardback: 978-1-80511-213-6
ISBN Digital (PDF): 978-1-80511-214-3
ISBN Digital ebook (EPUB): 978-1-80511-215-0
ISBN DIGITAL ebook (HTML): 978-1-80511-217-4

DOI: 10.11647/OBP.0388

Cover image: Ghardaïa, Algeria, UNESCO World Heritage Site. Photograph by Lilia Makhloufi (2007). All rights reserved.
Cover design by Jeevanjot Kaur Nagpal

Contents

III. LIVING HERITAGE AND CULTURAL TOURISM POTENTIAL

IV. HERITAGE SITES AND PRESERVATION CHALLENGES

Je dédie ce livre à mes parents,
pour m'avoir inculqué le sens de la responsabilité, ainsi que
l'importance de l'honnêteté et du travail bien fait.

This publication is a result of the research project 'Tangible and Intangible Heritage: Architecture, Design and Culture', conducted by Prof. Dr. Lilia Makhloufi and Prof. Dr. Ammar Abdulrahman, members of the Arab-German Young Academy of Sciences and Humanities (AGYA). The research project was funded by the Arab-German Young Academy of Sciences and Humanities (AGYA) based in the Berlin-Brandenburg Academy of Sciences and Humanities (BBAW) in Germany.

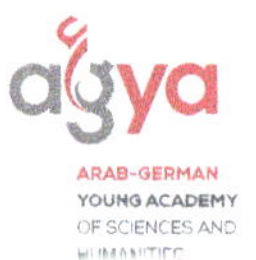

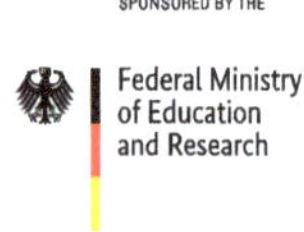

Scientific and review committees

All chapters have been evaluated by an international scientific committee and an international review committee consisting of researchers from various academic backgrounds.

Scientific coordinator and chair of the scientific and review committees

Dr. Lilia Makhloufi, Ecole Polytechnique d'Architecture et d'Urbanisme (EPAU), Algiers, Algeria. Member of the Arab-German Young Academy of Sciences and Humanities (AGYA), Berlin, Germany

Scientific committee members

Prof. Lalla Btissam Drissi, LPHE-Modeling & Simulations, Faculty of Science, Mohammed V University, Rabat, Morocco (AGYA Alumna)

Prof. Ahmad Sakhrieh, Mechanical and Industrial Engineering Department, School of Engineering, American University of Ras Al Khaimah, 10021, United Arab Emirates. Mechanical Engineering Department, the University of Jordan, Amman 11942, Jordan (AGYA Alumnus)

Dr. Alaa Aldin Alchomari, Islamische Abteilung an der Uni Tübingen, Tübingen, Germany.

Dr. Honey Fadaie, Department of Architecture, Faculty of Art and Architecture, Roudehen Branch, Islamic Azad University (RIAU), Roudehen, Tehran, Iran.

Dr. Fanny Gerbeaud, Higher National School of Architecture and Landscape Architecture (ENSAP), Bordeaux, France. PAVE Research Centre, Bordeaux, France.

Dr. Ikram Hili, University of Sousse, Tunisia (AGYA Member)

Dr. Nibal Muhesen, Cultural heritage expert at the Directorate general of antiquities and museums (DGAM), Damascus, Syria, and researcher at the University of Copenhagen, Denmark.

Review committee members

Prof. Khalid El Harrouni, Ecole Nationale d'Architecture, Rabat, Morocco.

Prof. Assia Lamzah, Institut National d'Aménagement et d'Urbanisme, Rabat, Morocco.

Dr. Ammar Abdulrahman, Institute for Ancient Near Eastern Studies of the Freie Universität Berlin, Germany (AGYA Alumnus)

Dr. Safa Achour, National School of Architecture and Urbanism of Tunis, Tunisia.

Dr. Aline Barlet, Higher National School of Architecture and Landscape Architecture (ENSAP), Bordeaux, France.

Dr. Honey Fadaie, Department of Architecture, Faculty of Art and Architecture, Roudehen Branch, Islamic Azad University (RIAU), Roudehen, Tehran, Iran.

Dr. Fanny Gerbeaud, Higher National School of Architecture and Landscape Architecture (ENSAP), Bordeaux, France. PAVE Research Centre, Bordeaux, France

Dr. Nibal Muhesen, Cultural heritage expert at the Directorate general of antiquities and museums (DGAM), Damascus, Syria, and researcher at the University of Copenhagen, Denmark.

Ms. Carmen Antuña Rozado, Senior Scientist, MSc (Arch), VTT Technical Research Centre of Finland, Helsinki, Finland.

Ms. Maryam Mirzaeii, Department of Architecture, Faculty of Art and Architecture, Roudehen Branch, Islamic Azad University (RIAU), Roudehen, Tehran, Iran.

Notes on contributors

Mohamed Amer holds a PhD in Heritage Marketing and Sustainable Cultural Tourism from Roma Tre Università, Italy. He is a HeritageForAll initiative founder and ICOMOS-ICTC member. He has an extensive background in heritage management and marketing and holds an MA in Heritage Conservation and Site Management from BTU Cottbus-Senftenberg and Helwan University (2015), and has taken part in many activities organised by UNESCO and other international organisations. He participated in Oecumene Studio, as a researcher, in the heritage project 'SIWI'. He led two international internship programs in 'Rural Heritage and Traditional Food' and 'Musealization of Cultural Identity'.

ORCID ID: 0000-0003-1471-3856

Meriem Ben Ammar is a PhD student in Architecture at the University of Cagliari Faculty of Civil Engineering and Architecture. She obtained both an undergraduate and master's degree in Architecture from the Tunis National School of Architecture and Urbanism and holds a second master's degree in Heritage Sciences: Islamic Archaeology from the Faculty of Humanities and Social Sciences of Tunis, where she prepared her master's thesis on Islamic legal manuscripts.

ORCID ID: 0009-0007-6861-6054

Mouenes Abd Elrrahmane Bouakar is an architect who obtained his master's degree at the Institute of Architecture and Urbanism, University of Batna-1, Algeria. He has participated in several projects, such as the elaboration of the Protection and Enhancement Plan of the archaeological site of Zemmouri el Bahri and its area, the study and the follow-up of the restoration of the Sidi Messaoud mosque in Oued Souf and thirty-three lots in the safeguarded sector of the Kasbah of Algiers (lots 03, 04, 06 and 31), and the elaboration of the Permanent

Development Plan of the Safeguarded Sector of the old town of Sidi el Houari in Oran.

ORCID ID: 0009-0000-2692-2837

Houda Driss obtained a doctorate in architecture in 2017, graduating from the Doctoral School of Architectural Sciences and Engineering at the National School of Architecture and Urbanism of Tunis (ENAU). She was university teacher from 2011 to 2015 at ENAU and from 2015 to 2021 at the Private Polytechnic School Ibn Khaldoun. She is a part of the research unit PAE3C (Architectural and Environmental Heritage: Knowledge, Understanding, Conservation) at ENAU, and a member of the Technical Referee Committee for the magazine *Sustainable Mediterranean Construction, Land Culture, Research and Technology*. She is also a consultant to the Tunisian Mediterranean Association for historical, social and economic studies.

ORCID ID: 0009-0001-9439-8886

Lemya Kacha is associate professor at the Institute of Architecture and Urbanism, University of Batna-1, Algeria. She received her PhD in engineering from Nagoya Institute of Technology, Japan. She contributed a chapter about the fractal measurements of morphological identity related to urban fabrics in the book *Villes, Réseaux et Transport, le défi fractal*, which was edited by Professor Gabriel Dupuy. In 2015, Lemya received the best paper award of the *Journal of Asian Architecture and Building Engineering*.

ORCID ID: 0000-0002-2527-5356

Heba Khairy is project coordinator at the Grand Egyptian Museum and a PhD candidate specialising in heritage and museum studies. She has participated in many international and national projects and studies focusing on the safeguarding of tangible and intangible cultural heritage, preservation, local community engagement and development. In 2016 she participated in the 'Memphis site management and Community development project' supported by the USAID and York University. In 2018 she participated in a study project aiming to safeguard the Syrian dance and musical performance 'Al A'rada', hosted in Egypt. In 2019 she participated in a study project aiming to safeguard the Egyptian traditional stitch handcraft known as 'Al Khayameia'.

ORCID ID: 0009-0000-8090-7945

Ayda Khaleghi is a researcher, architect, and 3D artist, with an interest in contemporary and classic architectural design, cultural heritage valorization, and historical restoration. She has been involved in multiple research projects related to historical renovations and mapping tangible and intangible heritage in the city of Mashhad. She has also been focused on the recent developments in Mashhad's city center and documentation of its rich historical values.

ORCID ID: 0009-0009-1001-0492

Assia Lamzah is a trained architect and holds a PhD in Landscape Architecture from the University of Illinois at Urbana Champaign (UIUC), USA. She is currently a professor at Ecole Nationale d'Architecture (ENA), Rabat, Morocco. She has experience in teaching and research in architecture, urban and regional planning and landscape architecture. Her recent research projects focus on urban and architectural cultural heritage management, smart design, the relationship between architecture, landscape and social culture, and postcolonial theory.

ORCID ID: 0000-0002-1875-8632

Lilia Makhloufi is an architect and urban planner. She obtained her magister's degree in urban planning in 2003, and her doctorate of science in territory planning in 2009 and her postdoctoral degree (habilitation) with accreditation to supervise research in 2019. As a teacher and researcher, she worked at the University of Constantine, the University of Jijel and since 2010 at Ecole Polytechnique d'Architecture et d'Urbanisme (EPAU) in Algiers. She is also a member of the Arab-German Young Academy of Sciences and Humanities (AGYA), based in the Berlin-Brandenburg Academy of Sciences and Humanities (BBAW) in Germany. Her main research experience and international collaborations are related to housing projects, public spaces, cities and sustainability.

ORCID ID: 0000-0002-8778-5132

Aliye Fatma Mataracı studied at Boğaziçi University, where she earned a PhD in history, an MA in sociology, and a BA in philosophy, as well as Istanbul Bilgi University, where she obtained an MA in film and TV studies. As a representative of Bosnia and Herzegovina, she actively participated in the project 'Heritage at War in the Mediterranean Region' carried out by the Ifpo Urban Observatory between 2015 and 2017. She also held several administrative roles at the International University of Sarajevo during her affiliation with Political Sciences Program from 2011 to 2023. Currently, she is as an associate professor in the School of Humanities and Social Sciences at Al Akhawayn University in Ifrane, Morocco.

ORCID ID: 0000-0001-8289-8763

Nibal Muhesen is a Syrian researcher in the field of archaeology and the protection of Syrian cultural heritage. He obtained a PhD from the University of Lyon II in Syrian archaeology in 2009. Since 2011, he has been involved in documenting the damage to Syrian cultural heritage and has participated in many international lectures and conferences aimed at protecting this heritage. He worked as an expert with the Syrian State Board of Antiquities where he took part in activities focusing on preserving and raising awareness about the importance of Syria's tangible and intangible heritage and advocating for community-driven reconstruction strategies. He is currently a member of the Department of Tourism Management at the University of Tartous Faculty of Tourism as a researcher in the field of archaeology and tourism.

ORCID ID: 0009-0009-6050-5303

Sasan Norouzi is an Iranian senior researcher at the department of Cultural Heritage at Samen Research Institute. In the past twenty years, Sasan has been teaching and lecturing at various universities and institutions of higher education in Iran. Adopting a humanistic, cultural, and innovative approach, Sasan has been leading projects that aim at conserving cultural heritage and revitalizing historic zones of urban areas including protecting and reusing water structures in ancient cities. His current research interests and activities include using cultural mapping tools and mitigation strategies to study the impact of social behavior, customs, and traditions on the conservation of urban heritage.

ORCID ID: 0009-0003-1401-0517

Joanes Rocha is an architectural historian and graduate research student at the University of Tokyo, Japan. Simultaneously, he holds the position of assistant professor of theory and history of architecture and is a visiting scholar at the Academia Sinica, Taipei. His research is centred on the Portuguese presence in East Asia from the sixteenth to the nineteenth centuries, with a primary focus on preserving and safeguarding this historical heritage.

ORCID ID: 0000-0002-4841-9658

Guillermo Rojas Alfaro is an architect (2012), MSc The Bartlett University College London (2015), and PhD candidate at the Melbourne School of Design (MSD). Before starting his PhD research in Atmospheres, Guillermo was an Assistant Professor of the MArch and Head of the Cultural Heritage Diploma at Pontificia Universidad Católica de Chile (PUC). For the past ten years, he has been an educator in architecture, teaching at several universities in Chile, Brazil, Germany, Belgium and Australia. His work as an architect has been awarded, published and presented in different exhibitions, such as the Venice Biennale and the Chilean Architecture Biennial. Currently, he teaches at the MSD and is a member of the PUC Heritage and Modernity Research Cluster.

ORCID ID: 0000-0003-2699-0930

Sepideh Shahamati is a PhD candidate at the Department of Geography, Planning and Environment at Concordia University, Canada. Her research focuses on identifying and documenting the intangible heritage of cities. With a particular interest in visual representations, she is developing a systematic mapping method to represent the invisible assets of urban areas. She holds an MA in Architecture, Planning and Landscape from Newcastle University and a BSc in Urban Planning from Azad University of Mashhad. Her previous work involves understanding and assessing the public perception of green urban landscapes.

ORCID ID: 0009-0006-1175-8249

Fabiola Solari Irribarra is an architect, Pontificia Universidad Católica de Chile (PUC) and Master of Urban and Cultural Heritage, University of Melbourne (UoM). Between 2013 and 2019, she taught design and research studios at the PUC School of Architecture, where she was coordinator and instructor of three versions of the Cultural Heritage Diploma. She worked as chief architect and coordinator of built heritage projects in the Chilean firm Tándem for four years, where she collaborated in multiple interdisciplinary public projects. She currently works for the Melbourne-based heritage firm Conservation Studio and is a member of the PUC Heritage and Modernity Research Cluster.

ORCID ID: 0009-0004-0799-6338

List of illustrations

Preface

Lilia Makhloufi

Tangible and Intangible Heritage in the Age of Globalisation considers heritage in different contexts from an interdisciplinary perspective, bringing together sixteen contributors from various fields. They include architects, urban planners, historians, sociologists and archaeologists, as well as heritage marketing, museum and cultural tourism professionals. These experts come from all over the world—Algeria, Canada, Chile, Egypt, Italy, Japan, Morocco, Syria, Tunisia and Türkiye—representing a diversity of scholarship which offers a broad range of insights on the topic of heritage.

The book is the outcome of an academic research project initiated and directed by Lilia Makhloufi under the title 'Tangible and Intangible Heritage: Architecture, Design and Culture'.[1] The research project was funded by the Arab–German Young Academy of Sciences and Humanities (AGYA) based in the Berlin–Brandenburg Academy of Sciences and Humanities (BBAW) in Germany. The scientific coordinator and the chair of the scientific and review committees would like to thank AGYA and the contributors to this volume as well as the members of the scientific and review committees for their comments during the review process to improve the submitted chapters. Their active contributions and their interesting recommendations on theoretical and practical approaches related to heritage contributed to the success of the publication project.

Dr. Lilia Makhloufi
Scientific coordinator
Scientific and review committees Chair

1 The project was run under grant 01DL20003 from the Federal Ministry of Education and Research (BMBF).

Introduction
Tangible and Intangible Heritage

Lilia Makhloufi

The old part of a city has always been a reference point in architecture, either from the urban perspective or from the building perspective. Traditional cities were shaped by a conceptual framework with conscious responses to environmental, urban and societal conditions. Over the centuries, this vernacular architecture encouraged a local style that manifested in ordinary houses with unified construction techniques and materials, and the harmonisation of the built framework and physical features.

This book analyses the architectural and urban spaces that shape cities' tangible heritage, considering the urban networks, residential spaces and materials and methods of construction. The book also examines the parameters governing societies' intangible heritage by defining: (i) individuals according to local identities, cultures and religions, (ii) behaviours rooted in local ways of life and social values, and (iii) practices including local customs, feasts and festivals.

Globalisation has developed the international standardisation of architecture and urban planning to the detriment of the representation of local identity and culture. In this sense, greater efforts have been made to protect local heritage and develop it through national and international organisations. However, the concepts of integrity and authenticity are challenged by international charters and academia. For instance, heritage sites are inscribed on the World Heritage List only if their integrity and authenticity are beyond question, ensuring their Outstanding Universal Value (OUV) in this way.

 https://doi.org/10.11647/OBP.0388.00

Today, heritage is subject to the transformation of cultures and the displacement of societies. Moreover, the number of studies on heritage has multiplied, as the currents of globalisation lend new exigence to its study and management. In this book, sixteen researchers from various disciplines—such as architecture, urban planning, landscape architecture, history, sociology, archaeology, heritage marketing, museum and cultural tourism—share their approaches to heritage, with perspectives on localities in the Middle East, North Africa, Eastern Europe, South America and Eastern Asia. More specifically, they focus on topics that will enrich the debate about the past, present and future of heritage in their respective countries and beyond.

Our collaboration on this book has sparked a fruitful exchange with the objective of redefining heritage as an interdisciplinary and intercultural concept. The contributors examine architectural, urban and cultural heritage, studying tangible and intangible parameters over time and discussing cultural challenges and opportunities. They analyse the conditions of the past with a focus on informing the present and the future. As a result, this book features case studies on Algeria, Bosnia and Herzegovina, Chile, Egypt, Iran, Japan, Morocco, Oman, Syria and Tunisia, which are presented over the course of eleven chapters, structured according to the following themes.

The first part of the book brings together architects who give their perspectives on built heritage in Tunisia. Reflecting on residential characteristics, these chapters explore social and spatial practices in traditional dwellings.

Houda Driss analyses ancestral ways of occupying and appropriating space within the 'troglodytic' dwellings in the village of Beni Zelten, located in southeast Tunisia. Her research examines this architecture with respect to its natural environment and historical longevity, before identifying and analysing the socio-spatial practices inside these living spaces. The combination of theoretical and practical aspects of troglodytic spaces enables her to enumerate the activities practised in this context, which she then classifies according to the user type, degree of privacy and frequency of practice. In this way, she demonstrates how the underground dwellings in the Tunisian village of Beni Zelten reflect and respond to the natural environment, social factors and cultural values.

Meriem Ben Ammar focuses on architecture and town planning in the medina of Tunis, highlighting norms and rules relevant to the spatial organisation of houses, the material separation between neighbours and the management of the city in general. She analyses an archived manuscript dating from the eighteenth century on Hanafi law, written by Tunisian jurist Muhammad bin Ḥusayn bin Ibrahim al-Bārūdīal-Ḥanafī. This manuscript offers fair solutions to conflicts over property ownership, construction forms and housing issues between inhabitants and their closest neighbours. Over many centuries, this intellectual heritage encouraged a unified system of construction in the walled medina of Tunis, an organisation of its urban network and the preservation of its neighbourhood relationships.

Housing is a social space and includes the material context of social life.[1] Yet, most of the time, housing is considered material data. However, we should be aware that housing is, above all, the product of a given society. This privileged place, in which people represent themselves and construct their lives, illustrates the codes of the society in which they live. By the intimacy that it preserves or the openness that it promotes, housing expresses a particular conception of social life. Moreover, the organisation of its spaces and the nature of its furniture represent a way of life and a culture, from which it is possible to discern the importance of the individual in every housing analysis.[2]

The second part of the book brings together architects, archaeologists and museum professionals, who give their perspectives on intangible components of cultural heritage in Iran, Egypt and Syria. More specifically, they examine local heritage, studying changes in collective memory over time, cultural challenges and opportunities.

In the twenty-first century, urban development effectively takes place according to socio-economic requirements. Local cultures, religious values and identities are increasingly neglected in decision-making

---

1 Lilia Makhloufi, 'Globalization Facing Identity: A Human Housing at Stake—Case of Bab Ezzouar in Algiers', in *Proceeding Book of ICONARCH II, International Congress of Architecture, Innovative Approaches in Architecture and Planning* (Konya: Selçuk University Faculty of Architecture, 2014), pp. 133–144 (p. 142).

2 Lilia Makhloufi, 'Inhabitants/Authorities: A Sustainable Housing at Stake—Case of Ali Mendjeli New Town in Constantine', in *Sustainable Architecture & Urban Development, SAUD 2010*, vol. 1, ed. by S. Lehmann, H. Al Waer & J. Al-Qawasmi (Amman: The Center for the Study of Architecture in the Arab Region & University of Dundee, 2010), pp. 367–383 (p. 372).

processes in favour of the measurable and quantifiable data available in architectural and urban projects. This has resulted in the transformation of neighbourhoods, the transfer of local populations and the loss of many traditions and other cultural practices for present and future generations.

In this context, Sepideh Shahamati, Ayda Khaleghi and Sasan Norouzi consider the case of the Iranian city of Mashhad. In the last decade, this city—and more precisely, its centre—has undergone different urban transformations, which have had a considerable impact on both its built and cultural heritage. The case of Mashhad's historic centre recalls the importance of reconceptualising intangible cultural heritage in decision-making processes and the challenges of its preservation in the twenty-first century, especially in the case of cities which were built and have developed according to spiritual and religious values.

Moreover, Heba Khairy analyses the museums of Egypt, a country renowned for its tangible and intangible heritage. Certainly, artefacts have been preserved in Egyptian museums since the twentieth century, but, to date, museum practice has been overwhelmingly concerned with tangible heritage, to the neglect of its intangible counterpart. As such, this research seeks to uncover viable solutions for the incorporation and development of intangible heritage in Egyptian museums. This is achieved by providing a conceptual prototype that will allow practitioners to safeguard and develop intangible cultural heritage, particularly in terms of living memory and communal identities.

Nibal Muhesen focuses on the case of intangible cultural heritage in Syria, which has suffered considerable destruction due to the conflicts of recent years. He underlines the importance of reviving all forms of local crafts, oral traditions, arts performance and old *Souqs,* with the objective of protecting the collective memory of communities and their cultural identities. He also suggests strategies for the protection of intangible cultural heritage, identifies challenges to its survival and emphasises the need for effective reconstruction efforts for all components of Syrian heritage.

The major obstacles to preserving tangible and intangible heritage in times of conflict are the subject of a great deal of contemporary discussion among researchers. They note the difficulties of safeguarding built heritage, on the one hand, and of protecting cultural heritage on the other. Indeed, several studies on archaeological sites, artefacts and historical monuments have been undertaken for the purposes of post-war damage assessment and the development of recovery policy. In the meantime, handicrafts, collective memories and cultural identities have suffered relatively less damage and could be more rapidly and easily revived.

The third part of the book brings together architects, historians and heritage management professionals who reflect on the cultural tourism potential in Oman, Algeria and Japan. They examine historic sites, studying the shape and content of their urban networks, buildings, infrastructure and spaces with respect to socio-cultural values.

Mohamed Amer examines the tangible and intangible heritage characteristics of the traditional market of Mutrah in Oman's capital city of Muscat. He assesses its interactive historic, architectural, urban, social, economic and cultural values alongside their managerial features, in order to identify practical measures for the enhancement of this living cultural heritage, the effective preservation of Omani cultural identity, avenues for local socio-economic empowerment and sustainable cultural tourism. Here, Strengths, Weaknesses, Opportunities and Threats (SWOT) analyses brought to light the internal and external factors that are favourable to achieving these objectives.

SWOT analyses have the potential to be a valuable tool in development processes and heritage conservation. Public spaces and streets in particular have a direct impact on the townscape, and their fundamental nature impacts the visual comfort of pedestrians (inhabitants, passers-by, tourists, merchants, etc.) and the attractiveness of the city for domestic and foreign visitors.

The historical and architectural significance of public spaces play an important role in preserving the identity of the heritage city. In this context, Lemya Kacha and Mouenes Abd Elrrahmane Bouakar investigate public spaces and their impact on the local community in the historic centre of Cherchell in Algeria, which has rich Punic, Roman, Arab-Andalusian, Ottoman and French heritage. The main objective of their analysis is to assess the perceptions and attractiveness of selected streetscapes among domestic tourists. Here, the Kansei Engineering method allowed them to quantify participants' perceptions of streetscapes based on panoramic photographs. Through this method, which has significant potential in the field of sustainable cultural tourism and heritage conservation, the researchers found that the originality of the materials and the construction techniques are the main factors that have led to the preservation of heritage value. Moreover, the attractiveness of architectural heritage will contribute to enhancing both cultural and heritage tourism in the long term.

The important role of historical and cultural richness in attracting tourism is also evident in Japan, which has excelled in dealing with the living heritage. The principal agency for preserving Japan's cultural properties has promoted churches as one of the region's leading tourism destinations and integrated museums and souvenir shops to encourage touristic activities around these cultural and religious sites of memory. The objective of this strategy is to restructure the leisure industry and to moderate the impact of tourism on the local community lifestyle.

In this context, Joanes Rocha explores the concept of the 'site of memory', with a comparative case study of the Japanese cities of Nagasaki and Amakusa, and their nomination for the World Heritage List. Although the study focuses on Catholic churches, it also considers local communities, their private sites and their significant contribution to the preservation of local history and religious practices and traditions. A comparative analysis allows different social, cultural and religious expressions of an intangible nature to be distinguished as a mechanism to strengthen local identity and to develop sustainable tourism in these historic and religious sites with their specific memorial aspects.

The fourth and final part of the book brings together architects and historians with perspectives on heritage sites in Morocco, Chile, and Bosnia and Herzegovina. The research in these chapters reveals the challenges faced when preserving cultural heritage within specific historical, environmental and political contexts.

Urban heritage, with its tangible and intangible components, is of vital importance for present and future generations as a source of social cohesion, cultural diversity, collective memory and identities. With this in mind, Assia Lamzah analyses the dualities between Orientalism and Occidentalism and their consequences for heritage in postcolonial Morocco. She questions the dichotomies long used in architecture and urban planning, such as traditional versus modern or oriental versus occidental, and discusses the ways they have been developed and normalised. This is done through a case study of Jemaa el-Fna Plaza in the Marrakesh medina, where precolonial conceptions and spatial construction have been continuously renewed to create a contemporary heritage site that corresponds to the needs of the local population and adapts to a dynamic Moroccan society.

Moreover, Fabiola Solari Irribarra and Guillermo Rojas Alfaro consider the vulnerability of urban and industrial constructions and their deterioration in arid climates. They question the authenticity of Humberstone and Santa Laura Salpeter Works in Chile according to the original fabrics and structures of this industrial heritage, the integrity of which has been harmed by the natural environment over time. In the last decade, several security measures and consolidation and stabilisation works were undertaken to conserve the tangible assets of this site. While conservation works partially compromised the original fabric and material aspects of the site, this change can be viewed as positive because the material decay of these mining complexes coexisted with efforts to keep them standing. In this way, these buildings and the choices made in conserving them bear witness to the key historical, industrial, and social processes associated with the heritage site.

Nowadays, heritage management and discourse are subject to contemporary challenges involving different actors, and the specific relationships of local populations and tourists to these heritage sites. For the local authorities as well as for researchers, these sites are important parts of national, historical and cultural heritage.

In this context, Aliye Fatma Mataracı analyses the National Museum of Bosnia and Herzegovina in Sarajevo and discusses the major challenges of preserving tangible and intangible heritage in war and post-war periods. She raises the difficulties of safeguarding and renovating the museum as a built heritage asset on the one hand, and of protecting and maintaining its collections as cultural heritage on the other. Particular attention is also given to the term 'national' and its usage in the English title of the museum, in reference to the former Austro-Hungarian and local appellations of the museum. This heritage site has been exposed to different political, social, economic and religious contexts. However, it promotes the expression and representation of the cultural heritage of people from Bosnia and Herzegovina and offers an alternative for the preservation and maintenance of the country's ethno-religious identities and cultures.

The publication process for this book has proven to be challenging, as it was necessarily carried out via emails during the COVID-19 pandemic, while contributors were in different countries and time zones. However, in overcoming these obstacles and seeing the publication through to its completion, I found my mind opened to other ways of thinking about tangible and intangible heritage, the significance of its theories and practices, and the ways cultures of heritage can be developed and fostered. I hope that this book will have a similar impact on the readership of Open Book Publishers.

I. BUILT HERITAGE AND RESIDENTIAL CHARACTERISTICS

1. Socio-Spatial Practices of a Community Living Beneath the Land in Beni Zelten, South-Eastern Tunisia

Houda Driss

Introduction

Architectural heritage is characterised by its physical and material features, which attract interest in the study of the intrinsic properties of the built framework. The study of space from a similar point of view allows us to understand the logic of its insertion in the urban context, to identify its geometrical characteristics and to define its materials and construction techniques. However, studying architectural heritage solely in terms of its physical materiality removes it from its content and meanings. The function of inhabited space is not limited to sheltering the human body and protecting it from external agents, but rather, over time, it acquires another abstract and immaterial dimension.

This chapter focuses on the study of socio-spatial practices in vertical troglodytic dwellings located in the village of Beni Zelten in south-eastern Tunisia, which constitute an important part of the region's intangible heritage. According to the Convention for the Safeguarding of the Intangible Cultural Heritage of the International Council on Monuments and Sites (ICOMOS), 'Social practices, rituals and festive events are habitual activities that structure the lives of communities and

 https://doi.org/10.11647/OBP.0388.01

groups and that are shared by and relevant to many of their members.[1] In this chapter, the author will identify and explore the spaces in which these practices, rituals and events took place and their significance to the community.

The first part of this study identifies the spaces belonging to these dwellings and the relationships that exist between the different spaces, using the methodologies of literature review, in situ observation (particularly the architectural survey technique) and other investigative methods. The second part consists of enumerating and analysing the activities practised in the studied dwellings through a historical and investigative approach which relies on direct interviews with several elderly individuals (women and men) native to and resident in the region. In the course of these interviews, the interviewees discussed the socio-spatial domestic practices of their ancestors. The collected data was then processed and classified according to the interlocutor's gender, degree of privacy and the frequency of specific activities (daily or occasional).

Spatial organisation of vertical troglodytic dwellings

The village of Beni Zelten is located in the Governorate of Gabès in south-east Tunisia. It was inhabited by Arabised Berbers who led a semi-nomadic lifestyle and were active in the agro-pastoral and artisanal sectors. Troglodytic architecture, which is characteristic of the architecture in the village, refers to habitable spaces that are dug out of geological formations. Trebbi and Bertholon add that it is 'an architecture in negative", dug in a mass, which favours the interior space obtained by subtraction of material.[2] They can be considered subterranean dwellings, which Golany defines as 'Structures located deep within the ground. The depth may vary. The soil cover functions not only as an insulator but

1 ICOMOS, Intangible Heritage, Convention for the Safeguarding of Intangible Cultural Heritage / Québec declaration on the preservation of the spirit of place / The ICOMOS charter for the interpretation and presentation of cultural heritage sites with a bibliography based on documents available at the UNESCO-ICOMOS Documentation Centre. August 2011, https://www.icomos.org/centre_documentation/bib/2011_intangible-heritage_complete.pdf

2 Jean Charles Trebbi and Patrick Bertholon, *Habiter le paysage* (Paris: Alternatives, 2007), p. 7.

also and primarily as a heat retainer. The subterranean system is usually found in a hot/dry climate'.[3]

The vertical troglodytic dwellings are occupied by extended families consisting of a father, mother and married male descendants. In this conservative and patriarchal society, the members of an extended family share the agricultural harvest and the available resources, under the predominant authority of the father. The houses are imperceptible at first glance. Only the patios, large circular or square holes dug at the top of the small hills, testify to the presence of an underground human settlement.

The dwellings are accessible through an entrance vestibule, which preserves the privacy of the inhabitants by shielding them from public view. Located on both sides of the access corridor (also underground) are barn(s) and storage area(s) for agricultural equipment. The vestibule leads to the patio, usually on the west side.

The open-air patio is the only source of air and light in the home. Its dimensions vary between six to ten metres in depth and five to ten metres in width. The depth of this central courtyard depends on the number of floors in the house. If the house has one or more granaries on the first floor, then greater depth is needed. The uncovered patio is sufficiently lit and airy, just as it would be in a dwelling built above ground. This patio is the site of various daily and occasional activities, especially those conducted by women, such as preparing meals, grinding grains, drying fruits and vegetables and laundry, etc. This central courtyard also allows passage between the different spaces—namely, the bedrooms, kitchen(s) and granary/-ies.

The houses have several rooms and no windows. They range from three to four metres wide and two to two-and-a-half metres high, and they have varying depths of four to eight metres. The roofs of these underground spaces are never flat. Rather, they take the form of a raised arch, a parabolic vault or a triangular shape. These are rigid structures. This configuration allows the distribution and transmission of load without the risk of collapse.

The rooms have multiple uses. The area closest to the door can house a loom and be furnished as a living room and a sleeping area for

3 Gideon Golany, *Earth Sheltered Dwellings in Tunisia: Ancient Lessons for Modern Design* (Newark: University of Deleware Press, 1988), p. 19.

children. However, the deepest, most intimate space is reserved for the couple. The back wall of some rooms has a small excavation that serves as an ablution space, often containing a shower. It is used exclusively to wash the body and never as a toilet. As André Louis observes, 'It should be noted that the troglodyte house does not have toilet facilities.[4] Toilets, considered impure, are not integrated into the dwelling. Instead, according to oral tradition, men go away from homes to perform these natural functions in the wild, whereas women make use of small, discreet excavations that are arranged outside the dwelling.

The cooking space may be a shallow excavation located on one of the walls of the patio. Alternatively, it can be a space bounded by a wall occupying a corner of the courtyard and covered by some tree branches. In the same dwelling, one can find up to four cooking spaces if the family inhabiting it is very large. The cooking spaces can be located to the right or left of the entrance vestibule opening on the patio and can occupy any position between two rooms.

The granary is a space used for storing olives. It opens onto the central courtyard, but it is raised a half or whole level above the patio floor. From the inside, it is accessible by carved notches or pieces of olive wood embedded in the wall, which function as a staircase. The granary occupies an elevated position compared with the other spaces that open onto the central courtyard, for two reasons. The first is to protect the contents of this space from thieves by making access difficult. The second relates to the symbolism of this space, which reflects the esteem and wealth of a family. The roof is equipped with a pipe that allows olives to be transferred into the granary from the outside without crossing the courtyard. According to Libaud, to fill the granary, 'the owner will only have to drive his camel on the hill (which is now the roof of the house) to the pipe and unload the olives directly from the outside.[5]

As the description above makes clear, vertical cave dwellings are not directly accessible. The organisation of the housing layout is not arbitrary; rather, the nature of spaces and the relationships between

4 André Louis, 'L'habitation troglodyte dans un village des Matmata', *Cahiers des Arts et Traditions Populaires*, 2 (1968), 33–60.

5 Geneviève Libaud, *Symbolique de l'espace et habitat chez les Beni-Aïssa du sud tunisien* (Paris: CNRS, 1986), p. 111.

them are dictated by well-defined social laws and cultural codes. As Pierre Robert Baduel explains,

> To produce a habitat, is first of all to develop societal relations, to organize proximities and distances, to draw boundaries between an inside and an outside. [... The] inhabited space is therefore oriented, and oriented specifically according to the reference culture.[6]

Privacy is only one such cultural concern that informs the layout of the troglodytic structures. The studied houses have two sets of spaces. The first contains the rooms, cooking spaces and granaries. The second consists of the service spaces (vestibule, barns and agricultural equipment depots), which are relatively far from the living spaces. This arrangement is a matter of health and hygiene, as it distances occupants from their animals. All the components of the house are part of the same enclosed perimeter because of the lack of security and the conflicts that have prevailed in this territory. As Eleb and Chatelet note, 'the division of the ground, as well as the distribution of the rooms of the dwelling qualify both the lifestyle [...] and the relationships between people.[7]

Socio-spatial practices in vertical troglodytic dwellings

Record of activities in vertical troglodytic dwellings

To understand the socio-spatial practices in vertical troglodytic dwellings, first we must collect information about how the local population used the different domestic spaces. The second task is to process the collected data to understand the different scenes of life in these underground spaces, by referencing the existing literature on the one hand and utilising investigative methodology on the other. Based on the inhabitants' speech, this study identified thirty-six domestic activities.

The activities are classified according to the gender of the user and the activities' periodicity. Female activities are performed only by

6 Pierre Robert Baduel, *Habitat–Etat–Société au Maghreb* (Paris: CNRS, 1988), p. 234.

7 Monique Eleb and Anne-Marie Chatelet, *Urbanité, sociabilité et intimité: Des logements d'aujourd'hui* (Paris: Epure, 1997), p. 350.

women, whereas male activities are performed only by men. Family activities are carried out by all family members (women and men). The second classification shows that daily activities are performed frequently throughout the year. While occasional activities take place in an irregular and seasonal manner, they have a religious, para-religious and ceremonial nature. Table 1.1 allows for the comparison of the data of the two established classifications.

Table 1.1 shows occasional activities, including those carried out by women, men and the entire family. For example, on the day of *Eid al-Adha*, men slaughter sheep and women clean and grill offal as they prepare couscous with lamb meat. Then, the whole family partakes in the meal.

Table 1.1 Classification of activities according to type and frequency.

		ACTIVITY TYPES		
		Female	**Male**	**Family**
periodicity of activities	**Daily activities**	Toileting, Tidying house, Preparing food, Making bread, Washing dishes, Putting away dishes, Washing laundry, Drying laundry, Grinding grains, Carding and spinning wool, Weaving wool, Receiving family, Milking sheep and goats, Processing milk	Maintaining farm equipment, Tidying farm equipment Sheltering cattle, Working alfa	Sleeping, Showering, Taking Meals
	Occasional activities	Drying figs, Storing dried figs, Shearing wool, Ritual of *Muharram*, Ritual of *Ashura*, Ritual of *Mawlid*, Ritual of *Eid al- Fitr*, Ritual of *Eid al-Adha*, Ritual of birth, Preparations for weddings, Ritual of circumcision, Ritual for funerals	Storing cereals (wheat, barley, etc.), Storing olives, Storing olive oil, Ritual of *Eid al-Adha*, Preparations for weddings, Ritual for funerals	Ritual of *Muharram*, Ritual of *Ashura*, Ritual of *Mawlid*, Ritual of *Eid al- Fitr*, Ritual of *Eid al-Adha*, Preparations for weddings, Ritual of circumcision, Ritual for funerals

The different activities can be further classified according to the degree of privacy of the space. The study first distinguishes private activities performed by a small family (a couple and their children) within a room. It then identifies semi-private activities carried out by members of the extended family (all occupants of the dwelling: grandparents, parents, aunts, uncles, cousins, etc.). Finally, it indicates the common activities carried out publicly, in the presence of guests and neighbours. This classification is presented in Table 1.2.

Table 1.2 Classification of activities according to the degree of privacy (private, semi-private, common).

Private activities	Semi-private activities	Common activities
Sleeping, Toileting, Showering, Ritual of birth	Tidying house, Preparing food, Taking meals, Making bread, Washing dishes, Putting away dishes, Washing laundry, Drying laundry, Grinding grains, Storing dried figs, Carding and spinning wool, Weaving wool, Milking sheep and goats, Processing milk, Ritual of *Muharram*, Ritual of *Ashura*, Ritual of *Mawlid*, Ritual of *Eid al- Fitr*, Ritual of *Eid al-Adha*	Storing cereals (wheat, barley, etc.), Drying figs, Storing olives, Storing olive oil, Maintaining farm equipment, Tidying farm equipment, Shearing wool, Receiving family, Sheltering cattle, Working alfa, Preparations for weddings, Ritual of circumcision, Ritual for funerals

Identifying activities in spaces

The obtained data on activity types (female, male and family), degree of privacy (private, semi-private and common), periodicity (daily or occasional) and the different spaces contribute to a better understanding of socio-spatial practices in studied homes.

Table 1.3 Identification of activities in spaces.

ACTIVITIES	SPACES									
	V	P	A	S	C	G	Ch	Chh	Ab	T
1		O					O			O
2	O									
3									O	
4	O	O			O		O			
5					O					
6		O					O			
7					O					
8					O					
9					O		O			
10		O								
11		O								
12		O				O				
13		O								
14										O
15						O				
16						O				
17						O				
18	O	O								
19				O						
20		O	O							
21		O					O			
22		O					O			
23	O									
24			O							
25		O								
26			O							
27		O					O			
28		O			O		O			
29		O			O		O			
30		O			O		O			
31		O			O		O			
32		O	O		O		O			
33					O		O			
34		O			O		O	O		O
35		O			O		O			
36		O			O		O	O		

O	Female activities		Private activities		Daily activities
O	Male activities		Semi-private activities		Occasional activities
O	Family activities		Common activities		

V: Vestibule, P: Patio, A: Barn, S: Equipment storage, C: Cooking space, G: Granary, Ch: Room, Chh: Guestroom, Ab: Ablution space/Shower, T: Terrace

In Table 1.3, each line represents an activity. The columns indicate the different spaces in the dwelling. The observed activity is marked by a circle in the corresponding box. The three circle colours correspond to the following significations:

- Red: female activities
- Blue: male activities
- Green: family activities

To indicate the periodicity of the activity, the boxes relating to daily activities are shaded in light grey and the occasional activities are shown in salmon colour. The degree of privacy is expressed by the boxes with dashed lines for private activities, fine lines for semi-private activities and bold lines for common activities.

Classification of spaces by number of activities

Based upon the information in the preceding tables, Figure 1 shows the percentage of the use of each space in vertical troglodytic dwellings.

This graph shows that the patio has the highest number of activities at 30%. Rooms and cooking spaces occupy the second rank, with a percentage close to 20% each. The other spaces are sparsely used and have rates below 6%.

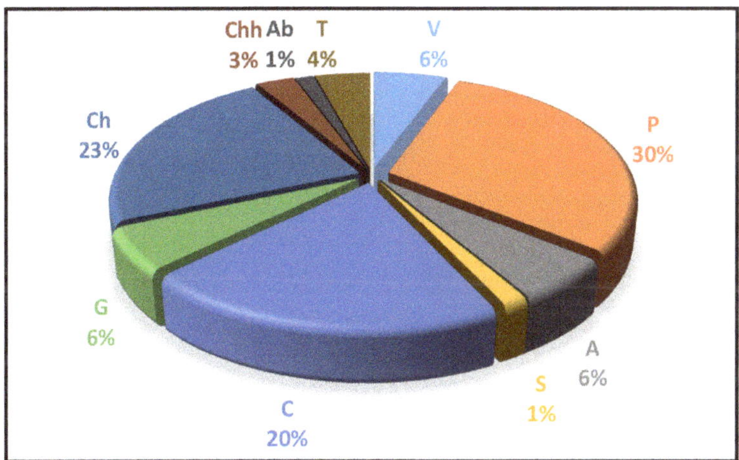

Fig. 1.1 Percentage of use of each space in vertical troglodytic dwellings (V: Vestibule, P: Patio, A: Barn, S: Equipment storage, C: Cooking space, G: Granary, Ch: Room, Chh: Guest room, Ab: Ablution space/Shower, T: Terrace). Author's graph, CC BY-NC-ND.

Spatial characteristics according to female, male and family practices

The digital data from Table 1.3 have been converted into graphs to better differentiate the type of user of the space (female, male and family). The kitchen contains 100% female activities (meal preparation, cooking), and men do not use this part of the house. The cooking space is the only space exclusively for female use. The storage space for agricultural equipment and the guest room (if it exists) is comprised of 100% male activities. The women do not engage in any activity in these two spaces that open onto the vestibule.

The ablution area houses 100% family activities. The family members (women and men) use the space to wash their bodies equally and without segregation. The barn includes 50% female activities and 50% male activities. Female and male activities take place in the same space but at different times of the day.

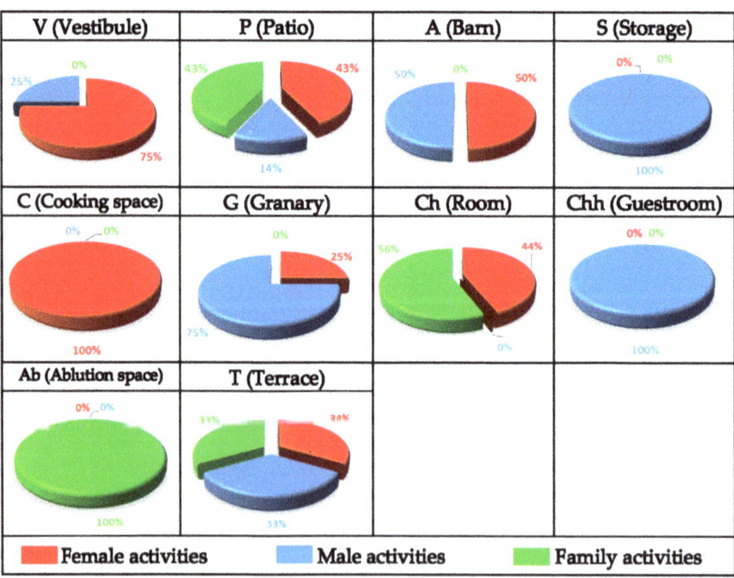

Fig. 1.2 Spatial characteristics according to female/male/family activity types. Author's graphs, CC BY-NC-ND.

The vestibule represents mostly female activities, with a percentage of 75%, whereas male activities account for only 25% of the activities. No family activity occurs in this space of transition between the interior and the exterior of the home. The granary houses only 25% female activities and 75% male activities. The graph shows no family activity in the storage space. In all rooms except the cooking space, guest room, granaries and terrace, 44% female activities and 56% family activities occur, but there are no exclusively male activities that take place there. The patio involves exclusively female activities, family activities and exclusively male activities. In this area, female and family activities are carried out at the same rate, each representing 43% of the activities. However, the rate for male activities is much lower, at 14%.

Spatial characteristics according to the degree of privacy (private, semi-private or common)

Figure 3 shows that the storage space for agricultural equipment, the guest room and the terrace allow common activities to be practised in front of different members of the extended family as well as people from outside the family. These spaces contain 100% common activities. The ablution space is used individually; it contains an intimate activity that is 100% private. The vestibule houses activities belonging to all three levels of privacy. Private activities and semi-private activities are equal in this area, at 25% each. The percentage of common activities is higher, at 50%.

The rooms, such as the vestibule, contain activities belonging to the three levels of privacy; however, the rates for practising each level are different. The activities are mostly semi-private, with a rate of 69%. Private activities have the lowest rate (12%), and the rate for common activities is 19%. The barn does not involve any private activity. Half the barn activities are semi-private (50%), and the other half are reserved for common activities. The patio houses 71% semi-private activities and only 29% common activities; no private activities are practised in this space.

Activities in the kitchen are mostly semi-private, with a rate of 79%. Only 21% of the activities are common, and no private ones are performed in this space. Seventy-five per cent of the activities in the granary are common, 25% are semi-private and no private activity takes place in this storage space.

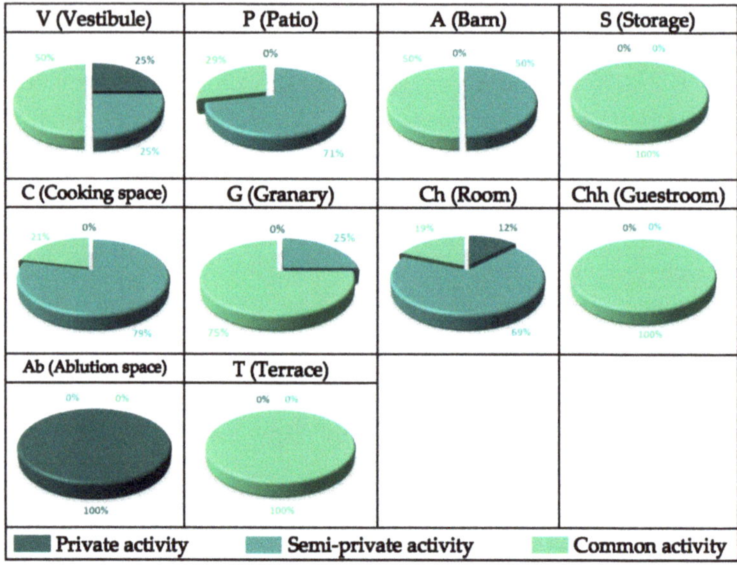

Fig. 1.3 Spatial characteristics according to the degree of privacy (private, semi-private and common). Author's graphs, CC BY-NC-ND.

Characteristics of socio-spatial practices in vertical troglodytic dwellings

According to Letesson, socio-spatial analysis reveals 'the intrinsic relationships between the social and the architectural aspects, between a human group and its built space'.[8] This study allows the detection of certain principles that govern the socio-cultural life of the inhabitants of Beni Zelten and that are inscribed in the architectural object by well-defined spatial organisation.

The entrance hall is a transitional space between the interior, the domain of the family's private life, and the exterior, the domain of the community's collective life. It is a common space for all users of the dwelling, but it is forbidden to those who do not reside in the dwelling, except with the inhabitants' permission. Depending on the time of day, the degree of privacy of this space may change. It preserves the intimacy

8 Quentin Letesson, *Du phénotype au génotype, analyse de la syntaxe spatiale en architecture minoenne* (*MMIIIB-MRIB*) (Belgium: Presses universitaires de Louvain, 2009), p. 5.

of the home and especially the privacy of women. The vestibule is in direct connection with the patio, the stable, the storage space for agricultural equipment, and, in some rare cases, the guest room.

On either side of the vestibule, we find excavations that are used to shelter domesticated animals and agricultural tools. These service spaces, located close to the entrance of the house, are far from the human spaces. The storage space and the barn are considered less 'noble' and less clean than the rest of the spaces, but they are essential to maintain the inhabitants' way of life. These service spaces house mostly common male activities. In some houses, the vestibule has a guest room, which is never arranged around the central courtyard of the dwelling. The guest room is intended to accommodate outside visitors who visit the family for wedding ceremonies or mourning. It is accessible through the vestibule to avoid interfering with the intimacy of the women of the house.

The patio houses activities mainly of a female and family nature, which are mostly semi-private. This space, which is especially utilised by women, is used for meeting family members, weaving, washing and drying laundry, grinding grain, taking meals and so on. However, the men occupy this space to repair the agricultural equipment, to work the alfa, for gatherings and other such activities. The rooms are multipurpose spaces where essentially private activities are carried out, especially by women. The kitchens are exclusively for female use and essentially qualified as semi-private. Most of the studied houses have one or more granaries. These spaces are used for the storage of the food supply (cereals, olives, dried figs, etc.), which can be rare and very valuable, especially during difficult years, when irregular rainfall impedes agricultural production in the area. These granaries, with their difficult access, are rarely used and represent areas for men to practice common activities.

The spatial practices in the studied houses are the result of the interaction between the natural context, represented by the available resources, and the particular socio-economic context. This interaction gave birth to an intangible heritage housed in a tangible heritage that is now abandoned. Since the 1950s and 1960s, the inhabitants of the village have occupied new forms of built housing where the old socio-spatial practices have mixed with new ones. These are dictated by the change in the sectors of activity of the population and by the adoption of new standards of modern life.

Conclusion

This study showed that in the troglodytic houses in Beni Zelten, South-Eastern Tunisia, the dwelling is the women's domain par excellence. There is a gendered spatial distribution that has also been found to manifest in several other societies. Men occupy the house during moments of rest or to carry out complementary activities to their agropastoral occupations on agricultural lands. Thus, the dwelling ensures the security and preserves the intimacy of the family and the privacy of women. As Zaied confirms, 'the idea of honour is linked to three entities: The tribe, the family and the woman. [...] This control is even more severe with regard to women. [...] She is even one of the symbols of honour'.[9] The village of Beni Zelten, like all *Jbelia* villages, has long suffered from insecurity and political conflicts between tribes. The houses were an adapted response to these situations that would allow inhabitants to contend with invaders and looters. The houses are underground dwellings that are difficult for enemies to spot. Access is provided through a transitional space (vestibule) and is never direct. Finally, the food supply is stored in granaries that are difficult to access.

The south-eastern region of Tunisia is strongly affected by the phenomenon of migration. Nasr speaks about 'a very ancient Dynamic for more than four centuries (organized emigration)'.[10] These migratory movements intensified around the middle of the twentieth century in the aftermath of World War II. Young people of working age then left their native regions for big cities in Tunisia or abroad in search of better paying jobs and better living conditions. The dwellings in the troglodytic villages were subsequently abandoned. They have been replaced by built houses that are better adapted to the standards of modern life, characterised by the standardisation of daily activities and

9 Abdesmad Zaïed, *Le monde des Ksours du sud tunisien* (Tunis: Centre de Publication Universitaire, 2006), pp. 151–53.

10 Noureddine Nasr, 'Agriculture et émigration dans les stratégies productives des jbalia du Sud-Est tunisien', in *Environnement et sociétés rurales en mutation: Approches alternatives*, ed. by Michel Picouet, Mongi Sghaier, Didier Genin et al. (Paris: IRD Editions, 2004), pp. 247–57.

current needs. Troglodytic dwellings as tangible heritage fell into ruin and gradually deteriorated over time.

What should we say about socio-spatial practices, considered to be intangible heritage, that fall completely into oblivion? According to the Convention for the Safeguarding of the Intangible Cultural Heritage 'Social practices, rituals and festive events are strongly affected by the changes communities undergo in modern societies. [...] Processes such as migration, individualisation, the general introduction of formal education [...] have a particularly marked effect on these practices.[11] Thus, this study represents an opportunity to reveal socio-spatial practices in troglodytic dwellings in the village of Beni Zelten as intangible heritage. It could be extended to other villages in the same region or to other regions. This troglodyte heritage reflects the identity of the region. It is time for politicians, heritage authorities and architects to take action to protect these sites and proceed with their registration as cultural heritage before it is too late.

11 ICOMOS, Intangible Heritage, Convention for the Safeguarding of Intangible Cultural Heritage / Québec declaration on the preservation of the spirit of place / The ICOMOS charter for the interpretation and presentation of cultural heritage sites with a bibliography based on documents available at the UNESCO-ICOMOS Documentation Centre. August 2011, https://www.icomos.org/centre_documentation/bib/2011_intangible-heritage_complete.pdf

Bibliography

Baduel, Pierre-Robert, *Habitat–Etat–Société au Maghreb* (Paris: CNRS, 1988).

Eleb, Monique and Chatelet, Anne-Marie, *Urbanité, sociabilité et intimité: Des logements d'aujourd'hui* (Paris: Epure, 1997).

Golany, Gideon, *Earth Sheltered Dwellings in Tunisia: Ancient Lessons for Modern Design* (Newark: University of Deleware Press, 1988).

ICOMOS, Intangible Heritage, Convention for the Safeguarding of Intangible Cultural Heritage / Québec declaration on the preservation of the spirit of place / The ICOMOS charter for the interpretation and presentation of cultural heritage sites with a bibliography based on documents available at the UNESCO-ICOMOS Documentation Centre. August 2011, https://www.icomos.org/centre_documentation/bib/2011_intangible-heritage_complete.pdf.

Letesson, Quentin, *Du phénotype au génotype, analyse de la syntaxe spatiale en architecture minoenne (MMIIIB-MRIB)* (Belgium: Presses universitaires de Louvain, 2009).

Libaud, Geneviève, *Symbolique de l'espace et habitat chez les Beni-Aïssa du sud tunisien* (Paris: CNRS, 1986).

Louis, André, 'L'habitation troglodyte dans un village des Matmata', *Cahiers des Arts et Traditions Populaires*, 2 (1968), 33–60.

Nasr, Noureddine, 'Agriculture et émigration dans les stratégies productives des jbalia du Sud-Est tunisien', in *Environnement et sociétés rurales en mutation: Approches alternatives*, ed. by Michel Picouet, Mongi Sghaier, Didier Genin et al. (Paris: IRD Editions, 2004), pp. 247–57.

Trebbi, Jean-Charles and Bertholon, Patrick, *Habiter le paysage* (Paris: Alternatives, 2007).

Zaïed, Abdesmad, *Le monde des Ksours du sud tunisien* (Tunis: Centre de Publication Universitaire, 2006).

2. Impact of Jurisprudential Heritage in the Organisation of the Medina of Tunis: Joint Ownership, Social Practices and Customs

Meriem Ben Ammar

Introduction

Since the beginning of Islam, Islamic law has ordered relations between Muslims and managed their lives, rights and duties. The city as a living environment was organised through numerous rules and laws, based on the Hadith of the prophet Mohammad, which state that harm should neither be inflicted nor reciprocated.

The neighbourhood is an important aspect of Muslim life and a special focus of both the Quran and the Sunnah, which emphasize unity and peace as distinctive elements of the Islamic neighbourhood. Religious tenets include notions of good neighbourliness and various rights and customs governing interactions between residents of the same neighbourhood. As Ali Safak notes, 'One of the most important of today's problems [for Muslims], about which questions are frequently asked, is the matter of ownership rights'.[1] This will be the subject of

1 Ali Safak, 'Urbanism and Family Residence in Islamic Law', *Ekistics*, 280 (1980), 21–25 (p. 21).

 https://doi.org/10.11647/OBP.0388.02

the current chapter. From the relationship between neighbours, various types of transactions are generated, such as joint ownership, the object of which can be a shop, land, a house or a contiguous wall, given the anatomy of the Islamic city and the layout of its dwellings.

According to some researchers, shared walls are a characteristic feature of the medina, or old town. Moncef M'halla considers the clustering and connecting of houses to be at the origin of the formation of the medina and its urban fabric, where the wall—as an important architectural element—is akin to its spinal column.[2] This feature is absent in contemporary cities, which adopt the European model as a development plan. As Mazzoli-Guintard states, we should not forget 'that among the remarkable morphological features of the city of the medieval Arab-Muslim world is that of the contiguity of the building'.[3] We can observe this omnipresent aspect in the medina of Tunis, registered since 1979 as a United Nations Educational, Scientific and Cultural Organization (UNESCO) World Heritage Site, with its weaving of houses surrounded by mosques, *souqs* [markets], mausoleums, *madrasas* [schools], *hammams* [bathhouses], *fondouks* [hotels] and so on.

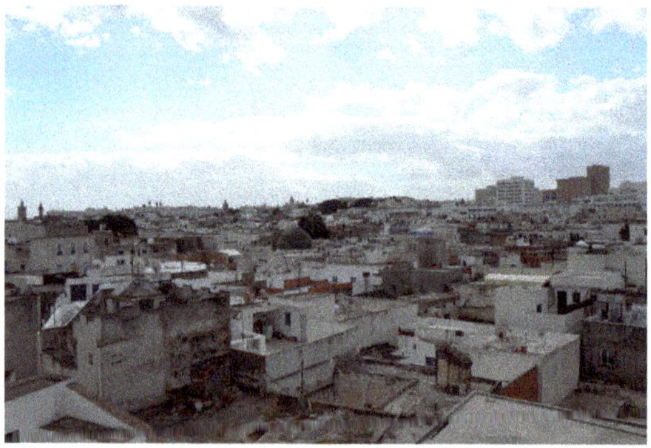

Fig. 2.1 Medina of Tunis, example of a party wall used by one of the neighbours as a support for its construction of an upper floor. Author's photograph, 2017, CC BY-NC-ND.

2 Moncef M'halla, 'La médina un art de bâtir', *Africa: Fouilles, monuments et collections archéologiques en Tunisie, Institut national du patrimoine de Tunis*, 12 (1998), 33–98 (see esp. p. 44, pp. 53–54), https://www.inp2020.tn/periodiques/atp/atp12.pdf

3 Christine Mazzoli Guintard, *Vivre à Cordoue au Moyen Âge: Solidarités citadines en terre d'Islam aux Xe-XIe siècles* (Rennes: Presses universitaires, 2015), p. 163, https://doi.org/10.4000/books.pur.17013

According to O'Meara, the city can be defined and determined by its walls. The basic building block was the *dar* [house], simply a walled enclosure or a cell. Thus, the medina's structure is defined by the enclosures' walls that set out and delineate the buildings and the streets.[4] Some owners could legally make changes to their private properties (extension, restoration, demolition, reconstruction of walls, etc.), but sometimes owners did so illegally, violating the regulating code of the medina[5] and disrupting the neighbourhood's harmony (Fig. 2.1).

To minimise the incidents and injustices caused by joint ownership and establish a legal framework to resolve these conflicts, Islamic jurisprudence sets out several rules that take into account social practices, relations between neighbours, construction techniques and materials. These long-established rules have since become customs. They were written by jurists, judges or even masons in the form of books or epistles under the heading 'Jurisprudence of Architecture and Urbanism' and are dedicated to discussing problems related to construction techniques and materials, neighbourhood conflicts, roads, town planning, lighting and so on.[6]

The study of the rules transmitted from one generation to another, here analysed and interpreted in a graphical way, constitutes a fundamental contribution to the knowledge of the structure of the contemporary Islamic city; it can be useful for the assessment of contemporary tangible heritage, and therefore, for making decisions regarding the protection and enhancement of the built environment in the light of tradition.

---

4 Simon O'Meara, *Space and Muslim Urban Life: At the Limits of the Labyrinth of Fez* (New York: Routledge, 2007), p. 15.

5 Plan d'aménagement urbain de la commune de Tunis, Règlement d'urbanisme [Urban development plan for the municipality of Tunis] (Commune-Tunis, January 2016), pp. 31–33, http://www.commune-tunis.gov.tn/publish/images/actualite/pdf/Reg-PACT-livre-enq%20publiqueh.pdf
The urban planning rules relating to the medina of Tunis occupy a chapter in this code, which presents the characteristics of the medina as a residential, economic real-estate space and monumental heritage with safeguarding standards.

6 Several classical books have been written in this field, such as the following (the titles of these books and of the epistle studied in this chapter have been translated from the Arabic by the present author): Issa bin Moussa al-Toutili, *The Book of the Wall* (tenth century); Al-Mourji al-Thaqafi, *The Book of the Walls* (tenth century); Al-Fursutaai al-Nafoussi, *The Book of the Division and the Origins of the Lands* (twelfth century); and *The Book of Advertisement of Judicial Provisions of Buildings* (fourteenth century) by the Tunisian mason Ibn al-Rami.

State of studies on Islamic urban planning

Since Islamic jurisprudence manages both religious and temporal aspects of believers' lives, it practically regulates all areas of existence. 'Jurisprudence of Architecture and Urbanism' can be defined as the set of rules and recommendations prescribed by Islamic law that govern everything related to architecture, town planning and the development of an Islamic city. It can also be considered a group of principles derived from the urban movement and its interaction with society. It provides answers to the Muslim community's concerns while respecting the interests of the individual and the public. These responses subsequently provide a reference for any problematic situation as well as a legally binding framework. The need for a legal guide has given rise to works and treatises that can be employed and developed according to rite, space and need.

Early research on the Islamic city was characterized by homogeneity, thanks to a structural model that was applied to all cities without taking into account the geographical, economic, social, and historical characteristics of each region.[7] Efforts have been made to revise this approach that account for these factors, as well as distinguishing towns from rural settlements. Giulia A. Neglia noted that, after 1970, studies have been oriented towards the role of religion in the codification of Islamic urban form and society, or on the structure of cities in different regions.[8]

The Islamic city with all its components is not the result of a singular generative mechanism, but a multidisciplinary process based on various parameters: legal, religious, political and cultural.[9] Dating from the

7 Henri Pirenne, *Les villes du moyen âge* (Brussels: Lamertin, 1927); Georges Marçais, 'L'urbanisme musulman', in *5e Congrès De la Fédération des Soc. Savantes d'Afrique du Nord, Tunis*, 6–8.4.1939 (Algiers, 1940), 13–34; Georges Marçais, 'La conception des villes dans l'Islâm', *Revue d'Alger*, 2 (1945), 517–33.

8 Giulia Annalinda Neglia, 'Some historiographical notes on the Islamic city with particular reference to the visual representation of the built city', in *The City in the Islamic World*, ed. by Salma K. Jayyusi, Renata Holod, Attilio Petruccioli and André Raymond (Leiden, Boston: Brill, 2008), pp. 3–46 (p.13).

9 *The Islamic City: A Colloquium*, ed. by Albert Habib Hourani and Samuel Miklos Stern (Oxford: University of Pennsylvania Press, 1970); *Islamic Architecture and Urbanism*, ed. by Aydin Germen (Dammam: King Faisal University, 1983); *The Middle East City: Ancient Traditions Confront a Modern World*, ed. by Abdelaziz Y. Saqqaf (New York: Paragon House, 1987); Janet L. Abu-Lughod, 'The Islamic City: Historic Myth, Islamic Essence, and Contemporary Relevance', *International Journal of Middle East Studies*, 2 (1987), 155–76.

eighteenth century, the book *An Epistle on Disputed Contiguous Walls* by Tunisian jurist Muhammad bin Hussain al-Baroudi al-Hanafi (d. 1801) focuses on cases of neighbourhood conflicts, using the provisions set out in the treaties of Hanafi law as a reference. This manuscript is devoted exclusively to neighbourhood conflicts, unlike previous works which have addressed this issue along with many other subjects, such as water, streets, impasses, and public and private property. The jurist tried to collect and cite all the rules relating to these conflicts, while providing accompanying commentary. Despite the rich potential of this legal literature, it has only been treated with minimal interest.[10] It is true that numerous manuscripts were transcribed, but this chapter is interested in analytical works focused on the study of sources of legislation related to the city and its architecture. More contemporary academic studies of this literature on Islamic law presented elements drawn from work on jurisprudence and the various questions relating to urbanism dealt with by Maliki jurists. They tried to show how religious laws and ethical values have been central to the creation and development of the city over time.[11] In examining the subject from various levels of analysis—from the city to the Muslim world,[12] and back to the neighbourhood—the contemporary academic study sheds light on the relationships between society, religion, and the construction of urban and architectural practices. This is done in an effort to demonstrate the application of the Islamic foundations in urban planning, and to explain how Islamic thought has affected urban strategy, roads, infrastructure, politics and social life.[13]More contemporary academic studies offering a new reading of the Maliki and Hanafi legal sources endeavour to understand the genesis of the medina by

10 To the best of the author's knowledge, unlike other manuscripts of architectural and urban planning jurisprudence, this epistle has not been analysed. The epistle has been consulted at the National Library of Tunis, in the form of a manuscript dating from the 18th century.

11 Robert Brunschvig, 'Urbanisme médiéval et droit musulman', *Revue des études islamiques*, XV (1947), 127–55; Besim Selim Hakim, *Arabic-Islamic Cities: Building and Planning Principles* (New York: Routledge, 2010); Jean-Pierre Van Staëvel, *Droit mālikite et habitat à Tunis au XIVe siècle. Conflits de voisinage et normes juridiques d'après le texte du maître-maçon Ibn al-Rāmī* (Cairo: Institut français d'archéologie, 2008).

12 Jamel Akbar, *A Crisis in the Built Environment: The Case of the Muslim City* (Leiden: E. J. Brill, 1988).

13 Khaled Azab, *Fiqh al-ᶜimāra al-Islāmiyya* [*Islamic Jurisprudence of Architecture*] (Egypt: University Publishing House, 1997); Muhammad Abd al-Sattar Uthman, *Al-Madīna al-Islāmiyya* [*The Islamic City*] (Cairo: Dar al-Afaq al-Arabiyah, 1999).

emphasising the role of the wall and the rules of the contiguity between joint ownership and donation of the wall. These are an attempt to find a link between Islamic legal techniques and modern cities by exploring how these sources can help to understand and solve present-day urban problems through emphasis on the phenomenon of contiguity.[14]

Presentation of the *Epistle*

Two copies of the *Epistle* were found at the National Library of Tunis; their characteristics are listed in Table 2.1.

Table 2.1 Characteristics of the two copies of the *Epistle*.

Nature	**Hanafi Fiqh**	
Number	09732	03933
State	Draft	Final copy
Source	Collection of legal questions (a set of 123 folio)	Independent booklet
Owner	Kheireddine pasha	Kheireddine pasha
Number of sheets	16 (from folio 32 to folio 47)	18
Date of writing	End of Shaaban in the year 1215H (January 1801)	Tuesday 9 dhu al-Qa'da in the year 1215H (23 March 1801)
Dimensions (cm)	20.8 * 15	21 * 15
Writing	Maghrebi script	Maghrebi script
Ink	Black	Black
Support quality	Parchment	Parchment
Binding	Cardboard covered with domino paper	Cardboard covered with Bordeaux red Morocco coating

14 Moncef M'halla, 'La médina un art de bâtir', *Africa: Fouilles, monuments et collections archéologiques en Tunisie, Institut national du patrimoine de Tunis*, 12 (1998), 33–98; Abdelmalek Houcine, 'La mitoyenneté dans la jurisprudence islamique', *Tracé (bulletin technique de la Suisse romande)*, 1 (2011), 6–15; Simon O'Meara, 'A Legal Aesthetic of Medieval and Pre-Modern Arab Muslim Urban Architectural Space', *Journal of Arabic and Islamic Studies*, 9 (2009), 1–17, https://doi.org/10.5617/jais.4594

The jurist, his approach and his sources

The jurist was descended from a family of Turkish scholars originally from Morea in Greece. His grandfather, Ibrahim al-Baroudi, a janissary specialist in the manufacture of gunpowder, arrived and settled in Tunis towards the end of the seventeenth century. His father was Hussain bin Ibrahim al-Baroudi (1700–1773), a renowned Hanafi jurist and theologian who held several important positions in the Tunisian Beylic. Muhammad bin Hussain bin Ibrahim al-Baroudi also became a renowned Hanafi jurist. He worked as a teacher at the great mosque and at *al-Chammaiya Madrasah*. In 1776, Ali Bey (1712–1782) appointed him as the third Hanafi *mufti*, and in 1780, he became *imam* and teacher at the Hammouda pasha mosque. He gained remarkable status under the rule of Hammouda pasha (1759–1814), including the title of *Cheikh al-Islam*, which he received around 1799 and held until his death in 1801.[15]

The text[16] is presented in a progressive manner with the absence of the classic layout of jurisprudence manuscripts (introduction, sections and chapters). Al-Baroudi starts by introducing the topic of neighbourhood conflicts, expressing his interest in this problem and encouraging jurists to pay special attention to it. We can discern the various cases of conflict thanks to his descriptive writing, which uses an informative tone and a hypothetical style to describe certain situations and enumerate their relative causes, the conditions and the different states on either side of the wall—each neighbour's property, the state of his walls, the roof, its composition, and the construction technique. Finally, Al-Baroudi presents the most suitable solution, accompanied by references from legal sources to support the judgement.

15 Hassan Hosni Abdelwaheb, *Kitāb al-ᶜumr fil-muṣannafāt wal-muʾallifīn al-tunisiyyīn* [*A Book on Tunisian Works and Authors*], 2 vols. (Tunis: Dar al-Gharb al-Islami, 1990), I, p. 930; Muhammad Mahfûz, *Tarājim al- muʾallifīn al-tunisiyyīn* [*Biographies of Tunisian Authors*], 5 vols. (Tunis: Dar al-Gharb al-Islami, 1994), I, p. 74; Muhammad al-Snussi, *Musāmarāt al-dharīf bi ḥusn al-taᶜrīf* [*Biographies of Tunisian authors*], ed. by Muhammad al-Chadli al-Nayfir, 4 vols. (Tunis: Dar al-Gharb al-Islami, 1994), II, p. 40.

16 In general, the Arabic is fluent and understandable; the text is rich in technical and legal terminology, but the jurist has provided definitions for difficult terms.

Throughout the manuscript, and to consolidate his opinions, Al-Baroudi mentions various sources that belong to the Hanafi rite. These include the works of the founder of the doctrine, Abu Hanifa, and his student and companion, Abu Yousuf. Two other works were mentioned several times—the *Imadian Decisive Arbiter*,[17] described as a valuable and comprehensive collection of all legal matters, and *Fatawa Qadi Khan*,[18] one of the most approved, widely known and ubiquitous *Fatwah* books among Hanafi jurists. Other than the general *Fiqh*,[19] Al-Baroudi relies on the most famous book of the Hanafi school on architecture and urbanism, the *Book of the Walls*.[20] This book covers a variety of issues related to shared walls—the right of use, connections between buildings, roofing, common ownership of a party wall, connected and raised beams, wall arrangements in the case of conflicts and multi-storey buildings, as well as issues relating to streets, water canals, irrigation and so on.

Cases of neighbourhood conflict

Al-Baroudi addresses the reader directly, informing them of disagreements between two neighbours concerning a contiguous wall where each claims ownership but without proof or avowal. The cases are grouped into two main categories, the first where the two contestants are equal in their pleas and neither has a valid argument that favours one person or side over the other. The second category includes cases where one or both parties have a reason that supports their claim.

17 Al-Imad Abu al-Fath Zainuddin Abd al-Rahimbin Abi Bakr Al-Marghinani (d. 670 C.E), *Al-Fuṣūl al-ᶜimādiyyah* [*The Imadian Decisive Arbiter*] in Yahya Mohammad Melhem, *The Imadian Decisive Arbiter* (Jordan: The University of Jordan, 1997).

18 Fakhr al-Din QadiKhan al-Hanafi (d. 592/1195), *Fatāwā Qādhī Khān* [*Legal opinions of Qadikhan*] (Mohamed Shahin Press, 1865).

19 Fiqh refers to Islamic jurisprudence and can be characterized as the means by which legal scholars extract guidelines, rules, and regulations from the foundational principles found in the Quran and the Sunnah.

20 The copy used here is not that of al-Thaqafi (see note 6) but that of the Hanafi jurist and judge Omar bin Abd al-Aziz bin Maza al-Bukhari (1090–1141). Al-Baroudi mentioned his recourse to this jurist and his work, which could be explained by the fact that Ibn Maza's copy contained the complete, annotated version of the book.

Division criteria

Types of connection

Al-Baroudi mentions two types of connection: a stretcher bond and an adjacency connection. The first is defined as the connection between the contested wall and another orthogonal one so that its masonry blocks overlap with those of the other. This is called squaring because it is built to form a square space with two other walls.

According to Al-Baroudi, if the construction is made of stone or brick, the half-blocks of the contested wall are interwoven with the half-blocks of the uncontested orthogonal wall, and if it is made of wood, each bar is inserted into the orthogonal wall (Fig. 2.2).[21] The second type of construction is the juxtaposition of two walls without overlapping, also called contiguity. According to jurists, this is a simple juxtaposition of two walls, without interference or sharing, and the neighbours each occupy and operate their building (Fig. 2.2).

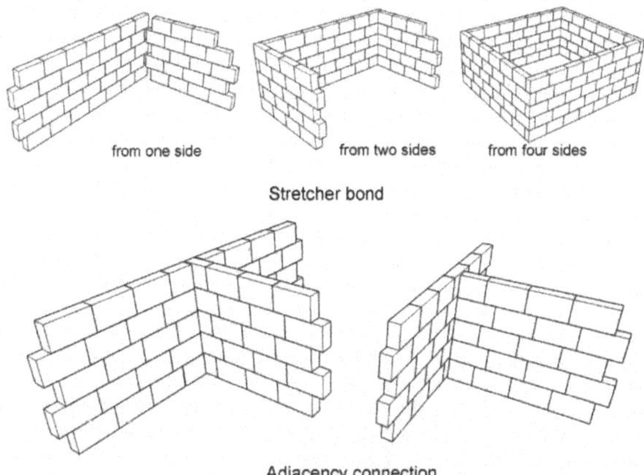

Fig. 2.2 Types of stretcher bond and adjacency connection. Author's illustration, CC BY-NC-ND.

21 The jurist explained how the construction material is laid in the case of a stretcher bond connection. Only the blocks' stretchers are visible, designated by the term 'half-blocks'; they are linked to the opposite wall by interweaving.

The method of use

The wall is presented as a partition wall between two distinct properties. It is a dividing wall commonly referred to as a contiguous wall. Al-Baroudi explains that it can be built in masonry composed of blocks of cohesive and viscous clay (that is, not mixed with sand), bricks, or even wood. He insists that the wall is only built to support the floor by sustaining its beams (palm trunks) and cannot be built to provide shade.

Precedence

An important criterion in determining the owner of the wall is distinguishing the person who has precedence in terms of use. This person has the right of ownership of the wall. Precedence is in the order of priority; in Islamic law, anything old corresponding to the law must be left intact unless there is evidence to the contrary because the persistence of something for a long time is proof that it is legitimate.[22] This criterion is also used in determining easements, the rights of the road, the right to water and so on.

Contiguous properties without tangible connection

Contiguous properties without concrete connection can be defined as a situation where the only connections between two contiguous properties are the neighbourhood and the party wall. The party wall can be the subject of a dispute between the owners of the two properties that adjoin it, especially in the absence of a proof of ownership or a declaration of non-ownership, or a recognition or cause of preference. There are two types of case described. The first is where the wall is not connected to the two properties either by a stretcher bond or by an adjacency connection and does not support palm beams. At this point, the wall must be divided between the two neighbours identically and with abandonment of cause (Fig. 2.3a).[23] The second case predicts that, despite the discontinuity

22 Ali Haydar, *Durar al-ḥukkām šarḥ majallat al-aḥkām* [*Explanation of the Journal of Provisions*], 4 vols. (Beirut: Dār al-Kutub Al-Ilmiyyah, 2018), I, p. 19.

23 This is reported in the text as a judgment that leaves things as they are, which means that the object of the conflict is to be left in the hands of the owner of the land. See Badr al-Din al-Aini, *Al-Bināya fī šarḥ al-hidāya* [*Explanation of the Guidance*], 13 vols. (Beirut: House of Scientific Books, 2000), XII, p. 309; Hervé

between the wall and the two neighbouring properties, there are beams supported by the wall that belong to the two parties. In this case, the situation is divided into several sub-cases (Fig. 2.3b).

If there is an equal number of beams on both sides, the wall is a common possession. Otherwise, if owner A has a beam placed higher than that of owner B, the latter would have ownership of the wall since he enjoys the right of precedence while maintaining A's beams on the condition that they do not damage the wall. If the beams are at the same height, there are three possibilities.

Firstly, each has three or more beams; the wall is a common possession; the abundance of beams does not change anything; and the two are equal in the mode of use since the wall is built to support the floor, which requires at least three beams.

Secondly, A has three beams and B has two. It could be that the wall is a common property; alternatively, it may simply be attributed to owner A. According to Al-Baroudi, the latter opinion is most suitable, considering the role of the wall as a support for the roof.

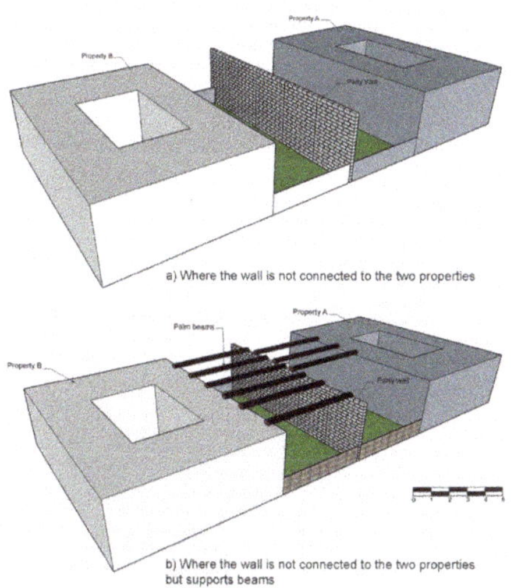

Fig. 2.3 Cases of contiguous properties without concrete connection. Author's illustration, CC BY-NC-ND.

Bleuchot, *Droit musulman*, 2 vols. (Marseille: Presses Universitaires d'Aix-Marseille, 2015), II, p. 470. The judge can prevent the plaintiff from going on with the trial, such as by instructing him: 'You have no right' or 'you are forbidden to claim' (Ali Haidar, *Explanation of the Journal of Provisions*, IV, p. 573).

Thirdly, A has three beams and B has only one. Al-Baroudi decides that the wall must be attributed to A but without removing the beams of B.[24] He also raises the question about the void above the wall attributed to A, since A already enjoys property rights to the wall, whereas B only has the right to support his beams.

Connection between the wall and adjacent buildings

A connection between the wall and adjacent buildings is characterised by the presence of a connection between the party wall and the two adjoining constructions, as well as several arguments that favour one side over the other. In fact, there are two conditions—either the wall is connected to the two parties' homes, or it is only connected to a single neighbour's dwelling. Several cases are distinguished for each situation.

The wall is connected to the two neighbouring houses

The first such case is if the wall is connected to the two houses on one, two or four sides by a stretcher bond or an adjacency connection without beams. Only one side is enough to confirm the liaison; therefore, the party wall is considered common property (Fig. 2.4a).

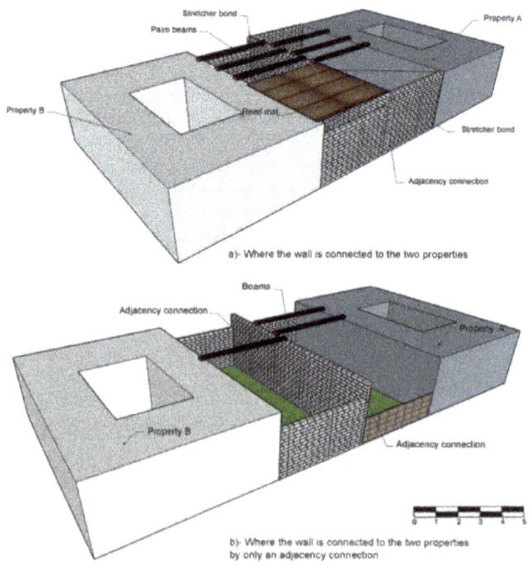

Fig. 2.4 Cases of connection to the two properties. Author's illustration, CC BY-NC-ND.

24 This is justified in that it is a judgment of an argument or a right to exception, a judgment based on the examination of the wall's situation and not for cancellation or revocation.

If the wall is connected to the two houses by a stretcher bond and only one of the two parties has beams hanging on it, the one that has the link has priority. However, if the wall is connected to both houses and each of them has beams placed on it, it will be divided evenly between them for equality of cause and confirmation of the use of the wall by both. It is also assigned to both evenly when the party wall is linked to A by a stretcher bond on one side and to B from two sides.

If the wall is connected to one property by a stretcher bond, while in the other property we find a reed mat placed on the wall for shade, ownership is then attributed to the stretcher bond holder because the presence or absence of the reed mat is equal and does not change anything. The party wall and the two houses are linked by an adjacency connection: if we find the same number of beams placed on either side, the wall is a common property of the two contestants. If the number is different, the judgement is made according to the basis of the three beams. If only one has beams, then he is the owner of the wall (Fig. 2.4b).

The wall is linked to a single property

If the party wall is linked to neighbour A by a stretcher bond from the four corners,[25] while A or B has beams, the wall ownership goes to the holder of the bond. If the wall is linked to A by an adjacency connection, while B has beams, the wall then reverts to B's ownership. However, if these beams belong to A, then the wall belongs to A absolutely (Fig. 2.5).

If the wall is linked to A by a stretcher bond and by an adjacency connection to B, the former has the right to the wall.

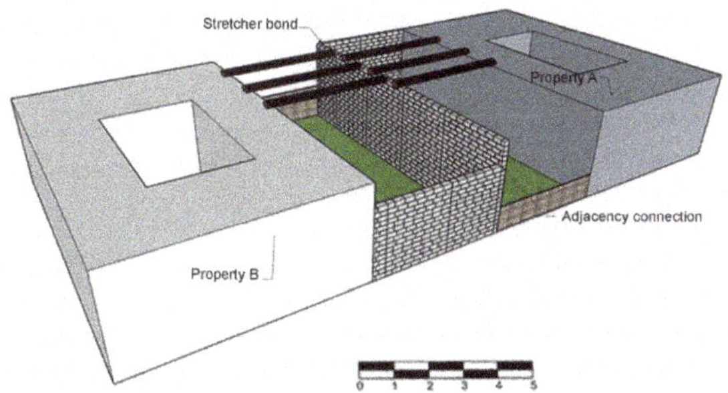

Fig. 2.5 Where the wall is connected to only one of the properties either by adjacency connection or stretcher bond. Author's illustration, CC BY-NC-ND.

25 The contested wall's masonry is linked by overlap to two other orthogonal walls, which are linked to a fourth wall.

Utility of jurisprudence heritage in the management of the medina

From this analysis, it can be seen that certain distinctive elements of the neighbourhood and party wall relationships could be beneficial to resolve current joint ownership and neighbourhood conflicts, or to help during the restoration phase. These are: the construction of storeys; the loan of the wall by its owner to the neighbour; an extension on the empty space of the adjacent street; the permitted height of the construction; the determination of the real owner of the wall; the mode, techniques and materials of construction used; the presence and number of beams; the existence of an opening; and the criterion of precedence. Based on observation and direct inspection of the building for a fair and equitable judgement: the party wall is a structural element whose only role is to lift and support the roof. An essential criterion in determining its owner is the inspection of the type of use, its nature, and its date. The person with precedent takes priority, especially when they have built something; this is a strongly endorsed argument.

A stretcher bond is a finished construction; therefore, the presence of a stretcher bond is considered valid evidence of the laying of the beams since the former preceded the latter. When beams are set on the wall, this is an act of preparation to build a roof, so it is more valuable than an adjacency connection. Assigning the wall to one of the neighbours does not give the neighbour the right to remove what the other has in terms of beams, parapets or reed mats on the wall. The person can continue to use it as long as it does not cause damage to the neighbour's property.

For jurists, the principles of not causing damage and helping neighbours were the main guides to regulate these relationships and resolve any conflict. Evolving over time and in relation to the requirements and nature of Islamic cities, several legal rules and behaviours developed over time, such as those mentioned in the *Epistle*.

Resolving wall conflicts requires a thorough knowledge of construction issues and their technology, which confirms the jurist's ability and legal and architectural knowledge. In general, this allowed jurists to carry out the task of controlling and organising the urban fabric of the medina of Tunis in the absence of the municipality at that time, given the fact that the first municipality was founded in Tunis in

1858. They based their task on the customary law, which examined the connection between the party wall and its surroundings.

The customary techniques and building materials used in this space, relating to the architectural culture passed down from one generation to another, have the potential to solve a variety of disputes between neighbours. While these rules have been passed down orally, this does not exclude the possibility that they may have been written down at some point in time, a supposition justified by the mention of several references that go back to the basis of the Hanafi doctrine. It also shows the evolving and flexible nature of Hanafi jurisprudence, allowing it to adapt to any period and situation as long as the public and private benefit is guaranteed. Although the regency had a Malikite majority, the Hanafi rite was used because Hanafi governance was in place, with seemingly clear influence at the level of the mosques and mausoleums, as well as at the level of the medina. Ibn Abi Dhiaf said that during the reign of Hammouda Pacha Bey (1759-1814), people eagerly moved towards agriculture, commerce and industries and the country experienced urban development, financial prosperity and wealth under some Ottoman rulers,[26] with urban extensions and constructions of new dwellings in the suburbs that potentially caused neighbourhhood conflicts requiring resolution. Even today, these customs continue to exist and operate in a tacit way but are recognised between neighbours (they include the customs of privacy, the prohibition of looking into your neighbour's house, the prohibition of illegal occupation of the street, restrictions on heights of buildings, etc.). This is true not only in the medinas (Tunis, Kairouan, Sousse, etc.) but also in new cities built since the 1980s with a similar (or even a different) configuration where the houses are isolated.

Hanafi jurisprudence largely inspired the Ottoman Urbanism Code called *Madjallah*,[27] which ceased to function after the Westernisation of Ottoman law. Following their colonisation[28], the Maghreb countries, including Tunisia, adopted the European model of development, which

---

26 Ibn Abi Dhiyaf, *Itḥāf ahl al-zamān bi akhbār mulūk Tūnis wa ʿahd al-amān* [*Present of the Men of our Time. Chronicles of the Kings of Tunis and the Fundamental Pact*], 8 vols., ed. by the Commission of Inquiry of the Ministry of Cultural Affairs (Tunis: Arabic House of the Book, 1999), III, p. 78.

27 This code was promulgated in 1882 by the Ottoman Empire as urban Islamic law.

28 Starting with the colonisation of Algeria in 1830, Tunisia in 1881and Libya in 1911.

involved an urban planning code. As Houcine has shown, technical and material innovations pursued by most of the provincial cities, especially the Maghreb cities and medinas, have always been accompanied by recourse to European laws and the abandonment of Islamic ones, which are better suited to Muslim life and spatial practices, especially in terms of contiguity and joint ownership.[29] Not only are these regulations able to resolve conflict issues, but they are also fundamental to understanding the traditional basis of the rules of neighbourhood conviviality in the whole medina. As Houcine notes, 'We have continued to adopt Western planning laws and instruments, without worrying about their inadequacies to the socio-cultural realities of Muslim nations'.[30]

According to Van Staëvel, by analysing the normative legal discourse devoted to the property regime, it becomes possible to outline some of the particular features of social practices and representations of space, both domestic and urban, in cities of the medieval Muslim Occident.[31]

European laws have failed to protect medinas from vandalism and the loss of homogeneity and uniformity.[32] With this study, we have aimed to demonstrate the utility of Islamic jurisprudence in future reforms of the legislation regulating Tunisian medinas, which are the subject of continual debates regarding the conservation and preservation of their identity. It is essential to understand the reasoning behind their creation and to consider the Islamic architectural and urban law in future processes of urban redevelopment. The medina is a historical urban space with a long and complex tradition. Its efficient management requires a functional grasp of the principles and urban

29 This has included even harmful redevelopment operations in historic centres, namely the '*éventrement*' or demolition of *cul-de-sacs* to control and connect the old and new cities (Tlemcen, Constantine and Tunis, with an unfinished project from 1957 providing for the opening of the medina by a boulevard connecting Bourguiba Street to the Kasbah district).

30 Abdelmalek Houcine, 'La mitoyenneté dans la jurisprudence islamique', *Tracé (bulletin technique de la Suisse romande)*, 1 (2011), 6–15 (p. 7).

31 Van Staëvel, *Droit mālikite et habitat à Tunis au XIVe siècle*, pp. 10–11.

32 The urban planning regulations of the Urban Development Plan of the Municipality of Tunis insist on respecting the medina as an important piece of heritage and maintaining the standards that regulate it: preservation of volumetric homogeneity, a fixed height, lighting thanks to the interior courtyard, etc. Despite the existence of this code, violations are observed in some neighbourhoods, including height overruns, volumetric breaks, pollution, graffiti, etc.

standards inspired by the ancient rules that historically generated and organised the medina.

The persistence of the medina's urban fabric reflects the area's history and suggests that these legal rules have proven their effectiveness. Many issues related to housing, property and joint ownership remain largely unchanged over time. Today, despite the presence of the relevant authorities and the Urban Code, transgressions are prevalent in the old cities and have no deterrents or solutions.

The manuscript *An Epistle on Disputed Contiguous Walls*, and the study of ancient jurisprudence in general, is useful to understand the laws governing the medina. A broader and more comprehensive look at this set of rules makes it possible to discern the vitality and complexity of the building processes of the past and to link them to the present. In this way, we can better understand which practices are best suited to preserve the architectural and urban heritage of spaces in historic centres, and what rules to apply to respect private and public property, especially the quality of the places in which we live. The past offers valuable insights for finding solutions in the present.

Conclusion

The interest of studying Muslim legal manuscripts lies in understanding the mechanisms of city formation through the discernment of social practices and constructive and legal customs that have persisted because of their effectiveness. This has created an opportunity to clarify, via the study of neighbourhood relationships, the mechanisms and parameters responsible for the functioning of the medina before the municipality (founded in 1858 in Tunis) replaced jurists, *qadis* and guilds. It is an attempt to determine their role and to understand how citizens shaped their living environment.

This study does not advocate the adoption of these manuscripts as a code of urbanism, but rather highlights their utility in resolving urban problems, many of which remain largely similar despite population growth and the evolution of needs, techniques and building materials. Such manuscripts thus provide valuable references for those developing the new rules governing the medina, but are nevertheless often considered outdated, and as such, neglected. By demonstrating their relevance, this study seeks to reverse this trend and encourage researchers to study them.

Though often overlooked, current practices of joint ownership constitute an important aspect of legal and cultural heritage, which can be observed in the urban fabric of the medina, where they continue to be functional despite the changes that have occurred over time. The restoration of some districts like the Hafsia Quarter have been undertaken in the image of the existing urban fabric, benefiting from elements discussed by Islamic laws—height restrictions, houses with courtyards, the prohibition of the obstruction of the street, non-opposing doors, respect for one's neighbour and so on. Throughout history, these laws have proven their effectiveness and adaptability, in addition to being a significant element of cultural and intellectual heritage. For these reasons, they must be preserved and incorporated into modern codes and laws.

Bibliography

Abdelmalek, Houcine, 'La mitoyenneté dans la jurisprudence islamique', *Tracé (bulletin technique de la Suisse romande)*, 1 (2011), 6–15.

Akbar, Jamel, *A Crisis in the Built Environment: The Case of the Muslim City* (Leiden: E. J. Brill, 1988).

Al-Baroudi, Muhammad bin Hussain bin Ibrahim, *Risālat Fatḥ al-Raḥman fī mas'lat al-Tanāz'u fī al-ḥitān* [*Epistle on Disputed Contiguous Walls*], Tunis, National Library, MS 03933, MS 09732.

Azab, Khaled, *Fiqh al-'imāra al-Islāmiyya* [*Islamic Jurisprudence of Architecture*] (Egypt: University Publishing House, 1997).

Hakim, Besim Selim, *Arabic-Islamic Cities: Building and Planning Principles* (New York: Routledge, 2010).

Jayyusi, Salma K., Holod, Renata, Petruccioli, Attilio, and Raymond, André, eds., *The City in the Islamic World* (Leiden, Boston: Brill, 2008).

M'halla, Moncef, 'La médina un art de bâtir', *Africa* (*Institut national du patrimoine de Tunis*), 12 (1998), 33–98, https://www.inp2020.tn/periodiques/atp/atp12.pdf

Mazzoli-Guintard, Christine, *Vivre à Cordoue au Moyen Âge: Solidarités citadines en terre d'Islam aux Xe-XIe siècles* (Rennes: Presses universitaires de Rennes, 2003), https://doi.org/10.4000/books.pur.17013

O'Meara, Simon, 'A Legal Aesthetic of Medieval and Pre-Modern Arab Muslim Urban Architectural Space', *Journal of Arabic and Islamic Studies*, 9 (2009), 1–17, https://doi.org/10.5617/jais.4594

Robert Brunschvig, 'Urbanisme médiéval et droit musulman', *Revue des études islamiques*, XV (1947), 127–55.

Safak, Ali, 'Urbanism and Family Residence in Islamic law', *Ekistics*, 280 (1980), 21–25.

Uthman, Muhammad Abd al-Sattar, *Al-Madīna al-Islāmiyya* [*The Islamic City*] (Cairo: Dar al-Afaq al-Arabiyah, 1999).

Van Staëvel, Jean Pierre, *Droit mālikite et habitat à Tunis au XIVe siècle. Conflits de voisinage et normes juridiques d'après le texte du maître-maçon Ibn al-Rāmī* (Cairo: Institut français d'archéologie, 2008).

II. CULTURAL HERITAGE AND INTANGIBLE COMPONENTS

3. Revisiting Definitions and Challenges of Intangible Cultural Heritage: The Case of the Old Centre of Mashhad

Sepideh Shahamati, Ayda Khaleghi and Sasan Norouzi

Introduction

Urban areas are currently facing powerful processes of change and transformation. The rising challenges of the twenty-first century, such as the exponential increase in urbanisation and the growing number of urban development projects, globalisation and its homogenisation processes, and the changing role of cities as drivers of economic activity and development, have had major impacts on the physical and social character of cities. Such processes are continuously reshaping urban areas and have led to numerous threats to cultural diversity and pluralism.[1]

Because of these growing threats, safeguarding the identity and diversity of communities and urban areas has been identified as a matter of emergency by the United Nations Educational, Scientific and Cultural

1 Francesco Bandarin and Ron Van Oers, *The Historic Urban Landscape: Managing Heritage in an Urban Century* (Oxford: John Wiley & Sons, 2012).

 https://doi.org/10.11647/OBP.0388.03

Organization (UNESCO) in the last three decades.[2] This in turn has given rise to various charters and conventions[3] which not only provide guidelines and policies for protecting the identity of communities, but encompass a more universally accepted understanding of heritage and its complexities. As a result, heritage has come to be conceptualised globally based not only on its tangible and monumental forms, but also its humanistic value.[4]

Based on UNESCO's definition, cultural heritage consists of both tangible and intangible assets. Tangible heritage includes monuments, artefacts and the built environment, while intangible heritage is characterised as an invisible dimension[5] which can take the form of songs, myths, beliefs, superstitions, oral poetry, memories, performing arts and other types of social practices. Because intangible heritage is often deeply connected to collective identities and a sense of place,[6] it is an important aspect of safeguarding cultural diversity in cities that are increasingly threatened by globalisation and its homogenising processes.[7] Although the recognition of the intangible dimensions of culture has heightened the attention given to cultural diversity and social values, there are still various challenges to achieving a more comprehensive understanding of such values in cities. UNESCO recognised intangible heritage via an official nomination and recognition process based on specific criteria.[8] Yet, most of the invisible assets of local areas face difficulties in being recognised through such processes.

---

2 Noriko Aikawa, 'A Historical Overview of the Preparation of the UNESCO International Convention for the Safeguarding of the Intangible Cultural Heritage', *Museum International*, 56:1–2 (2004), 137–149.

3 D. Fairchild Ruggles and Helaine Silverman, 'From Tangible to Intangible Heritage', in *Intangible Heritage Embodied*, ed. by Helaine Silverman and D. Fairchild Ruggles (New York: Springer, 2009), pp. 1–14.

4 Richard Kurin, 'Safeguarding Intangible Cultural Heritage in the 2003 UNESCO Convention: A Critical Appraisal', *Museum International*, 56:1–2 (2004), 66–77.

5 Barbara Kirshenblatt-Gimblett, 'Intangible Heritage as Metacultural Production 1', *Museum International*, 56:1–2 (2004), 52–65.

6 Alys Longley and Nancy Duxbury 'Introduction: Mapping Cultural Intangibles', *City, Culture and Society*, 7:1 (2016), 1–7; Rohit Jigyasu, 'The Intangible Dimension of Urban Heritage', in *Reconnecting the City: The Historic Urban Landscape Approach and the Future of Urban Heritage*, ed. by Francesco Bandarin, Francesco and Ron Van Oers (Chichester: John Wiley & Sons, 2014), pp. 129–160; Longley and Duxbury, 'Introduction: Mapping Cultural Intangibles', pp. 1–7.

7 Longley and Duxbury, 'Introduction: Mapping Cultural Intangibles'.

8 Caroline Bertorelli, 'The Challenges of UNESCO Intangible Cultural Heritage', 観光学研究= *Journal of Tourism Studies*, 17 (2018), 91–117.

With the current emphasis on measurable and quantifiable aspects of cities in urban planning practice and research, the marginalisation of the 'soft' and subjective elements that are otherwise known as intangible is inevitable.[9] The importance placed on measurable features of urban areas has led to decisions that prioritise the values of the built environment at the dire expense of the social environment. Relevant examples of such decisions can be seen in various urban redevelopment projects that have resulted in the displacement of residents through the gentrification process or forced eviction.[10]

Urban interventions have contributed to the modification of the urban fabric without considering the accumulated identity of places and their cultural, social and historical complexities. Even when mainstream planning practices acknowledge cultural heritage, they tend to be limited to what is embedded in the built environment. Cultural maps designed for planning purposes are systematically limited to sites, monuments and buildings that can be precisely pinpointed in the physical environment, while dismissing any intangible dimensions that cannot be easily measured or clearly circumscribed spatially.[11] These maps contribute to the erasure of intangible heritage in our collective memories. Because of its invisible nature, these intangible dimensions are often in danger of disappearance and destruction. This problem is heightened in historic towns or boroughs built on intangible values.

To investigate this subject in greater depth, this chapter looks at a historic city built on intangible values—the city of Mashhad in northeast Iran. With a population of roughly three million people, Mashhad is the second largest city in the country after Tehran, and has been built around a holy shrine for Shia Muslims. The Holy Shrine has historically determined the socio-economic conditions of the city as well as its architectural emphasis on religious values, such as humbleness. The story of Mashhad shows that intangible values that have survived for centuries are now endangered by the growing threats of globalisation and urban revitalisation. In focusing on this story, this

9 Darko Radovic, 'Measuring the Non-Measurable: On Mapping Subjectivities in Urban Research', *City, Culture and Society*, 7:1 (2016), 17–24.

10 Ted Grevstad-Nordbrock and Igor Vojnovic, 'Heritage-Fueled Gentrification: A Cautionary Tale from Chicago', *Journal of Cultural Heritage*, 38 (2019), 261–70.

11 Sharon M. Jeannotte, 'Story-Telling About Place: Engaging Citizens in Cultural Mapping', *City, Culture and Society*, 7:1 (2016), 35–41.

chapter highlights the importance of reconceptualising intangible heritage not only in international charters but also in research and practice. This study seeks a reconceptualisation of cultural heritage that can lead to more innovative and concrete ways of integrating these assets in decision making.

Redefining intangible heritage

UNESCO has played a leading role in heightening the level of global attention paid to the intangible dimension of culture. UNESCO's approach to intangible cultural heritage is rooted primarily in the Convention for the Safeguarding of Intangible Cultural Heritage (2003), followed by the Convention on the Protection and Promotion of the Diversity of Cultural Expressions (2005).[12] Even before the 2003 Convention, UNESCO initiated other activities for promoting intangible cultural heritage worldwide, including the Recommendation on the Safeguarding of Traditional Culture and Folklore (1989), the Living Human Treasure System (1993) and the Proclamation of Masterpieces of the Oral and Intangible Heritage of Humans (1998).[13]

The Convention for the Safeguarding of Intangible Cultural Heritage (2003) was a decisive point in the conceptual understanding of intangible heritage. It reflected the efforts made by the international community to define intangible heritage and provided a series of recommendations for safeguarding these assets against deterioration and disappearance. Based on the definition of the Convention, intangible cultural heritage includes oral traditions, languages, performing arts, social practices, traditional knowledge and practices concerning nature and the universe, as well as traditional artisanship.[14] More specifically, Article 2.1 of the Convention defines 'intangible cultural heritage' as the 'practices, representations, expressions

12 Longley and Duxbury, 'Introduction: Mapping Cultural Intangibles'.

13 Laurajane Smith and Natsuko Akagawa, *Intangible Heritage* (London: Routledge, 2009).

14 Henrietta Marrie, 'The UNESCO Convention for the Safeguarding of the Intangible Cultural Heritage and the Protection and Maintenance of the Intangible Cultural Heritage of Indigenous Peoples', in *Intangible Heritage,* ed. by Laurajane Smith and Natsuko Akagawa (New York: Routledge, 2009), p. 169.

and skills as well as the instruments, objects, artefacts and cultural spaces associated with communities and groups that are constantly being recreated by communities in response to their environment and provides them with a sense of identity and continuity'.[15]

UNESCO's definition of intangible heritage laid the groundwork for a better understanding of this concept, providing a comprehensive conceptualization of its meaning and an enumeration of its different forms and representations. However, this approach to intangible cultural heritage has also been met with a range of criticisms. One major criticism of this Convention and of UNESCO's approach relates to the use of lists and inventories for identifying, recognising and valorising cultural traditions and dividing them into material and immaterial traditions.[16] UNESCO's differentiation between tangible (material) and intangible (immaterial) culture reflects a Eurocentric view of cultural heritage and thus is inappropriate for interpreting the cultures of many groups. In the definition provided by UNESCO, intangible heritage is characterised as an invisible part of cultural heritage that is separate from what we consider tangible heritage, such as monuments and artefacts. However, the interconnection of intangible, tangible and natural heritages[17] must not be overlooked.[18] Taking natural heritage into consideration, it can be argued that the 'land is not only interwoven by biodiversity, habitat and ecosystem but also our senses, emotions and connections to one

---

15 UNESCO, 'Text of the Convention for the Safeguarding of Intangible Cultural Heritage' General Conference of the United Nations Educational, Scientific and Cultural Organization, thirty-second session, Paris, September 29–October 17 (2003).

16 Walter Leimgruber, 'Switzerland and the UNESCO Convention on Intangible Cultural Heritage', *Journal of Folklore Research: An International Journal of Folklore and Ethnomusicology*, 47:1–2 (2010), 161–196; Valdimar Hafstein, 'Intangible Heritage as a List: From Masterpieces to Representation', in *Intangible Heritage*, ed. by Laurajane Smith and Natsuko Akagawa (New York: Routledge, 2009), pp. 93–111; Kumi Kato, 'Community, Connection and Conservation: Intangible Cultural Values in Natural Heritage—the Case of Shirakami-sanchi World Heritage Area', *International Journal of Heritage Studies*, 12:5 (2006), 458–473 (93–111).

17 Natural heritage refers to natural features, geological and physiographical formations and delineated areas that constitute the habitat of threatened species of animals and plants and natural sites of value from the point of view of science, conservation or natural beauty (UNESCO, 1972).

18 Kirshenblatt-Gimblett, 'Intangible Heritage as Metacultural Production 1'.

another'.[19] The conservation practices of many communities have been developed through their cultural values and understandings, which have reshaped the natural landscapes over time.[20] Thus, it is relevant to reconceptualise natural heritage through its interconnectedness with intangible heritage.

Similarly, intangible heritage can be considered inseparable from material and tangible heritage. The separation of tangible and intangible heritage is inherently imprecise, as the construction and use of tangible heritage is often reliant on intangible heritage such as certain skills, traditional knowledge or social practices.[21] More specifically, tangible heritage can be considered slow events created via specific processes and skills with particular values and meanings to the community.[22] From this perspective, material culture gets its significance from socially attributed meanings rather than physical characteristics. Ise Jingu, the sacred shrine in Japan, is rebuilt every twenty years without undergoing any material changes or any changes in its use. The process of rebuilding the shrine takes eight years and has been carried out sixty-one times since the shrine's creation by local carpenters who remember and try to pass on their knowledge. Therefore, Ise Jingu is a slow event related to the meanings, knowledge, skills and values that intertwine with the physical aspect of the building.[23] This example challenges the validity of separating tangible and intangible heritage as suggested by international organisations[24] as this would neglect the essence of the concept of heritage and its inherent complexities.

A second issue with the definition of intangible heritage adopted by UNESCO and others is that it implies a direct connection with communities. UNESCO's definition is structured around preserving the cultural practices of communities. Although the relationship between intangible heritage and communities is important, the definition of community becomes blurrier in the urban context. Because of the dynamic and flexible nature of the concept of community in cities, people might

19 Kato, 'Community, Connection and Conservation', 67.
20 Ibid.
21 Kirshenblatt-Gimblett, 'Intangible Heritage as Metacultural Production 1'.
22 Marilena Vecco, 'A Definition of Cultural Heritage: From the Tangible to the Intangible', *Journal of Cultural Heritage*, 11:3 (2010), 321–324.
23 Kirshenblatt-Gimblett, 'Intangible Heritage as Metacultural Production 1'.
24 Silverman and Fairchild, 'From Tangible to Intangible Heritage'.

belong to various groups and communities temporarily based on shared interests, such as music, lifestyle or even sexual orientation. Therefore, by definition, communities may be temporary, highly complex and interrelated. The community-centric approach to intangible heritage can also be criticised as biased towards well-organised groups that can better promote their roles and perspectives.[25]

Viewing heritage through the lens of communities can also limit its scope to social practices. In other words, the intangible heritage of communities may be viewed as separate from places and mostly contingent on the human bearers of tradition. Based on this perspective, some might defend the problematic assertion that the displacement of communities does not necessarily affect their intangible heritage. Given these concerns, it is beneficial to rethink the conceptualisation of communities within common definitions of intangible cultural heritage, particularly as they relate to the significance on the places in which the traditions are practiced.

Places and landscapes[26] offer an interesting framework for examining the relationships between people and cultural heritage. As a theoretical concept, landscapes can be understood as 'produced and lived in an everyday, practical, very material and repetitively reaffirming sense'.[27] This concept can be characterised by social practices embedded in a spatial context.[28] The landscape approach in heritage studies envisions urban landscapes as accumulations of the multiplicity of meanings, significance and collective and individual relevance to the past, present and future.[29] This approach highlights the importance of spatiality and meanings in different contexts, supporting the idea that individuals

---

25 Arno Van der Hoeven, 'Networked Practices of Intangible Urban Heritage: The Changing Public Role of Dutch Heritage Professionals', *International Journal of Cultural Policy*, 25:2 (2019), 232–45.

26 Grete Swensen, Gro B Jerpåsen, Oddrun Sæter, and Mari Sundli Tveit, 'Capturing the Intangible and Tangible Aspects of Heritage: Personal Versus Official Perspectives in Cultural Heritage Management', *Landscape Research*, 38:2 (2013), 203–21.

27 James Duncan and Nancy Duncan, 'Can't Live with Them, Can't Landscape without Them: Racism and the Pastoral Aesthetic in Suburban New York,' *Landscape Journal*, 22:2 (2003), 88–98 (p. 7).

28 Swensen et al., 'Capturing the intangible and tangible aspects of heritage'.

29 Loes Veldpaus, Ana R. Pereira Roders, and Bernard J.F. Colenbrander, 'Urban Heritage: Putting the Past into the Future', *The Historic Environment: Policy & Practice*, 4:1 (2013), 3–18.

and groups are inseparable from the places where they live.[30] As Relph emphasises, 'an individual is not distinct from his place; he is that place'.[31] The daily lives of individuals and groups shape the places they inhabit and vice versa. Understanding intangible heritage in an urban context, which is often characterised by the multiplicity of communities and social groups, can be achieved through the study of the lives of its inhabitants and of their relationships with the built environment. In other words, rather than viewing intangible heritage as cultural expressions created by and dependent upon communities, we can look at the relationship between places and people regardless of the communities they might often be associated with. This is not to say that identifying communities and their cultural expressions should not be a priority; rather, it is to acknowledge places as valuable sources of knowledge that can help us better understand intangible assets. By examining places and the various processes that have shaped them, we can more clearly identify their intangible assets.[32]

As mentioned earlier, in order to understand intangible heritage, it is essential to pay attention to the continuous interaction between people and the physical environment.[33] Intangible heritage can be considered an inclusive dimension of culture derived from the meanings and values people give to the environment. Based on this understanding, intangible heritage can be reconceptualised as heritage that emerges through the continuous interaction of people with their physical environment over time. It is embodied in people and is connected to places, objects and natural landscapes. Intangible cultural heritage can be manifested in values, beliefs, representations, skills, knowledge and social connections. This understanding diverges from the mainstream conceptualisation of tangible and intangible that confines them to certain forms. Reconceptualising heritage as an accumulation of tangible and intangible dimensions that have been interwoven into places has the potential to broaden our understanding of historic towns and centres.

The next section of this chapter delves into the history of the Iranian city of Mashhad, a city built on religious values. Based on archival

30 Swensen et al., 'Capturing the intangible and tangible aspects of heritage'.
31 Edward Relph, *Place and Placelessness*, vol. 67 (London: Pion, 1976), p. 43.
32 Ibid.
33 Swensen et al., 'Capturing the intangible and tangible aspects of heritage'.

studies, two years of direct observations in the area and individual interviews with residents, business owners and pilgrims, this research outlines the importance of intangible religious values in the formation and evolution of Mashhad and the manifestations of such values in the built environment in relation to the growing challenges of the twenty-first century.

The story of Mashhad: A city built on intangible values

Intangible heritages have played an important role in the development of the city of Mashhad since its origins in the ninth century. Mashhad began to expand and flourish following the death of Imam Reza in the year 818 AD (the eighth Shia Imam). Historically, there was a town in the vicinity of Imam Reza's burial tomb named Sanabad. Over time, the number of pilgrims visiting the grave from Sanabad and other towns increased, leading to the creation of the first structure of Mashhad, which was a bazaar[34] built on the road linking Sanabad to Imam Reza's tomb.[35] Thus, it can be argued that the first structure of the city was built as a direct result of religious visitors. With an increase in the number of pilgrims, many structures and buildings were constructed in the immediate vicinity. Over time, this growth led to the emergence of Mashhad as an independent city.

The growing importance of religious beliefs of Shias during the Safavid dynasty (the sixteenth to the eighteenth centuries) brought various urban elements, including numerous *karavansara* (equivalent to modern day hotels), bazaars, mosques and main transport routes.[36] As such, the city's roots, as well as its subsequent development were shaped by intangible values—as a result of people's affection for Imam Reza. The Holy Shrine and the tradition of pilgrimage not only created this city but also led to its growth. Religious values affected various

34 Alireza Rezvani, *Dar jostojuye howeyate šahre Mašhad* [*In Search for Mashhad's Identity*] (Tehran: Ministry of Housing and Urban Planning, 2005).

35 Ahmad Mahavan, *Târixe Mašhadol Rezâ* [*Mashhad's History*] (Mashhad: Mahavan, 2004); Rezvani, *Dar jostojuye howeyate šahre Mašhad.*

36 Ibid.; Maryam Mirahmadi, *Dino Dowlat* [*Religion and the State*] (Tehran: Amir Kabir, 1990).

dimensions of urban development in Mashhad, including its physical, economic, social and even environmental character.[37]

The economic character of the city has been built and reinforced through pilgrims and the culture of pilgrimage. Over time, not only has trade with pilgrims strengthened the economic development of Mashhad but the importance of souvenirs during pilgrimage has also contributed to the economic vitality and survival of this city.[38] Moreover, the culture of devotion has played an important role in its economic development. The religious value of donating wealth for the public good has always been influential in the growth of Mashhad. Various schools, mosques, gardens, cemeteries, hammams, mausoleums, qanats, bazaars and hospitals have been built as a gift from the wealthy families of the city to the public.[39] The religious character of the city has also been reflected in its social assets. Numerous social activities and relations have been shaped by religious traditions and celebrations, such as Ashura, Moharram and Ramazan. Mosques have been the centres of such religious activities during specific months and have created a strong social setting for residents and pilgrims. Despite all the recent developments, such cultural connections can still be seen in the centre of the city.

The most important aspect of Mashhad's character that has affected its current situation is its physical dimension, which, like its other aspects, was also based on religious values. Etemado Alsaltaneh described the exteriors and facades of buildings as extremely simple and modest, originating from the religious values of humility and equality.[40] One of the earliest Western visitors to Mashhad, James Bailie Fraser, also described the city's humble physical character, noting that this simplicity is one of

37 Vahid Tavassoli, 'Arzešhâye târixiye harame motahhare razavi dar šekl giri va tose'eye šahre Mašhade moqadas' [Historical Values of Creation and Development of Mashhad], International Congress on Revising Islamic Cultural Civilization and Islamic Cities with Focus on Mashhad (Mashhad: 2017).

38 Mahdi Seyedi, *Târixe šahre Mašhad* [*Mashhad's History*] (Tehran: Jami, 1999); Tavassoli 'Arzešhâye târixiye harame motahhare razavi dar šekl giri va tose'eye šahre Mašhade moqadas'.

39 Seyedi, *Târixe šahre Mašhad*.

40 Etemado Alsaltane, *Matlaelšams* [*Sunrise*] (Tehran: Farhangsara Publications: 1983).

the most striking features for visitors.[41] These qualities within the built environment, inspired by religious values, make Mashhad a city that has evolved based on the invisible and intangible values of spirituality, and demonstrate the necessity of recognising invisible values of heritage in historical assessments.

Intangible assets of Mashhad

Constructed based on intangible values, Mashhad has maintained its religious identity over the centuries. Furthermore, the built environment of the city has always had distinctive architectural qualities as compared with other historic Iranian towns, such as Yazd, Isfahan and Shiraz. A short description of its numerous intangible heritage assets is given below. These assets, while often overlooked by city planners and decision makers, make Mashhad an exemplar of a historic town based on intangible values.

Mashhad's centre is home to a rich variety of tradition bearers that sustained cultural continuity through their local knowledge, oral history and craftsmanship. As emphasised by UNESCO (2003), the tradition bearers play a vital role in the survival of the tangible and intangible assets of communities. Recognition of these figures contributes to the expansion of knowledge regarding the cultural assets of communities. In Mashhad, apart from their role in sustaining oral history and different forms of local knowledge, they have also been involved in constructing traditional institutions as settings for social activities in different neighbourhoods. Mahdiye Abedzadeh, one of Mashhad's important cultural institutions, was built and owned by the renown religious philanthropist Ali Asghar Abedzadeh. Over time, the institution has expanded in size, coming to encompass a number of buildings donated by Abedzadeh for cultural and religious purposes. The institution has become a social setting in the heart of various neighbourhoods for people to gather for religious or political debates, educational activities and other special events.

Certain places in each of the city's neighbourhoods are designated for meetings and social gatherings among residents. A study on the

41 James Bailie Fraser, *Safarnâmeye Fraser* [*Fraser's Travel Diary*], translated by Manouchehr Amiri (Tehran: Toos, 1821).

historic neighbourhoods of Mashhad by the Samen Research Institute[42] shows that each of the historic neighbourhoods has a centre where residents gather and socialise. These are often informal places known only by long-term residents. Yet, these places, which have been shaped through social connections, are threatened not only by redevelopment and construction projects but also by growing evictions of the residents and the loss of their social interactions.

Events play a significant role in the cultural survival of this city. Religious events in particular have shaped Mashhad's physical environment. Seven major religious events take place each year in Mashhad and they are integral to the physical and social character of the city. These special events, where people traditionally distribute food, drink and gifts, are an important part of Mashhad's spiritual and social vitality.

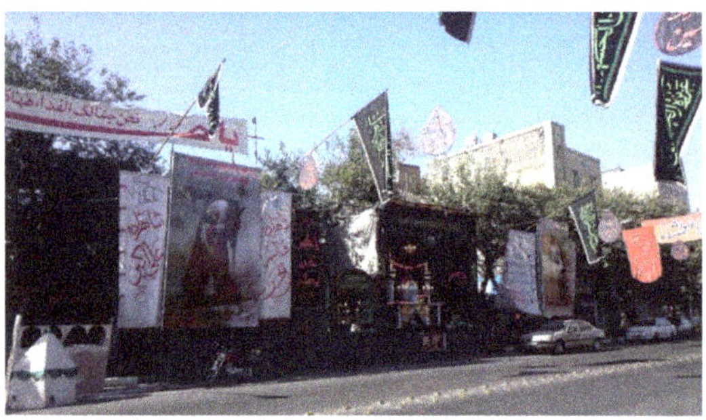

Fig. 3.1 Street installations for free food distribution during the month of Moharram, Mashhad. Author's photograph, 2016, CC BY-NC-ND.

There are yearly religious marches that take place in the streets leading to the Holy Shrine. During Tasua and Ashura, which are the two most important religious days for Shias, all the streets leading to the holy shrine are full of devout citizens. These groups come from Mashhad and all around the country to be in the vicinity of Imam Reza on these special days. Apart from the religious events held in the mosques, there are three important houses that have hosted the celebrants of Ashura and Tasua for over one hundred years. These houses are not listed officially as places of religious events, but they are well known by all the residents of surrounding neighbourhoods.

42 Samen Research Institute, *Asarâte tarhe tose'eye mantaqeye sâmen* [*Impacts of the Development Plan of Samen District*] (Mashhad: Samen Research Institute, 2018).

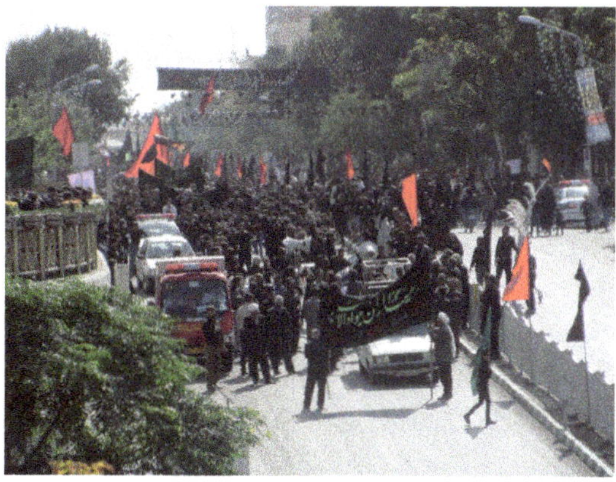

Fig. 3.2 Street marches towards the Holy Shrine during the Month of Moharram, Mashhad. Author's photograph, 2016, CC BY-NC-ND.

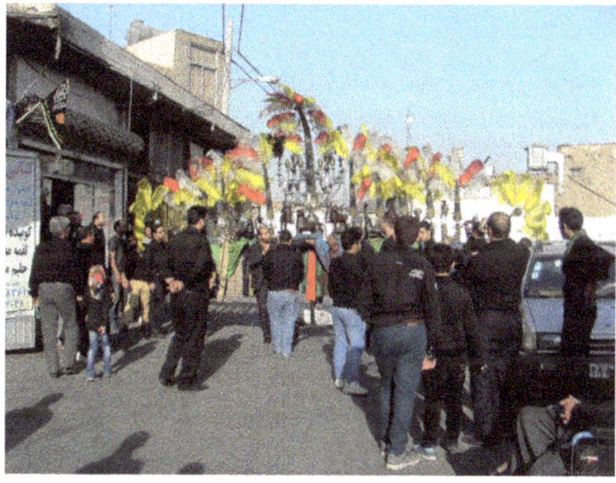

Fig. 3.3 Street performance during Moharram, Mashhad. Author's photograph, 2016, CC BY-NC-ND.

Religious performances have also been a source of cultural vitality in this area. These performances, inspired by historic events, have been conducted in special places that have been well-known in local knowledge and collective memory for one hundred years. Mashhad once housed ten such historic performance venues, but because of the neglect of these assets, only two of these locally important locations remain.

Food is also a significant part of the cultural identity of Mashhad. Not only does the city have a unique culture of distributing free food, but the distinctive dish of Mashhad, Sholeh,[43] is iconic for its traditional preparation methods. The making of this dish, which has been listed as intangible heritage in Iran, entails a convergence of spirituality, devotion and cultural values.[44] Still, although the recipe and the process of making Sholeh have been listed as national intangible heritage, the places in which this tradition takes place remain unrecognised. Every year, specific houses in the area cook this food and distribute it to the public. These houses, which have intangible values for residents, are often not prioritised in decision-making processes.

The aforementioned examples are just some of the rich cultural inheritances of the city of Mashhad—a city whose development has been shaped by religious traditions and values. However, Mashhad's intangible heritage assets have been neglected by both the Iranian National Heritage Listing and UNESCO lists, as well as by the city's decision makers and developers. As we will see in the following section, this negligence has resulted in massive transformations in the area that have threatened and destroyed both invisible and visible heritage.

The neglect of intangible heritage in the urban development plans of Mashhad

As mentioned above, the rich intangible cultural heritage of Mashhad has not been prioritised by decision makers and urban planners. The historic centre of the city, 360 hectares in size,[45] has witnessed massive transformations in different historical periods from the Safavid era (the sixteenth to the eighteenth century) to the present. Its first redevelopment programme led to the construction of many courtyards and passageways to the shrine in the Timurid (the fourteenth to the sixteenth centuries) and Safavid eras. The programme continued in the Pahlavi era (1925–1979) and later resulted in the disconnection of

43 Šole [Sholeh] is the traditional food of Mashhad, which is made of meat, beans and spices.

44 Isna, *Sabte melliye šoleye Mašhad* [*National Listing of Mashhad's Sholeh*] (Isna.ir, 2017), https://www.isna.ir/news/96071005128/

45 Elnaz Sarkheyli, Mojtaba Rafieian, and Ali Akbar Taghvaee, 'Assessing the Convergence Effects of Religious and Economic Forces on the Contemporary Changes of Form and Shape of Samen Region in Mashhad', *Motaleat Shahri*, 12 (2015), 87–101.

the bazaar from the Shrine and the construction of a large roundabout. These redevelopments were followed by a total relocation of the bazaar and extensive clearance around the shrine, which led to the destruction of many houses and retail stores during the second half of the twentieth century.[46]

One of the most controversial interventions in the historic centre of Mashhad and around the Holy Shrine was the renewal plan in 1966 proposed by the renowned Iranian architect, Borbor. This plan crucially overlooked the historic value of the area with the exception of a few buildings and proposed massive transformations of the built environment.[47] Further plans, especially the one implemented by Abdolazim Valian in 1973, led to the destruction of the urban fabric within 320 metres of the shrine.[48] However, the most impactful redevelopment and transformations in this district happened in 1992,[49] when a renewal plan stressed this area's inefficiency and lack of urban and architectural value, and proposed massive demolitions and reconstructions.

The plan defined its goals as follows: (i) improving the role and importance of the religious character of the city as a hub for Islam and Muslim pilgrims and (ii) increasing the economic competitiveness of the city at local, regional and international levels. The second goal involved a focus on the religious role of the city when amending the physical environment, satisfying the needs of pilgrims and providing opportunities for investment.[50] The plan proposed major transformations in the area; based on the recommendations, a large part of the centre had to be demolished and rebuilt. New forms of blocks and road

46 Elnaz Sarkheyli, Mojtaba Rafieian, and Ali Akbar Taghvaee, 'Qualitative Sustainability Assessment of the Large-Scale Redevelopment Plan in Samen District of Mashhad', *International Journal of Architecture and Urban Development*, 6:2 (2016), 49–58; Sarkheyli et al., 'Assessing the Convergence Effects of Religious and Economic forces on the Contemporary Changes of Form and Shape of Samen Region in Mashhad'.

47 Mostafa Akbari Motlagh, 'Barrasiye tajrobeye modâxele dar bâfte markaziye šahre mašhad' [Assessing Transformations in Mashhad's Central District], Sepidar Urban Planning and Architecture Research Institute (2014).

48 Sarkheyli et al., 'Qualitative Sustainability Assessment of the Large-Scale Redevelopment Plan in Samen District of Mashhad'.

49 Sarkheyli et al., 'Assessing the Convergence Effects of Religious and Economic forces on the Contemporary Changes of Form and Shape of Samen Region in Mashhad'.

50 Tash Consultant Engineers, *Tarhe nosâzi va bâzsâziye bâfte pirâmune harame motahhar* [*Regeneration of Holy Shrine's Surrounding District*] (Mashhad: MHDCC, 1994).

networks were built without consideration for the historic fabric of the area and mostly for the usage of short-term residents and tourists. This led to the dislocation of a high proportion of the original residents and the massive destruction of an urban fabric with a rich history. A large part of Mashhad's centre, which had residential infrastructure prior to the redevelopment proposals, was replaced by commercial and retail infrastructure. The decrease in the population of the area, from ~58,000 in 1991 to 32,851 in 2011, is also an indication of dislocation of residents from this area.[51]

In the aforementioned redevelopment plans, the historic value of this centre was assessed by the architectural value of the buildings. As mentioned above, the centre of Mashhad has been built upon religious values of humility and equity and did not have the common architectural qualities of Iranian historic centres. This led to the neglect of its intangible heritage value and as a result, to the destruction of its built as well as its intangible heritage.

Conclusion: The importance of reconceptualising intangible heritage in decision making

Cities are filled with cultural assets that may extend beyond the built environment and tangible manifestations. Historic urban environments are built on both material and immaterial elements. These invisible assets impact not only the daily lives of inhabitants, but also the designs and development of built landscapes.

The story of the evolution and development of Mashhad, as well as the challenges it is facing in the twenty-first century, shows the necessity of a reconceptualised perspective on intangible heritage. As a city built on intangible religious values, it is facing numerous challenges to the preservation and valorisation of its assets. The story of Mashhad shows that our current perspective towards listing tangible and intangible

51 Ahmad Reza Asgharpour Masule and Hossein Behravan, 'Cârcubi mafhumi barâye tahlile jâm'ešenâxti hamkâri miyane konešgarân dar barnâme nosâziye bâftahâye farsude bâ takid bar mantaqe sâmene mašhad' [A Conceptual Framework for Sociological Assessment of Cooperation between Actors in Redevelopment of Distressed Area Focusing on Samen District in Mashhad], *Mashhad Pazuhi*, 5 (2010), 35–56.

heritage is insufficient, and that there is a growing need for new tools and frameworks to better recognise and integrate these assets. Although novel theoretical frameworks and guidelines for a comprehensive understanding and representation of tangible and intangible assets have been introduced in the last two decades, the negligence of invisible assets in wider decision-making processes remains a significant problem. Whereas new methods, such as cultural mapping, seem to be a promising approach for identification and representation of tangible and intangible cultural assets, there are still various challenges related to them.[52]

Cultural mapping methods focus on processual approaches involving communities in defining and representing their cultural assets. Although the cultural mapping approach highlights the necessity of mapping both tangible and intangible assets, it is mostly focused on quantifiable and material resources while its treatment of intangible elements is often ambiguous.[53]

These challenges not only necessitate a new approach for identifying and representing intangible heritage with a fresh definition built on a place-related concepts, but they also call attention to the importance of a systematic method for wider planning and decision-making purposes. In the twenty-first century, the need to develop a systematic methodology capable of capturing and systematically representing the invisible essence of cultural heritage for urban researchers and decision makers is crucial. The methodological innovations should be primarily based on a revised concept of urban heritage, which liberates the notion from the constraints of listings and inventories and acknowledges the interconnectedness of visible and invisible assets. This reconceptualisation is an important step for the protection of the cultural identity of cities.

52 Nancy Duxbury, W. F. Garrett-Petts, and David MacLennan. *Cultural Mapping as Cultural Inquiry: Introduction to an Emerging Field of Practice* (New York: Routledge, 2015).

53 Duxbury et al., *Cultural Mapping as Cultural Inquiry*, p. 22.

Bibliography

Aikawa, Noriko, 'A Historical Overview of the Preparation of the UNESCO International Convention for the Safeguarding of the Intangible Cultural Heritage', *Museum International,* 56:1–2 (2004), 137–49, https://doi.org/10.1111/j.1350-0775.2004.00468.x.

Akbari Motlagh, Mostafa, 'Barrasiye tajrobeye modâxele dar bâfte markaziye šahre mašhad' [Assessing Transformations in Mashhad's Central District], Sepidar Urban Planning and Architecture Research Institute (2014).

Asgharpour Masule, Ahmad Reza and Behravan, Hossein, 'Cârcubi mafhumi barâye tahlile jâm'ešenâxti hamkâri miyane konešgarân dar barnâme nosâziye bâftahâye farsude bâ takid bar mantaqe sâmene mašhad' [A Conceptual Framework for Sociological Assessment of Cooperation between Actors in Redevelopment of Distressed Area Focusing on Samen District in Mashhad], *Mashhad Pazuhi,* 5 (2010), 35–56.

Bailie Fraser, James, *Safarnâmeye Fraser* [*Fraser's Travel Diary*], translated by Amiri, Manouchehr (Tehran: Toos, 1821).

Bandarin, Francesco, and Van Oers, Ron, *The Historic Urban Landscape: Managing Heritage in an Urban Century* (Oxford: John Wiley & Sons, 2012), https://doi.org/10.1002/9781119968115

Bertorelli, Caroline, 'The Challenges of UNESCO Intangible Cultural Heritage', 観光学研究= *Journal of Tourism Studies,* 17 (2018), 91–117

Duncan, James and Duncan, Nancy, 'Can't Live with Them, Can't Landscape without Them: Racism and the Pastoral Aesthetic in Suburban New York,' *Landscape Journal,* 22:2 (2003), 88–98, https://doi.org/10.3368/lj.22.2.88

Duxbury, Nancy, Garrett-Petts, W. F. and MacLennan, David, *Cultural Mapping as Cultural Inquiry: Introduction to an Emerging Field of Practice* (New York: Routledge, 2015), https://doi.org/10.4324/9781315743066

Etemado Alsaltane, *Matlaelšams* [*Sunrise*] (Tehran: Farhangsara Publications: 1983).

Grevstad-Nordbrock, Ted and Vojnovic, Igor, 'Heritage-Fueled Gentrification: A Cautionary Tale from Chicago', *Journal of Cultural Heritage,* 38 (2019), 261–270, https://doi.org/10.1016/j.culher.2018.08.004

Hafstein, Valdimar, 'Intangible Heritage as a List: From Masterpieces to Representation', in *Intangible Heritage,* ed. by Laurajane Smith and Natsuko Akagawa (London: Routledge, 2009), pp. 93–111.

Isna, *'Sabte melliye šoleye Mašhad'* [*National Listing of Mashhad's Sholeh*] (Isna.ir, 2017), https://www.isna.ir/news/96071005128/

Jeannotte, Sharon M., 'Story-telling about Place: Engaging Citizens in Cultural Mapping', *City, Culture and Society,* 7:1 (2016), 35–41, https://doi.org/10.1016/j.ccs.2015.07.004

Jigyasu, Rohit, 'The Intangible Dimension of Cities', in *Reconnecting the City: The Historic Urban Landscape Approach and the Future of Urban Heritage,* ed. by Franceso Bandarin and Ron Van Oers (Chichester: John Wiley & Sons, 2014).

Kato, Kumi, 'Community, Connection and Conservation: Intangible Cultural Values in Natural Heritage—The Case of Shirakami-sanchi World Heritage Area', *International Journal of Heritage Studies,* 12:5 (2006), 458–473, https://doi.org/10.1080/13527250600821670

Kirshenblatt-Gimblett, Barbara, 'Intangible Heritage as Metacultural Production 1', *Museum International,* 56:1–2 (2004), 52–65, https://doi.org/10.1111/j.1350-0775.2004.00458.x

Kurin, Richard, 'Safeguarding Intangible Cultural Heritage in the 2003 UNESCO Convention: A Critical Appraisal', *Museum International,* 56:1–2 (2004), 66–77, https://doi.org/10.1111/j.1350-0775.2004.00459.x

Leimgruber, Walter, 'Switzerland and the UNESCO Convention on Intangible Cultural Heritage', *Journal of Folklore Research: An International Journal of Folklore and Ethnomusicology,* 47:1–2 (2010), 161–196, https://doi.org/10.2979/jfr.2010.47.1-2.161

Longley, Alys, and Duxbury, Nancy, 'Introduction: Mapping Cultural Intangibles,' *City, Culture and Society,* 7:1 (2016), 1–7, http://dx.doi.org/10.1016/j.ccs.2015.12.006

Mahavan, Ahmad, *Târixe Mašhadol Rezâ* [*Mashhad's History*] (Mashhad: Mahavan, 2004).

Marrie, Henrietta, 'The UNESCO Convention for the Safeguarding of the Intangible Cultural Heritage and the Protection and Maintenance of the Intangible Cultural Heritage of Indigenous Peoples', in *Intangible Heritage,* ed. by Laurajane Smith and Natsuko Akagawa (London: Routledge, 2009).

Radovic, Darko, 'Measuring the Non-Measurable: On Mapping Subjectivities in Urban Research', *City, Culture and Society,* 7:1 (2016), 17–24, https://doi.org/10.1016/j.ccs.2015.10.003

Relph, Edward, *Place and Placelessness,* vol. 67 (London: Pion, 1976).

Rezvani, Alireza, *Dar jostojuye howeyate šahre Mašhad* [*In Search for Mashhad's Identity*] (Tehran: Ministry of Housing and Urban Planning, 2005).

Ruggles, D. Fairchild and Silverman, Helaine, 'From Tangible to Intangible Heritage', in *Intangible Heritage Embodied,* ed. by Helaine Silverman and D. Fairchild Ruggles (New York: Springer, 2009), pp. 1–14, https://doi.org/10.1007/978-1-4419-0072-2

Samen Research Institute, *Asarâte tarhe tose'eye mantaqeye sâmen* [*Impacts of the Development Plan of Samen District*] (Mashhad: Samen Research Institute, 2018).

Sarkheyli, Elnaz, Rafieian, Mojtaba, and Taghvaee, Ali Akbar, 'Assessing the Convergence Effects of Religious and Economic Forces on the Contemporary Changes of Form and Shape of Samen Region in Mashhad', *Motaleat Shahri,* 12 (2015), 87–101.

Sarkheyli, Elnaz, Rafieian, Mojtaba, and Taghvaee, Ali Akbar, 'Qualitative Sustainability Assessment of the Large-Scale Redevelopment Plan in Samen District of Mashhad', *International Journal of Architecture and Urban Development,* 6:2 (2016), 49–58.

Seyedi, Mahdi, *Târixe šahre Mašhad* [*Mashhad's History*] (Tehran: Jami, 1999).

Smith, Laurajane and Akagawa, Natsuko, eds., *Intangible Heritage* (London: Routledge, 2009), https://doi.org/10.4324/9780203884973

Swensen, Grete, Jerpåsen, Gro B, Sæter, Oddrun, and Tveit, Sundli Mari, 'Capturing the Intangible and Tangible Aspects of Heritage: Personal Versus Official Perspectives in Cultural Heritage Management', *Landscape Research,* 38:2 (2013), 203–221, https://doi.org/10.1080/01426397.2011.642346

Tash Consultant Engineers, 'Tarhe nosâzi va bâzsâziye bâfte pirâmune harame motahhar' [Regeneration of Holy Shrine's surrounding district], Mashhad: MHDCC (1994).

Tavassoli, Vahid, 'Arzešhâye târixiye harame motahhare razavi dar šekl giri va tose'eye šahre Mašhade moqadas' [Historical Values of Creation and Development of Mashhad], International Congress on Revising Islamic Cultural Civilization and Islamic Cities with Focus on Mashhad (Mashhad: 2017).

UNESCO, 'Text of the Convention for the Safeguarding of Intangible Cultural Heritage', General Conference of the United Nations Educational, Scientific and Cultural Organization, Thirty-Second Session, Paris, September 29–October 17 (2003), https://ich.unesco.org/en/conventio.

Van der Hoeven, Arno, 'Networked Practices of Intangible Urban Heritage: The Changing Public Role of Dutch Heritage Professionals', *International Journal of Cultural Policy,* 25:2 (2019), 232–245, https://doi.org/10.1080/10286632.2016.1253686

Vecco, Marilena, 'A Definition of Cultural Heritage: From the Tangible to the Intangible', *Journal of Cultural Heritage,* 11:3 (2010), 321–324, https://doi.org/10.1016/j.culher.2010.01.006

Veldpaus, Loes, Pereira Roders, Ana R., and Colenbrander, Bernard J. F., 'Urban Heritage: Putting the Past into the Future', *The Historic Environment: Policy & Practice,* 4:1 (2013), 3–18, https://doi.org/10.1179/1756750513Z.00000000022

4. Promoting the Role of Egyptian Museums in Nurturing and Safeguarding Intangible Cultural Heritage

Heba Khairy

Introduction

Egyptian heritage is rooted in the earliest eras of ancient Egypt, when Egyptians recorded scenes from their daily lives and traditions on the walls of temples and tombs, including scenes of agriculture, dance performances, arts, industry, and religious rituals. Traditional handicrafts were an important part of these murals, which depicted the making of papyrus, pottery, jewellery, glass, and textiles as well as stone, metals, wood, and leather making. This heritage evolved and expanded through time due to cultural accumulation and the exchange of influence and knowledge with other cultures and civilizations neighbouring Egypt. As a result, the country became renowned among nations for its rich intangible cultural heritage (ICH), characterized by an originality, creativity, and diversity which reflects the depth and continuity of Egypt's various unique communities and groups.

Egyptian tangible heritage is considerably less endangered by the threats of deterioration and extinction than its intangible counterpart, likely as a result of the country's numerous museums, which have made preserving tangible heritage their priority. Since these museums

 https://doi.org/10.11647/OBP.0388.04

began to be established at the beginning of the twentieth century, they have successfully dealt with material artifacts, with little awareness or attention paid to the importance of preserving ICH. This chapter aims to provide a prototype for how Egyptian museums can evolve their functions and operations in order to take on a greater role in the safeguarding of living heritage, while engaging heritage practitioners and bearers in this process.

Globalisation of intangible heritage

The twenty-first century has already witnessed many conflicts, critical events and changes that have strongly affected human intellectual production and identity. The rapid growth of globalisation, industrialisation and modernity has made these processes an inescapable destiny for communities worldwide.[1] The objectives of globalization are characterized as positive in terms of outward impact, as the world has become more connected than ever before through technological advancements and economic integration. However, it has proved negative in terms of inward impact, as it has increased income inequality and substandard working conditions in developing countries that produce goods for wealthier nations, which accordingly affects traditional handicraft production. Globalisation has also been characterised as having hidden consequences, which include the elimination of intellectual, cultural, and human interactions between groups belonging to one place and civilisation.[2] It is widely acknowledged that globalisation has given traditional craftsmen and their handicrafts access to new technology and increased product quality, but surprisingly, many concerns have been raised over the impact on employment and the deterioration in the quality of jobs. So, it has been suggested that globalisation has also brought about 'negative inclusion,' since economic exclusion is linked to exclusion from

1 Iyan Septiyana and Defbry Margiansyah, 'Globalization of Intangible Cultural Heritage: Strengthening Preservation of Indonesia's Endangered Languages in Globalized World', in *Proceedings of the International Conference on Contemporary Social and Political Affairs (IcoCSPA 2017)* (Dordrecht: Atlantis Press, 2018), pp. 8–10, http://doi.org/10.2991/icocspa-17.2018.23

2 Mercy U. Nwegbu, Cyril C. Eze and Brendan E. Asogwa, 'Globalization of Cultural Heritage: Issues, Impacts, and Inevitable Challenges for Nigeria', *Library Philosophy and Practice Journal* (2011), 2–4.

the limited public space that remained accessible for discussion and negotiation. Globalisation has adversely affected the heritage practitioners' engagement, participation, transparency, accessibility, and accountability.[3] This has led to a widening gap between individuals and their communal identities, as well as the gradual disappearance of inherited traditions, values, and intellectual creativity.[4] In Egypt, most handicrafts are facing a fierce struggle for survival as human capital is replaced by modern industrial machinery. Currently, Egyptian artisans are fighting against the tide of industrial mechanics, synthetic fibres, and plastic products—materials which are not used to create new forms but merely imitations of traditional artisan work. The result is a hybrid product that lacks the soul of the Egyptian cultural tradition while pretending to have integrity and authenticity. Accordingly, traditional artisans experience increasing difficulty in finding their raw materials, preparing them, making tools, and finding ways to overcome modern obstacles.[5]

The negative consequences of globalization have become a global issue urgently requiring action by international and national organisations as well as museums to develop strategies, policies and measures to confront the erosion of traditions.[6] To this end, the International Committee of Museums (ICOM) added the concept of 'intangible heritage' to its definition of museums, leading to a notable shift in museum practices.

Museums worldwide, particularly Asian and European museums, have taken important steps towards increasing their involvement in the safeguarding of ICH. They have transformed from guardians of the past to cultural and educational institutions which enshrine the meaning of societies' transformations. From 2017 to 2020, museums in Belgium, Switzerland, the Netherlands, France and Italy cooperated to create the Intangible Cultural Heritage and Museums Project (IMP),

3 Hilal W. Ahmad, 'Impact of Globalization on World Culture', *Research Journal of Humanities and Social Sciences*, 2:2 (2011), 1–4.

4 Salwa M. Eladway, Yousri A. Azzam and Khalid S. al-Hagla, 'Role of Public Participation in Heritage Tourism Development in Egypt: A Case Study of Fuwah City', *WIT Transactions on Ecology and the Environment Journal* (2020), 27–43, http://doi.org/10.2495/SDP200031

5 Menha El-Batraoui, *The Traditional Crafts of Egypt* (Cairo: The American University Press, 2016), pp. 1–2.

6 Maha N. Khairbek, *Challenges of Globalization and its Relation with the Global Culture Heritage and Modernity* (Tahawolat.net, 2014), http://www.tahawolat.net/MagazineArticleDetails.aspx?Id=825

which explored the various practices and approaches of museums to safeguarding intangible heritage. The participating museums provided mutual assistance in the protection of ICH while working alongside its practitioners. IMP helped museums to support heritage communities, groups and individual practitioners in transmitting their cultural practices to future generations. The project succeeded in making living heritage an integral part of future museum practices and policies through the participation and engagement of the practitioners within the museum programmes, galleries and different activities. Additionally, IMP helped to build and develop the capacities of museum professionals by providing them opportunities to exchange knowledge and experiences such as at workshops and conferences.[7]

Egypt's intangible heritage domains

Egypt's modern history is an endless narrative of social, cultural and political innovations drawing on the experiences of the people who settled in the narrow valley in the middle of the Egyptian desert.[8] Looking at the relics, reliefs, and monuments of ancient Egypt, we cannot help but notice how much of the ancient heritage of the pharaohs is still reflected in present-day life in Egypt. Egyptians are conservative and keen to safeguard old rituals and inherited traditions which give modern Egyptians a sense of stability, belonging and continuity.[9]

Oral traditions and expressions

Although the national language of Egypt is Arabic, there are many other ethnic and indigenous languages widely spoken among the ethnic communities (e.g., the Amazigh, Nubian and Bedouin tribes). These

7 Tamara Nikolić Derić, Jorijn Neyrinck, Eveline Seghers, and Evdokia Tsakiridis, *Museums and Intangible Cultural Heritage: Towards a Third Space in the Heritage Sector: A Companion to Discover Transformative Heritage Practices for the 21st Century* (Bruges: Werkplaats immaterieel erfgoed, 2020), pp. 3–15.

8 Molefi Kete, *Culture and Customs of Egypt* (Westport: Greenwood Publishing Group, 2002), pp. 1–3.

9 Samia Abdennour, *Egyptian Customs and Festivals* (Cairo: American University Press, 2007), p. 12.

languages express an enduring living legacy and are harmonious and overlapping with the oral expressions of Egyptians from thousands of years ago.[10]

Performing arts

Upper Egypt and the Delta Region have a unique and authentic musical and performing heritage[11] which includes distinctive dances. For example, Al Tahteeb is a traditional dance of Upper Egypt performed by men wielding long sticks, sometimes on horseback. The dance of Zagal is an individual or communal dance performed by men in the Siwa Oasis which consists of continuous rolling and spinning in circles to the rhythm of drums and traditional musical instruments.[12]

Social practices, rituals, and festive events

Whether they are Copts or Muslims, Egyptians celebrate birthdays or anniversaries to honour saints or holy men in ceremonies known as Mulid which date back to ancient Egyptian traditions honouring kings and gods. In Egypt, almost every city, neighbourhood or town has its 'holy man' buried under a dome or tree.[13]

Knowledge and practices concerning nature and the universe

The belief in both good and bad luck has persisted from ancient Egypt. Today, Egyptians still endeavour to predict their good days, bad days and future events by reading shells, palms and the stars. Many believe blue-eye amulets, touching wood or repeating certain phrases or spells offers protection against the evil eye and envious spirits.[14]

---

10 Mokhtar Khalil, *The Nubian Language: How to Write It* (Khartoum: Nubian Studies and Documentation Centre, 2008), pp. 21–24.

11 Egypt State Information Service, *Egyptian Heritage* (Sis.gov, 2019) https://www.sis.gov.eg/section/10/1517?lang=ar

12 Mustafa Gad, *Treasure of the Intangible Culture Heritage Part 2* (Sharjah: Sharjah Institute for Heritage Publications, 2019), pp. 866–70.

13 Abdennour, *Egyptian Customs and Festivals*, p. 22.

14 Gad, *Treasure of the Intangible Culture Heritage Part* 2, pp. 358–59.

Crafts and traditional handicrafts

Many traditional handicrafts practised in contemporary Egypt date back hundreds or thousands of years. Looking at the scenes and reliefs depicted on the walls of ancient Egyptian temples and tombs, we can see ancient Egyptians represented while making pottery, spinning fabric, making papyri or carving stones and wood.

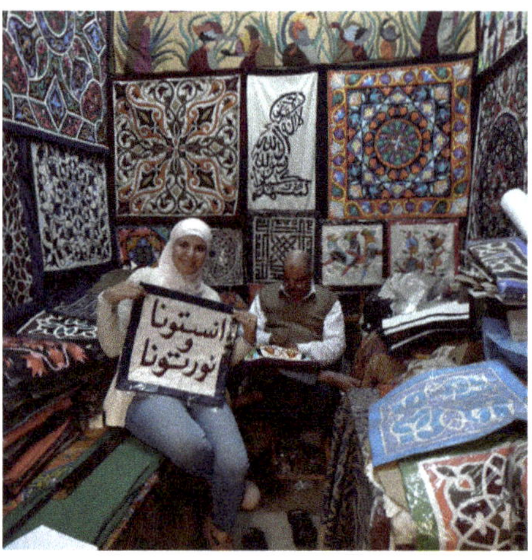

Fig. 4.1 Egyptian artist weaving a hand stitch portrait, Al-Khayameia traditional market, historical Cairo, Egypt. Author's photograph, 2019, CC BY-NC-ND.

Egyptian cities are also rich in traditional handicrafts. These include copper, glass, and wooden artwork, jewellery, carpets and hand-woven textiles, as well as pottery, which is one of the oldest crafts in Egypt. Pottery is distinctive in various parts of Egypt, such as Fustat in Cairo, Fayoum City, Damietta and many cities and villages of Upper Egypt.[15]

Inscribed intangible heritage of Egypt

Egypt was one of the first states to adopt the 2003 Convention for the Safeguarding of ICH. As a result, Egypt succeeded in inscribing seven elements of its intangible heritage on the lists of the United Nations Educational, Scientific and Cultural Organization (UNESCO): three elements on the representative list and two elements on the urgent safeguarding list. However, it is worth noting that this is a relatively

15 El-Batraoui, *The Traditional Crafts of Egypt*, pp.1–2.

small number considering the richness of Egyptian ICH. Accordingly, Egypt must take decisive measures to ensure that more elements of its living heritage are inscribed.

Festivals related to the Journey of the Holy Family

Every year, Christian and Muslim Egyptians of all ages celebrate the feast of the Journey of the Holy Family to Egypt and the birth of the Virgin Mary. These celebrations include singing, traditional games, re-enactments of the journey, religious processions, artistic performances, and the sharing of traditional foods. The celebrations are filled with social functions and cultural meanings, including the unified social and cultural fabric among Christians and Muslims.

Arabic calligraphy

Arabic calligraphy is considered a symbol of the Arab-Islamic world. The artistic practice of writing Arabic calligraphy expresses the harmony and beauty between the letters of the Arabic language. The fluidity of Arabic calligraphy provides unlimited possibilities for writing letters and transforming them in many ways to create different forms of the same word. Unfortunately, many Arabs no longer write by hand due to technological advances, which has led to a sharp decline in the number of specialized Arabic calligraphy artists.

Handmade weaving in Upper Egypt

The famous tradition of hand-weaving in Upper Egypt has been practised since the Pharaonic eras up to the present. It is distinguished across various governorates of Upper Egypt by the use of different types of looms, such as *Akhmimi* weaving in Sohag, *Farka* in Naqada Qena and *Adawi kilim* in Assiut. Additionally, hand-weaving tools and practices differ from one governorate to another, resulting in a diverse textile heritage across the country. For instance, Assiut kilims are different that those in Marsa Matrouh, and looms differ from one place to another.[16]

---

16 UNESCO, *Handmade Weaving in Upper Egypt (Sa'eed)* (Ich. unesco.org, 2021), https://ich.unesco.org/en/USL/handmade-weaving-in-upper-egypt-sa-eed-01605?USL=01605

Date palm, knowledge, skills, traditions and practices

Date palm practices have special industrial, culinary and religious importance in Egypt. Date palm was initially cultivated thousands of years ago in the Nile Valley. It was given various names in Ancient Egypt including *Bni*, *Buno* and *Benrt*. In ancient as well as modern Egypt, date palm leaves have been used for basket making, while the trunks have been used to make roofing for houses in rural areas.[17]

Al-Aragoz traditional hand puppetry

Al-Aragoz is a form of traditional Egyptian puppet theatre, involving glove dolls. Some researchers claim that this traditional puppet theatre has been passed down from ancient Egyptian heritage, whereas others trace it back to the Mamluk period.[18]

Tahteeb (stick game)

Tahteeb is a form of individual martial and dance art that was practised in ancient Egypt and is still practised today; however, while it retains some of its original symbolism, in modern times it has become more of a festive game. It is performed in front of a public audience by two male rivals wielding sticks in a non-violent competition.[19]

Al-Sirah Al-Hilaliyyah

Al-Sirah Al-Hilaliyyah, also known as the Al-Hilaly Epic, tells the story of the Bedouin tribe of Bani Hilal, which migrated from the Arab Peninsula to North Africa in the tenth century. The biography of Al-Hilaly, which disappeared everywhere except Egypt, is considered

17 Annamalai Manickavasagan, M. Mohamed Essa and Ethirajan Sukumar, *Dates: Production, Processing, Food, and Medicinal Values* (Boca Raton: CRC Press, 2012), pp.5–6, https://doi.org/10.1201/b11874

18 UNESCO, *Traditional Hand Puppetry* (Ich.unesco.org, 2018), https://ich.unesco.org/en/USL/traditional-hand-puppetry-01376

19 UNESCO, *Tahteeb, Stick Game* (Ich.unesco.org, 2016), https://ich.unesco.org/en/RL/tahteeb-stick-game-01189

one of the most important epic poems, which emerged as folk art in its musical form.[20]

Egyptian museums from a heritage perspective

Egyptian heritage has dazzled the world,[21] attracting the curiosity of researchers and amateurs alike. Accordingly, museums all over the globe are keen to acquire, display, preserve and study Egyptian antiquities within their museums and institutions.[22]

Egypt was the first country in the Middle East to create museums to collect and conserve the country's ancient treasures and express its temporal, civilisational and spatial identity. Egypt is renowned for its antiquities, which are displayed in dozens of museums that constitute major cultural wealth.[23]

Nevertheless, Egyptian museums are archaeological museums concerned with artefacts from ancient Egypt. These museums have a traditional function in terms of representing the country's national identity and history, through the preservation and study of the Egyptian antiquities.[24] As a result, these museums have neglected interpretive elements which would shed light on the specificity of Egyptian living heritage and link contemporary Egyptian society with its ancient past through inherited and continued practices. Thus, Egyptian museums may be losing their opportunity to be the premier supporters and interpreters of their communities' identities and beliefs. Today, Egyptian museums are stressing the need to develop deliberate policies for the advancement and marketing of museums at home and abroad.

The historical and multicultural city of Cairo is considered an open museum, reflecting thousands of years of history, heritage and

---

20 UNESCO, *Al-Sirah Al-Hilaliyyah Epic* (Ich.unesco.org, 2008), https://ich.unesco.org/en/RL/al-sirah-al-hilaliyyah-epic-00075

21 Barry J. Kemp, *Ancient Egypt: Anatomy of a Civilization* (London: Psychology Press, 2006), p. 23, https://doi.org/10.2307/530011

22 Christina Riggs, 'Colonial Visions: Egyptian Antiquities and Contested Histories in the Cairo Museum', *Museum Worlds*, 1:1 (2013), 65–84, https://doi.org/10.3167/armw.2013.010105

23 Mohamed Gamal, *Museology, its Creation, Branches and Impacts* (Cairo: Al Araby Publications, 2019), pp. 27–30.

24 Mohamed Gamal, 'The Museums of Egypt Speak for Whom?', *CIPEG Journal: Ancient Egyptian & Sudanese Collections and Museums*, 1 (2017), 1–11.

civilisations. As the capital of Egypt, Cairo is home to the country's major museums, which are regarded as among the most appealing attractions for visitors interested in Egyptian heritage, whether foreign or local. Based on interviews and surveys, the present research found that compared with other museums in Egypt, Cairo's museums are the most active in terms of the programmes and activities they offer to visitors.[25]

Egyptian museums and the community

The placement of objects at the centre of Egyptian museums' concerns and core functions has created barriers between the Egyptian museums and their local visitors, local communities and living heritage. Egyptian museums do not reflect the challenges and changes that have occurred in Egyptian society in the last ten years, and as such, they do not meet the needs and expectations of Egyptian communities. Local communities are likewise not adequately incorporated into museums' programmes and activities,[26] nor are heritage practitioners involved in museums' efforts to preserve and ensure the sustainability of living heritage.

Nevertheless, some Egyptian museums have made attempts in recent years to incorporate living heritage through programmes, activities and temporary exhibitions aimed at providing interactive and educational experiences through which Egyptian communities can learn about their heritage. Some of these programmes and activities have revolved around traditional handicrafts and folk performances. These attempts constitute a commendable step towards implementing new practices within Egyptian museums for presenting Egyptian living heritage.[27] Notably among these efforts are those that have been made by the Cairo Egyptian Museum and the National Museum of Egyptian Civilisation through their children's museum and educational department. This has included numerous educational programmes and

25 European Union External Action, *European and Egyptian Cooperation to Transform the Egyptian Museum of Cairo, Supported by the EU* (Eeas.europa.eu, 2019), https://south.euneighbours.eu/news/european-and-egyptian-cooperation-transform-egyptian-museum-cairo/

26 Mohamed Gamal, *Museology, its Creation, Branches and Impacts* (Cairo: Al Araby Publications, 2019), pp. 27–30.

27 Mohamed Gamal, 'The Museums of Egypt after the 2011 Revolution', *Museum International* (2015), 125–31, https://doi.org/10.1111/muse.12089

activities led and performed by heritage practitioners and artisans, such as tactile tours, handicrafts workshops and art performances. These programs and activities aim to extract the intangible heritage value from the museum objects. Another example is a temporary exhibition developed by the National Museum for Egyptian Civilization entitled 'Egyptian Handicrafts Across the Ages', which focused on the historical development of Egyptian traditional crafts.[28]

The Nubian Museum in Aswan provides an interesting experience based on the Nubian community traditions and folk lifestyle, using dioramas and real contemporary Nubian objects from the community.[29] Between 2014 and 2019, the Egyptian Textile Museum also held several programmes and lectures raising awareness about Egyptian traditional handicrafts as part of its annual World Heritage Day celebrations. Likewise, every year, the Egyptian Textile Museum also celebrates the Egyptian Heritage Festival.[30]

Unfortunately, the efforts described above lack continuity, effectiveness and creativity because they do not encourage the engagement and integration of heritage carriers (i.e. the heritage practitioners and heritage custodians). Moreover, Egyptian museums lack financial and professional capacities, effective strategies, communication tools and plans to deal with all domains of Egyptian intangible heritage and their practitioners. These factors have put Egyptian museums decades behind their international counterparts, who have made great strides in the last decade towards engaging with local communities to reflect their living identity and contemporary challenges.

Towards new models of museums functions in Egypt

Egypt's museums can effectively contribute to safeguarding and supporting intangible heritage, as well as the country's communities and individual practitioners who are keen to pass on their cultural practices

28 National Museum of Egyptian Civilization, *Events* (Nmec.gov.eg, 2023), https://nmec.gov.eg/ar/past/

29 Wendy Doyon, 'The Poetics of Egyptian Museum Practice', *British Museum Studies in Ancient Egypt and Sudan*, 10 (2008), 1–37.

30 Yomna El-Saeed, 'The Egyptian Textile Museum', *Daily News Egypt*, 1 October 2013, https://dailynewsegypt.com/2013/10/01/antique-fabrics-at-the-egyptian-textile-museum/

to future generations. The measures outlined below are ways museums can protect and nurture living heritage, namely through its integration in practice and policies, as well as the adoption of participatory and people-centred approaches.[31]

Adaption of laws and legislation

Egypt has passed many laws on the protection and preservation of cultural heritage, but these have focused only on tangible heritage without mentioning any of the intangible forms of Egyptian culture. This means that the Egyptian state has not yet considered any legal measures to ensure the protection of intangible materials.[32]

The Egyptian Constitution, ratified in 2014, includes several provisions that confirm the state's commitment to protecting the identity and cultural diversity of its communities. However, the term 'intangible' was not explicitly mentioned in these provisions. Thus, there is a need for legislation which explicitly affirms the state's obligation to protect ICH and the ethnic communities that live within the country's borders. The Egyptian government must develop practical instruments and theoretical guidelines that can contribute to protecting and supporting intangible heritage and its practitioners.[33]

Documenting and collecting ICH

The procedures for documenting artefacts and objects within Egyptian museums are different from creating an inventory of intangible heritage.[34] Therefore, Egyptian museums should develop documentation policies

---

31 *Between the Visible and the Invisible: The Intangible Cultural Heritage and the Museum*, ed. by Mila Santova, Iveta Todorova-Pirgova and Mirena Staneva (Sofia: Publishing House of the Bulgarian Academy of Sciences, 2018), pp. 2–8.

32 Ministry of Antiquities, *Antiquities Protection Act and Its Executive Regulations* (Mota.gov.eg, 2022), https://mota.gov.eg/media/yafbwufg/%D9%82%D8%A7%D9%86%D9%88%D9%86-%D8%AD%D9%85%D8%A7%D9%8A%D8%A9-%D8%A7%D9%84%D8%A2%D8%AB%D8%A7%D8%B1-2022.pdf

33 Nivine N. Zakaria, 'What "Intangible" May Encompass in The Egyptian Cultural Heritage Context? Legal Provisions, Sustainable Measures and Future Directions', *International Journal for Heritage and Museum Studies*, 1:1 (2019), 17–18, http://10.21608/ijhms.2019.119038

34 Marilena Alivizatou, *Intangible Heritage and the Museum: New Perspectives on Cultural Preservation* (London: Routledge, 2016), p. 22, http://10.1080/13527258.2014.913343

and standards that reflect and are more relevant to the Egyptian characteristics of their living heritage. This can be done by combining both methodologies, generating an enriched approach to heritage documentation via the following measures:[35] linking community-based heritage inventories to object-identification systems, moving from object collecting to collecting heritage stories within the Egyptian community, and creating a databank to be integrated into existing museum databases for the intangible elements that are collected.[36] These measures could be successfully implemented through cooperation with the Centre for the Documentation of Cultural and Natural Heritage, which is developing projects to document the ICH of Egypt in line with its mission to document Egyptian traditions from Egyptians' daily lives.[37]

Collaboration with stakeholders

There is national collaboration between many governmental organisations, including the Higher Institute for Folklore and the Art House for Folklore and Performing Arts, and non-governmental organisations (NGOs), such as the Egyptian Archives of Folk Life and Folk Traditions and Egyptian Society for Folk Traditions. Collaborating globally, in particular with UNESCO and ICOM as leading international organisations, can also provide technical support for the safeguarding of Egyptian heritage through various programmes and workshops focused on exchanging expertise gained through previous successful experiences, strategies and projects in international museums.

Building capacities

Capacity building that is relevant to safeguarding living heritage must target heritage practitioners and museum professionals alike. Training ensures that an effective and qualified workforce can be maintained inside Egyptian museums, promoting dialogue and co-creation activities.

35 ICOM, *Shanghai Charter* (Icom.museum 2018), https://icom.museum/wp-content/uploads/2018/07/Shanghay_Charter_Eng.pdf

36 UNESCO, *Text of the Convention for the Safeguarding of the Intangible Cultural Heritage* (Ich.unesco.org, 2022), https://ich.unesco.org/en/convention

37 Centre for Documentation of Cultural and Natural Heritage, *Briefing about CULTNAT* (Cultnat.org, 2020), https://www.cultnat.org/About

Measures to build the capacities of Egyptian museum professionals should have the following aims:[38]

- To deepen their sense of social responsibility for safeguarding and nurturing living heritage.
- To strengthen their knowledge about the forms of heritage that exist within their society.
- To develop their working relationships with intangible heritage bearers using sociology and anthropology workshops and sessions, as well as through participatory tasks with heritage practitioners.

Museum education: Object/heritage-based education

Education is central to the function and practices of museums, and both formal and non-formal education is of great importance for the transmission of intangible heritage. Incorporating the artefacts and collections of Egyptian museums into educational programmes to teach Egyptian heritage and history has strong potential to attract visitors and encourage their engagement, as artefacts embody the stories of real people from the past and shed light on cultural inheritances from past generations.

Building trust and creating spaces for heritage practitioners

Strong relationships between museums and heritage custodians are the result of frequent and continued interaction and emotional engagement based on reciprocity. Weak relationships can prohibit access to new information that evokes creativity and innovation.[39] Museums can cultivate a trusting relationship with heritage custodians through dialogue based on the appreciation of their values and practices, and measures such as those outlined below which aim to help them revive their endangered traditions.

38 ICOM, *Shanghai Charter*.

39 Tamara Nikolić Derić, Jorijn Neyrinck, Eveline Seghers, and Evdokia Tsakiridis, *Museums and Intangible Cultural Heritage: Towards a Third Space in the Heritage Sector* (Bruges: Werkplaats immaterieel erfgoed, 2020), p. 13.

In addition, museums can support artists financially by providing them space to sell their handicrafts in museum shops and retail spaces.[40] Outreach programmes can likewise be developed for museum professionals to support and engage with practitioners in their local communities. Most importantly, heritage practitioners should be assisted in safeguarding and transmitting their cultural traditions and skills in a contemporary context by focusing on cultural revival rather than archival documentation.

Traditional handcraft workshops in the museum campus

Training programmes, workshops and sessions can be led by heritage practitioners, giving space and opportunity for artisans and crafters to practice their trades and confirm the artistic value in this field in a historical, creative and modern environment. For example, each artisan can produce heritage products related to the museum's collections as displayed to visitors in the galleries. At the end of the museum tour, each visitor can request a particular piece that they liked from the collection to take home as part of the tour. Through this interactive approach, visitors can experience the stories behind the pieces, representing the intangible side of Egyptian culture.[41]

Community-based exhibitions

Egyptian museums must go beyond their conventional role as mere places for the display of artifacts and become community-based spaces. By adopting a participatory approach that highlights their community and its values, they can act as stakeholders who have the authority to interpret the objects they display. The community exhibition approach aims to ensure community cohesion and well-being, by highlighting the distinctive heritage among the community members through the participation of these members in choosing the theme of the exhibition and the collection, in addition to writing the narratives of the

40 UNESCO, *Text of the Convention for the Safeguarding of the Intangible Cultural Heritage* (Ich.unesco.org, 2022), https://ich.unesco.org/en/convention.

41 Naohiro Nakamura, 'Managing the Cultural Promotion of Indigenous People in a Community-Based Museum: the Ainu Culture Cluster Project at the Nibutani Ainu Culture Museum, Japan', *Museum and Society Journal*, 3 (2007), 148–67.

exhibition to present their collective identity and memories. In this case, exhibitions can involve the practitioners of that heritage and the forms of knowledge and values linked to it.[42] This promises to strengthen the relationship between museums and communities, providing the latter with a sense of inclusion and the opportunity to express themselves through storytelling and gallery talks.

Exhibitions can be developed about living heritage communities, which depend on practitioners as 'first-person interpreters', where sharing their story, values and culture serves as an interpretation tool. Additionally, videos and records accompanying the display can be used as an interactive approach to gallery interpretation. This will generate a dialogue, enabling visitors and museum professionals to connect personally and emotionally with the intangible stories of the museum collections.

Conclusion

Society has changed rapidly in the twenty-first century as a result of social transitions, economic and technological shifts, and the spread of globalisation and mass tourism. These all contribute to the contemporary challenges to the preservation of heritage, which have led to the destruction and loss of many cultural values and practices found within local communities. Globally, many institutions and organisations dealing with heritage, especially museums, have taken steps towards safeguarding and nurturing ICH and its communities. These steps have manifested in many approaches and forms ranging from developing strategies and plans to creating exhibitions and human/heritage-based activities.

Egypt is a country of tremendous diversity and unique intangible heritage and values. This heritage is notable for its integrity and authenticity, having been formed and passed down over thousands of years and influenced by other cultures and civilisations through both cultural integration and exchange. The lack of awareness about the forms and values of Egyptian living heritage, in addition to the lack

---

42 Marta Wieczorek, 'Postmodern Exhibition Discourse: Anthropological Study of an Art Display Case', *Journal of Science and Technology of the Arts*, 2 (2015), 19–24, https://doi.org/10.7559/citarj.v7i2.139

of institutional engagement in ensuring the sustainability of Egyptian ICH, has a deeply detrimental impact on the stability and continuity of these forms and values. Furthermore, Egyptian museums have failed to reflect their heritage communities and the challenges they have been facing for decades.

Museums in Egypt still play their traditional role as institutions that preserve and display artefacts. However, in order to confront the threats to their country's heritage and the challenges facing Egyptian communities, they must rethink and redefine this role, adopting more inclusive and participatory approaches. Effective efforts to safeguard their country's living heritage in the twenty-first century will require museums to shift their focus from objects to human experience by integrating intangible heritage within their displays, functions and programmes. These measures are the surest means of protecting and supporting Egypt's threatened cultural heritage.

Bibliography

Abdennour, Samia, *Egyptian Customs and Festivals* (Cairo: American University Press, 2007).

Ahmad, Hilal W., 'Impact of Globalization on World Culture', *Research Journal of Humanities and Social Sciences*, 2 (2011), 1–4.

Alivizatou, Marilena, *Intangible Heritage and the Museum: New Perspectives on Cultural Preservation* (London: Routledge, 2016), http://10.1080/13527258.2014.913343.

Centre for Documentation of Cultural and Natural Heritage, *Briefing about CULTNAT* (Cultnat.org, 2020), https://www.cultnat.org/About.

Derić, Tamara N., Neyrinck, J., Seghers, E., and Tsakiridis, E., *Museums and Intangible Cultural Heritage: Towards a Third Space in the Heritage Sector: A Companion to Discover Transformative Heritage Practices for the 21st Century* (Bruges: Werkplaats immaterieel erfgoed, 2020).

Doyon, Wendy, 'The Poetics of Egyptian Museum Practice', *British Museum Studies in Ancient Egypt and Sudan*, 10 (2008), 1–37.

Egypt State Information Service, *Egyptian Heritage* (Sis.gov, 2019), https://www.sis.gov.eg/section/10/1517?lang=ar.

Eladway, Salwa M., Azzam, Yousri A., and Al-Hagla, Khalid S., 'Role of Public Participation in Heritage Tourism Development in Egypt: A Case Study of

Fuwah City', WIT Transactions on Ecology and the Environment Journal (2020), 27–43, http://doi.org/10.2495/SDP200031

El-Batraoui, Menha, *The Traditional Crafts of Egypt* (Cairo: The American University Press, 2016).

El-Saeed, Yomna, 'The Egyptian Textile Museum', *Daily News Egypt*, 1 October 2013, https://dailynewsegypt.com/2013/10/01/antique-fabrics-at-the-egyptian-textile-museum/.

European Union External Action, *European and Egyptian Cooperation to Transform the Egyptian Museum of Cairo, Supported by the EU* (Eeas.europa.eu, 2019), https://south.euneighbours.eu/news/european-and-egyptian-cooperation-transform-egyptian-museum-cairo/

Gad, Mustafa, *Treasure of the Intangible Culture Heritage Part 2* (Sharjah: Sharjah Institute for Heritage Publications, 2019).

Gamal, Mohamed, 'The Museums of Egypt after the 2011 Revolution', *Museum International* (2015), 125–31, https://doi.org/10.1111/muse.12089

Gamal, Mohamed, 'The Museums of Egypt Speak for Whom?', *CIPEG Journal: Ancient Egyptian & Sudanese Collections and Museums*, 1 (2017), 1–11.

Gamal, Mohamed, *Museology, its Creation, Branches and Impacts* (Cairo: Al Araby Publications, 2019).

ICOM, *Shanghai Charter* (Icom.museum 2018), https://icom.museum/wp-content/uploads/2018/07/Shanghay_Charter_Eng.pdf

Kemp, Barry J., *Ancient Egypt: Anatomy of a Civilization* (London: Psychology Press, 2006), https://doi.org/10.2307/530011

Kete, Molefi, *Culture and Customs of Egypt* (Westport: Greenwood Publishing Group, 2002).

Khairbek, Maha N., *Challenges of Globalization and its Relation with the Global Culture Heritage and Modernity* (Tahawlat.net, 2014), http://www.tahawolat.net/MagazineArticleDetails.aspx?Id=825

Khalil, Mokhtar, *The Nubian Language: How to Write It* (Khartoum: Nubian Studies and Documentation Centre, 2008).

Manickavasagan, A., Essa, M. Mohamed and Sukumar, E., eds., *Dates: Production, Processing, Food, and Medicinal Value*s (Boca Raton: CRC Press, 2012), https://doi.org/10.1201/b11874.

Ministry of Antiquities, *Antiquities Protection Act and Its Executive Regulations* (Mota.gov.eg, 2022), https://mota.gov.eg/media/yafbwufg/%D9%82%D8%A7%D9%86%D9%88%D9%86-%D8%AD%D9%85%D8%A7%D9%8A%D8%A9-%D8%A7%D9%84%D8%A2%D8%AB%D8%A7%D8%B1-2022.pdf

Nakamura, Naohiro, 'Managing the Cultural Promotion of Indigenous People in a Community-Based Museum: The Ainu Culture Cluster Project at the

Nibutani Ainu Culture Museum, Japan', *Museum and Society Journal*, 3 (2007), 148–67.

National Museum of Egyptian Civilization, *Events* (Nmec.gov.eg 2023), https://nmec.gov.eg/ar/past/.

Nwegbu, Mercy U., Eze, Cyril C. and Asogwa, Brendan E., 'Globalization of Cultural Heritage: Issues, Impacts, and Inevitable Challenges for Nigeria', *Library Philosophy and Practice Journal* (2011), 2–4.

Riggs, Christina, 'Colonial Visions: Egyptian Antiquities and Contested Histories in the Cairo Museum', *Museum Worlds*, 1:1 (2013), 65–84, https://doi.org/10.3167/armw.2013.010105

Santova, Mila, Todorova-Pirgova, Iveta, and Staneva, Mirena, eds., *Between the Visible and the Invisible: The Intangible Cultural Heritage and the Museum* (Sofia: Publishing House of the Bulgarian Academy of Sciences, 2018).

Septiyana, Iyan and Margiansyah, Defbry, 'Globalization of Intangible Cultural Heritage: Strengthening Preservation of Indonesia's Endangered Languages in Globalized World' in *Proceedings of the International Conference on Contemporary Social and Political Affairs* (Dordrecht: Atlantis Press, 2018), pp. 8–10, http://doi.org/10.2991/icocspa-17.2018.23

UNESCO, *Al-Sirah Al-Hilaliyyah Epic* (Ich.unesco.org, 2008), https://ich.unesco.org/en/RL/al-sirah-al-hilaliyyah-epic-00075

UNESCO, *Handmade Weaving in Upper Egypt (Sa'eed)* (Ich.unesco.org, 2021), https://ich.unesco.org/en/USL/handmade-weaving-in-upper-egypt-sa-eed-01605?USL=01605

UNESCO, *Tahteeb, Stick Game* (Ich.unesco.org, 2016), https://ich.unesco.org/en/RL/tahteeb-stick-game-01189

UNESCO, *Text of the Convention for the Safeguarding of the Intangible Cultural Heritage* (Ich.unesco.org, 2022), https://ich.unesco.org/en/convention

UNESCO, *Text of the Convention for the Safeguarding of the Intangible Cultural Heritage* (Ich.unesco.org, 2022), https://ich.unesco.org/en/convention

UNESCO, *Traditional Hand Puppetry* (Ich.unesco.org, 2018), https://ich.unesco.org/en/USL/traditional-hand-puppetry-01376

Wieczorek,, Marta 'Postmodern Exhibition Discourse: Anthropological Study of an Art Display Case', *Journal of Science and Technology of the Arts*, 2 (2015), 19–24, https://doi.org/10.7559/citarj.v7i2.139

Zakaria, Nivine N., 'What "Intangible" May Encompass in The Egyptian Cultural Heritage Context? Legal Provisions, Sustainable Measures and Future Directions', *International Journal for Heritage and Museum Studies*, 1:1 (2019), 17–18, http://10.21608/ijhms.2019.119038

5. Syrian Intangible Cultural Heritage: Characteristics and Challenges of Preservation[1]

Nibal Muhesen

Introduction

The current chapter follows the general description of intangible cultural heritage as framed by scientific and legal writings such as the general UNESCO convention labeled ICHC. Although many of the concepts developed here are meant to be considered in the Syrian context, one cannot ignore the increasing importance of this topic acrosss the Arabic region, for example, in Egypt and Lebanon. In fact, the interaction between all components of heritage in the Middle Eastern context is far more complex than is accounted for in traditional Western frameworks. This is because across the Arab region, and in Syria in particular, heritage is a part of everyday life and cannot exist separately from it.

Intangible heritage is considered the first means of expressing the culture of the community because it originates in its local environment and is closely related to its composition. Intangible or immaterial heritage here does not refer to physical entities; it is seen as the repository of people's cultural identity and the reflection of their collective memory. Taking such an assumption as a starting point, a difference arises

1 My sincere thanks go to Dr. Lilia Makhloufi and Dr. Ammar Abdulrahman for extending me this kind invitation and for their intellectual contributions to the debate on the topic. I am also grateful to my colleagues in Syria for their help.

 https://doi.org/10.11647/OBP.0388.05

between the physical and nonphysical aspects of heritage. The current study attempts to respond to this by drawing clear borders between the two following types of heritage:

1. The 'official heritage' existing under the shadow of official institutions and legally protected; this is perceived as being more material or physical, stable across time, durable and present in people's minds and in the official media outputs by institutions. Under this category comes the Authorized Heritage Discourse (AHD).[2] Notably, this study perceives tangible cultural heritage reflected in sites, monuments and urban agglomerations to belong to this type.
2. The 'folklore' related more to the German concept of *Volkskunde*, meaning the knowledge of nations. This could also be labelled 'public heritage', as opposed to official heritage, and is related to societies' emotional and social changes. Here, heritage manifests in a more fragile way than tangible cultural heritage. I perceive intangible cultural heritage to be the most representative of this category, where it is the faithful reflection of societal upheavals and can easily vanish or be relegated to oblivion in the face of conflicts, modernity and social changes. Its preservation is more complex than the protection of endangered sites or buildings.

The scope and definition of Syrian intangible cultural heritage

At this stage, the scope of Syrian intangible heritage has to be defined and its distinguishing features explained. Indeed, this topic is governed by several factors:

1. It is of purely local use and perception, made by people and for the service of people; moreover, it is part of the Eastern Mediterranean regional framework, and it is included under the universal and global values of heritage. In other words, it has both national and international dimensions.

2 Laurajane Smith, *Uses of Heritage* (New York: Routledge, 2006), p. 36.

2. Syrian intangible heritage expresses a unique and close connection between physical and nonphysical heritage as it appears in the concept of 'cultural spaces', such as mosques and churches, bazaars and *Khans Caravanserai*, which enshrine both official heritage through their monumental structure and public traditions and crafts via their public access.
3. It reflects the rich diversity of the religious, ethnic and cultural fabric of society, best conveying the concept of 'cultural diversity'—a key concept in the veritable melting pot that is Syria. This is why such heritage forms a common cultural identity for all Syrians from all parts of society.
4. It is surrounded by a substantial emotional dimension, which makes it sensitive and vulnerable to the encroachment of modernity and growth of capital.
5. It expresses living voices; many groups still adhere to it, and thus, it could be described as 'living heritage' par excellence where its elements interact with the daily lives of the population.
6. It boosts the national economy through the income generated by tourism activities.
7. It also plays an important part in the economy via its integral role in advancing the United Nations Sustainable Development Goals (SDGs) in Syria, particularly goal 11.4 on 'Sustainable cities and communities' in a direct sense, as well as goal 3 in an indirect sense.
8. It has a transnational aspect since many regions that are far from each other still share the same elements of intangible heritage, such as textile practices, metalcrafts, and oral storytelling shared by the coast and southern and northern Syria. Thus, heritage here cannot be delineated geographically.
9. It must be stressed that intangible heritage contributes significantly to the instrumentalisation of heritage as such, by generating a more diverse, inclusive and continuous cultural identity in the country; moreover, it is an element in the larger picture of the cultural revival in Syria after years of violence

and clashing narratives about heritage. It is clear that the preservation of old districts, mosques and traditional houses is also a means of preserving intangible heritage because these places are the holders of local crafts and traditions.

Intangible cultural heritage in the international discourse

It is useful to define the initial concepts related to intangible cultural heritage as reflected in the international discourse. In fact, the concept of intangible heritage is contained in the text of the Convention for the Safeguarding of the Intangible Heritage of United Nations Educational, Scientific and Cultural Organization (UNESCO; called ICHC), which was adopted in Paris in 2003 and ratified and signed by Syria in 2005. In the convention, ICH is defined as follows:

> The practices, representations, expressions, knowledge, skills—as well as the instruments, objects, artefacts and cultural spaces associated therewith—that communities, groups and, in some cases, individuals recognize as part of their cultural heritage. This intangible cultural heritage, transmitted from generation to generation, is constantly recreated by communities and groups in response to their environments, their interaction with nature and their history, and provides them with a sense of identity and continuity, thus promoting respect for cultural diversity and human creativity.[3]

The agreement clarifies that heritage includes the following main categories: oral traditions and expressions, including language as a vehicle for the expression of intangible cultural heritage, and performing arts and rituals. It also mentions arts and traditions of performances, social practices, rituals and celebrations, knowledge and practices relating to nature and the universe, and finally, skills associated with traditional craftsmanship. It is worth commenting on what is meant by 'preservation' in the Convention. Preservation refers to measures aimed at ensuring the sustainability of intangible cultural heritage, including

3 UNESCO, *Text of the Convention for the Safeguarding of the Intangible Cultural Heritage* (Ich.unesco.org, 2003), https://ich.unesco.org/en/convention

the identification, documentation, research, preservation, protection, promotion, visibility and transmission of this heritage.

Another important issue that has been stressed by researchers is that the ICHC has come to adjust the 'dominant heritage paradigm', since heritage was seen mainly from a Western perspective and the notions of intangible cultural heritage are associated with more non-Western frameworks of understanding and using heritage. By adopting the ICHC, the International Heritage Committee foregrounded living traditions and local crafts or oral traditions, leaving monumental structures and archaeological sites in the background.[4]

Depending on the ICHC text, intangible heritage is closely bound with cultural identity, which affects and is affected by intangible heritage and delineates its angles and scope. Moreover, intangible cultural heritage forms the shared memory that shapes the emergence of perceptions and forms of expression. Intangible cultural heritage also represents inherited knowledge and its continuity across the structures of society. Notably, in the text of the Convention, ICH is related to laws consistent with the Charter of Human Rights and rights covenants. In addition, the Convention observes safeguarding measures and procedures, including documentation and protection.

Intangible cultural heritage in the local discourse

Although there is no clear-cut definition of intangible cultural heritage among Syrians, this study considers التراث الشعبي (public heritage) as the signifier of any discourse about intangible cultural heritage. In fact, the trend towards intangible heritage is recent in Syria; the efforts made in this field, as well as the official involvement in those efforts, are evident in the work of many official and non-official bodies, including non-governmental organisations (NGOs) and associations, which inspire feelings of pride and optimism.

The efforts to document and preserve heritage date back to the 1970s, when the Ministry of Culture established an office of 'public tradition', understood in Arabic as التقاليد الشعبية. The interest in gathering the local

4 *Intangible Heritage*, ed. by Laurajane Smith and Natsuko Akagawa (London and New York: Routledge, 2008).

crafts, arts and oral narratives or stories of each Syrian city was apparent in issuing journals dedicated to the topic (in Iraq first and then in Syria).[5] Such trends were also visible in earlier periods in the construction of museums or conversion of traditional Arabic houses into museums for folk traditions, such as the Azm Palace which was converted into a folk traditions museum in 1954.

Intangible cultural heritage, in Arabic called التراث الثقافي اللامادي, is the expression of a postcolonial narrative about community development and is intrinsically linked to the Syrian identity. It would be more appropriate for that identity to become inclusive of the whole community and to allow cultural, ethnic and religious pluralism. This would secure continuity and transmission over the generations and prevent distortion and breakage of the traditions.

One of the most active organisations in preserving intangible cultural heritage is the Syria Trust for Development, which contributes to the safeguarding of intangible cultural heritage as an NGO accredited by UNESCO. This body is tasked with preparing forms for nominating intangible cultural heritage elements to UNESCO lists, participating in the documentation of ICH elements and developing the national inventory and its digitalisation, as well as implementing community-based projects to safeguard ICH, such as 'Syrian Handicrafts' and 'Living Heritage'.[6] The efforts made by this NGO have had significant results on the international stage, including in relation to the elements inscribed on the UNESCO ICH list:

- Aleppo's traditional songs known as *Al Qudoud Al Halabia* were listed in 2021.
- The practices and craftsmanship associated with the Damascene rose, mainly practised by farmers and families in Al-Mrah village in rural Damascus, were listed in 2019.
- Shadow play, which is a traditional art consisting of handmade puppets moving behind a thin translucent curtain or screen inside a dark theatre, now practised mainly in Damascus, was listed in 2018.

---

5 Cf. Abdulhamid Younes, *Folk Traditions* (Cairo: Cairo Publication House, 2007), p. 139.

6 Syria Trust for Development, 'Cultural Identity and Living Heritage', 2021.

- The shadow theatre was also placed on the urgent conservation list in 2018.
- Falconry, associated with nature conservation, cultural heritage and social engagement within and among communities, was listed in 2016. Notably, Syria shares this element with other Arabic and non-Arabic countries, such as Saudi Arabia, Jordan and Italy.
- Crafting and playing the musical instrument *Oud* (the lute) was listed jointly for Iran and Syria in 2022.

It is also worth mentioning the work of a Syrian NGO called Homeland Document, which focuses on collecting war-related testimonies or records from various sections of Syrian society, forming a sort of database of conflict-related oral history—a step that will have an impact on the reshaping of both individual and collective memories. Also, several field studies were carried out by this NGO to document traditional local crafts, such as the Damascene mosaic profession, as well as ecclesiastical heritage, including elements such as architectural styles, rituals, manuscripts or religious hymns (cf. Homeland Document 2021).[7]

The Syrian cultural legacy has deep historical roots stretching back to ancient times, and many cultural landmarks attest to this, including the Umayyad Mosques in Aleppo and Damascus, covered markets, ancient churches, schools and castles. Before the Syrian crisis in 2011, the cultural monuments in many regions were visited by both local and international tourists and considered precious architectural and cultural pearls of Syria. Before the war, traditional houses were built in some Syrian cities that embraced a large part of the cities' traditions and memory, where documents, manuscripts, forms of popular art and traditions were displayed. Clear examples are the *Dar Ghazaleh* and *Beit Ajqbash*, which were both erected during the Ottoman period and were severely damaged in the recent conflict.

Syrian cities used to enjoy the benefits of the strong interest in intangible heritage felt by their inhabitants; Aleppo residents were known

7 Homeland Document, *Oral History Recordings Projects in Syria* (Wathiqat-watten. org, 2021), https://wathiqat-wattan.org/category/oral-history

to be very interested in their city's culture and heritage, evidenced by the work of heritage committees and associations inside the city, which gathered its intellectual elite and made a concerted effort to document the traditions of the city, such as the *'adiyat* (Annales of Aleppo). In Homs and Damascus, similar bodies tasked with preserving popular heritage also existed.

Damascus has famous sword and silk factories, the products of which made their way across both the West and the East, and Homs is well known for its ornamented carpets and looms. The skills of Syrian crafters have been popularised around the globe by many products, crafts and handicrafts. Intangible heritage or public heritage in Syria has many aspects, including the following:

- Local traditional industries, such as making laurel soap in the city of Aleppo;
- Silk and textiles, historically related to the famous old 'Silk Road'; many caravansaries dedicated to this type of commerce were dispersed across Syrian land, as in Damascus, Aleppo and Homs;
- Knitting arts, such as carpet weaving and embroidery;
- Local performing arts and dance, such as the *Al-Samah* Sufi dance widely associated with Aleppo;
- Various metal crafts, such as gold and silver crafting;[8]
- Performing arts, such as the various local musical arts, especially *Al-Qudood Al-Halabia* (local songs rooted in Andalusian music) and several *Inshad* practices (religious singing groups); Syria also has a rich and diverse musical heritage related to Christianity and liturgical music;
- Local oral traditions, such as folk proverbs and traditional stories;
- Inherited knowledge and experiences in the field of traditional architecture and building materials;

8 Moheb Chanesaz, Ella Dardaillon and Jean-Claude David, *L'artisanat du métal à Alep: Héritage et postérité* (*Enquêtes réalisées entre 2004 et 2009*) (IFPO Press and UNESCO Publications, 2018).

- The art of glazing and inlay furniture and shells;
- Various wedding rituals, feasts and spiritual celebrations; many Syrian ethnic groups celebrate distinct festivals, such as the Spring festival in north-eastern Syria;
- Many elements associated with social engagement within and amongst communities; in Syria, heritage moves with people, transcending regional boundaries and resisting clear geographic delineation.

Types of damage to intangible Syrian heritage

The destruction in recent years has had serious and devastating repercussions for various forms of intangible heritage across the country. Instances of damage can be categorised as full or partial, as they vary in severity and breadth. The following types of damage have occurred in several cities, with effects on intangible heritage:

- The destruction and burning of most traditional markets, places of worship and public spaces, which are incubators of intangible heritage;
- Most workshops, factories and craft shops have gone out of service and closed as a result of either looting or war;
- Loss of human capital due to immigration or people switching to other occupations;
- Weak financial support for traditional professions;
- Globalisation and mechanisation, which have pitted the survival of intangible Syrian heritage in many cities in a race against time;
- A lack of youth interest; rather than continuing the traditions of their forebears and ensuring the persistence and prosperity of traditional professions and local crafts, young people have gravitated *en masse* to other jobs that provide better income;
- Misleading interpretations and commentary on an academic level or provided by other influential sectors/elite actors of

society; public heritage has been characterized by the elite as backwards or *Baladi*, thus assigning it negative connotations.[9]

Recommendations for reviving public heritage

The task of reviving Syrian public heritage is by no means an easy one. Syria is still gradually recovering from the pain of its recent past, and it is necessary to develop current and future policies and procedures regarding the protection and promotion of heritage, and intangible heritage in particular. The needs of local communities must be prioritised in a way that neither hinders construction and development nor overlooks the pillars of the country's identity, antiquities and rich diversity of living and renewable heritage. With this in mind, this study arrives at the following proposals to protect and preserve Syria's intangible heritage:

- Raising awareness of the importance of protecting this heritage through popular and governmental awareness campaigns;
- Securing the necessary financial support to launch related activities;
- Implementing and adapting the necessary legal protections;
- Amending the laws and regulations related to work, and granting licences to facilitate trade and handcraft activity, as the first stage of economic revival and the preservation of heritage skills;
- Continuation of research and academic activities at the highest level related to the inventory, study and documentation of the various forms of intangible heritage;
- Delegating the responsibility for documenting and protecting heritage in all its forms to several government agencies, rather than any one exclusively;

9 This point deserves more attention from the experts, as the duality between public (*Baladi*) and official heritage (*Rasmi*) raises the important question of which social model to follow and underlines the eternal debate on authenticity (*Asala*) vs modernity (*Hadatha*). See Younes, *Folk Traditions*, p. 454.

- Promoting the objective historical and cultural value of Syrian heritage worldwide and counteracting false and harmful narratives that aim to distort the relationship of the Syrian people with their land and environment.

Conclusion

This research has sought to contribute to the growing debate about intangible heritage in the Arab region. The chapter has shown that the discourse about intangible heritage in Syria is historically situated, starting with the postcolonial context in which interest in heritage emerged and took shape, extending to the more nationalistic discourses which emerged in the period of the country's independence. It has demonstrated that intangible heritage entails an enormous emotional dimension on account of its integral relation to collective and individual memory, as well as multiple facets of a rich and composite cultural identity. It has aimed to underscore the fact that the preservation of public heritage is critical to the survival of affected communities and the transfer of knowledge to future generations in Syria. Furthermore, this research reiterates that any division between material and immaterial heritage in this context could be justified only to the extent that it facilitates the study and classification of their components. Through its diversity and richness, intangible heritage represents a sensitive intersection between the past, which echoes in the remains of sites of heritage, and the present, which is enacted in the daily lives of Syria's inhabitants.

The best-case scenario for the revival of Syrian intangible heritage would secure its future by allocating necessary funds to engage youth interest in traditional professions, whilst preserving the memory of the past. There should be a special focus on preserving oral traditions that translate the knowledge, memory, and local cultural and social identities of previous generations. Public authorities tasked with overseeing cultural heritage have to join forces with NGOs and civil society representatives. The successful protection and preservation of intangible heritage components would thus be a reflection of responsible and effective policies towards the cultural revival across Syria, including in cities such as Aleppo. Such policies would likewise have tremendous economic and social benefits for affected communities.

It should be noted that compared with tangible heritage, intangible heritage in Syria has suffered relatively less damage and could be revived faster and with much less funding. As such, strategic investment in its preservation, including in reviving crafts and tools associated with local traditions, would lead to the revival of tourism, boosting the Syrian economy. In addition, protection strategies should be a primary focus in the course of reconstruction, and they should be carried out in tandem with a national strategy to raise awareness about the importance of Syria's intangible heritage. This would pave the way to position support for local populations at the heart of any discourse about cultural heritage in all its aspects in the country. Thus, this chapter advocates strongly for the close cooperation between public authorities and locals who must be reengaged with their heritage. The protection of this heritage, marked though it is by massive displacement and the sufferings of war, also holds the promise of securing a better future.

Bibliography

Chanesaz, Moheb, Dardaillon, Ella and David, Jean-Claude, eds., *L'artisanat du métal à Alep: Héritage et postérité (Enquêtes réalisées entre 2004 et 2009)* (IFPO Press and UNESCO Publications, 2018).

Homeland Document, *Oral History Recordings Projects in Syria* (Wathiqat-watten.org, 2021), https://wathiqat-wattan.org/category/oral-history.

ICOMOS, Intangible Heritage, Convention for the Safeguarding of Intangible Cultural Heritage / Québec Declaration on the Preservation of the Spirit of Place / The ICOMOS Charter for the Interpretation and Presentation of Cultural Heritage Sites.

Smith, Laurajane, *Uses of Heritage* (New York: Routledge, 2006).

Smith, Laurajane and Akagawa, Natsuko, eds., *Intangible Heritage* (London and New York: Routledge, 2008).

Syria Trust for Development, 'Cultural Identity and Living Heritage', 2021.

UNESCO, *Text of the Convention for the Safeguarding of the Intangible Cultural Heritage* (Ich.unesco.org, 2003), https://ich.unesco.org/en/convention.

Younes Abdulhamid, *Folk Traditions* (Cairo: Cairo Publication House, 2007).

III. LIVING HERITAGE AND CULTURAL TOURISM POTENTIAL

6. Mutrah Old Market, Oman: Analysis to Enhance a Living Heritage Site[1]

Mohamed Amer

Introduction

Culture and heritage are a means of conserving the inherited past, enabling it to inform the present and develop a future vision. This is achieved through tangible and intangible transmitted cultural heritage expressions and the community.[2] Heritage cities serve to transmit cultural identity while accounting for the community's contemporary needs and promoting creativity.[3] According to the Hangzhou Declaration,[4] from a socio-economic perspective, heritage supported by urban planning also

1 This research was conducted at the Department of Logistics, Tourism, and Service Management, Faculty of Business and Economics, German University of Technology in Oman (GUtech), which is affiliated with RWTH Aachen University, during the Winter Semester 2018–2019. The author appreciates the cooperative effort of Professor Heba Aziz, Dean of Faculty.

2 Uzi Baram, 'Marketing Heritage', in *Encyclopaedia of Global Archaeology*, ed. by Claire Smith (New York: Springer, 2014); Shashi Misiura, *Heritage Marketing*, 1st ed. (London: Routledge, 2006); Roberta Cauchi Santoro, 'Mapping Community Identity: Safeguarding the Memories of a City's Downtown Core', *City, Culture and Society*, 7 (2016), 43–54.

3 Laurajane Smith, 'Theorizing Museum and Heritage Visiting', in *The International Handbooks of Museum Studies: Museum Theory*, vol. 1, ed. by Andrea Witcomb and Kylie Message (Chichester, West Sussex: John Wiley & Sons, 2015); Laurajane Smith, *The Uses of Heritage* (London: Routledge, 2006).

4 UNESCO, *The Hangzhou Declaration: Placing Culture at the Heart of Sustainable Development Policies*, 2013.

 https://doi.org/10.11647/OBP.0388.06

encourages sustainability, cultural diversity and inclusion. Furthermore, as 'nodes of economic activities for the creative industries',[5] they play a significant role in providing employment opportunities and generating local revenue.[6]

Mutrah old market, as a cultural heritage space, is a focal point of Omani living heritage. This chapter reviews the market's cultural significance, highlighting its potential to serve as a key driver of sustainable development. For this research method, the chapter employs a Strengths, Weaknesses, Opportunities and Threats (SWOT) analysis, using qualitative methods such as direct observation and interview. The chapter examines the current situation of Mutrah old market as a case study on the preservation of authentic heritage value and assurance of integrity.

Living heritage and the community

In the United Nations Educational, Scientific and Cultural Organization (UNESCO) recognition of cultural landscape (2013), certain authentic values valorise an interactive context between the human being and the surrounding cultural assets, both material and immaterial, to preserve 'traditional techniques of [sustainable] land use and maintaining [cultural] diversity'.[7] These processes of interaction within urban spaces create emotional connections with cultural meaning, continually reviving the lifelong learning memory of the community. Thus, cultural identity contributes to the city's public image, which highlights the transmitted living heritage by creating 'a mental map' of the city's

---

5 Jyoti Hosagrahar, Jeffrey Soule, Luigi Fusco Girard, and Andrew Potts, 'Cultural Heritage, the UN Sustainable Development Goals, and the New Urban Agenda', *ICOMOS Concept Note for the United Nations Agenda 2030 and the Third United Nations Conference on Housing and Sustainable Urban Development* (*HABITAT III*) (Quito, Ecuador: International Council on Monuments and Sites (ICOMOS), February 15, 2016).

6 UNESCO, *Culture: Urban Future. Global Report on Culture for Sustainable Urban Development* (Paris: UNESCO, 2016).

7 Justin B. Cranshaw, Kurt Luther, Patrick Gage Kelley, and Norman Sadeh, 'Curated City: Capturing Individual City Guides through Social Curation', in *CHI '14- Proceedings of the SIGCHI Conference on Human Factors in Computing Systems* (SIGCHI Conference on Human Factors in Computing Systems, Toronto, Canada: Association for Computing Machinery, 2014), pp. 3249–58.

memorable spaces and experiences. This offers a means of 'allowing the city's public image to emerge through social curation'.[8]

As stated in a 2015 UNESCO document, 'a living heritage site is a measure to evaluate the depth of communication or interaction between cultural properties and the populations [...] or what motivates the population to co-operate in achieving their common future visions'.[9] In defining the characteristics of a living heritage site, it is necessary to consider the heritage context to identify the modifications in the community-based cultural heritage fabric over time, including 'changes in the function, the space, and the community's presence, in response to the changing circumstances in society'.

The significant role of the community in preserving living heritage was aptly summarized in 2003, at the first meeting of the Living Heritage Programme of the International Centre for the Study of the Preservation and Restoration of Cultural Property (ICCROM):

> Heritage does not belong to experts, or to governments [...] which leave the public out of the process of defining their heritage and the most appropriate means to care for that heritage risk failure. Heritage belongs to the members of society whose values are reflected in the definition of heritage.[10]

Considering reflections on living heritage, Dr. Rhiannon Mason, a senior lecturer in museum, gallery and heritage studies at the International Centre for Cultural and Heritage Studies at Newcastle University, connects the cultural heritage and the cultural identity of local communities with the expression 'sense of the place', denoting

8 Gabriel Victor Caballero, 'Crossing Boundaries: Linking Intangible Heritage, Cultural Landscapes, and Identity', in *Pagtib-Ong: UP Visayas International Conference on Intangible Heritage* (UP Visayas International Conference on Intangible Heritage, Iloilo City, Philippines, 2017); Kevin Lynch, *The Image of the City* (Cambridge: Massachusetts Institute of Technology, 1960); Smith, *The Uses of Heritage*.

9 UNESCO, 'Policy Document for the Integration of a Sustainable Development Perspective into the Processes of the World Heritage Convention' (UNESCO, 2015).

10 ICCROM, 'Background Paper Prepared for the First Strategy Meeting of ICCROM's Living Heritage Sites Programme', in *The ICCROM's Living Heritage Sites Programme First Strategy Meeting* (Rome: ICCROM, 2003), p. 1; Keiko Miura, 'Conservation of a "Living Heritage Site": A Contradiction in Terms? A Case Study of Angkor World Heritage Site', *Conservation and Management of Archaeological Sites*, 7:1 (2005), 3–18.

an emotional rapport between the urban heritage space and the local community.[11] This rapport can be observed in local efforts to preserve the authentic value of heritage sites and ensure their integrity via a triangle of communities—communities of place, communities of interest and communities of practice.[12]

Thus, living heritage is mainly an engine for the continuity of the local community which preserves it and sustains its values.[13] The rapport between the community and its 'tangible and intangible' heritage should be enhanced by all key stakeholders, as should the community's motivation and desire to preserve and safeguard expressions of heritage. This will generate new added value, mitigating human-induced impacts such as the effects of tourism, development projects, and new facilities and amenities. As a people-centred conservative management approach, it aims to sustain the main function of heritage buildings and the urban fabric by creating a link between the cultural identity and tangible forms of heritage space and empowering the local communities to actively participate in heritage conservation progress. This link strengthens the sense of ownership or custodianship that drives the local community to conserve its heritage.[14]

Heritage values of Mutrah old market

Investigating the traditional markets and their culture in the Arabian region, the term 'market' conceptually refers to 'the place where baggage and goods are brought for sale and procurement... a point of convergence that gets people closer and translates [...] the social rituals

---

11 Rhiannon Mason, 'Heritage and Identity: What Makes Us Who We Are?', *The Heritage Alliance*, 5 November 2014.

12 Sarah Court and Gamini Wijesuriya, *People-Centred Approaches to the Conservation of Cultural Heritage: Living Heritage* (Rome: ICCROM, 2015).

13 'Emphasis is on the present, since "the past is in the present". The present is seen as the continuation of the past into the future, and thus past and present-future are unified into an ongoing present (continuity).' Ioannis Poulios, 'Discussing Strategy in Heritage Conservation: Living Heritage Approach as an Example of Strategic Innovation,' *Journal of Cultural Heritage Management and Sustainable Development*, 4:1 (2014), 16–34.

14 Poulios, 'Discussing Strategy in Heritage Conservation'.; UNESCO, 'Operational Guideline for the Implementation of the World Heritage Convention,' Organization, UNESCO World Heritage Centre, 2013.

that they practice'.[15] The significance of these traditional markets, as spaces of communities of practice, is not limited to their sold products; rather, these places also represent both tangible and intangible heritage and the authentic cultural knowledge of the local community. As a holistic recreational hub, the market represents a unique social, cultural and economic interactive living space that is perhaps the main tool for preserving the socio-cultural values and harmony of the Arabian community. Gradually, as a result of the cultural and economic pressures of globalisation, the role of the traditional market has diminished; the market has struggled to compete with contemporary 'shopping' culture, and at the same time, many historical market sites have deteriorated.[16]

Historically, Oman is considered one of the main examples of culturally mixed markets in coastal communities. The country's high level of commercial activities gave traders an understanding of other cultures, allowing them to export and import traditional goods with foreign countries with permanent markets.[17] Mutrah old market is located in the province of Mutrah, in the south of Muscat Governorate. It is a central commercial centre for Omani people, especially those who are living in Muscat. Although it is part of Omani culture and heritage, it brings together diverse cultures and traditions.

The attributes of Mutrah old market include the main road for traditional commercial activities; the Hindi Mosque; el-Zakwany House; the Arab American Mission complex (hospital/house/church) that was built in 1948; historic houses (al-Khonji Boutique Hotel Project); the 'al-Lowatya' enclosure wall; and the Mutrah Fort, gate and tower.

15 Ahood Abdullah Al-Maimani, 'Socio-Spatial Study of Traditional Souqs in the Arabian Peninsula, the Decline of Traditional Souqs: the Case of Souq Mutrah, Muscat, Oman' (Master of Science/Arts, Doha, Qatar University, 2014); Ahood Al-Maimani, Ashraf M. Salama, and Fodil Fadli, 'Exploring Socio-Spatial Aspects of Traditional Souqs: the Case of Souq Mutrah, Oman,' *International Journal of Architectural Research* (*Archnet-IJAR*), 8:1 (2014), 50–65.

16 Ibid.

17 Al-Maimani, Salama, and Fadli, 'Exploring Socio-Spatial Aspects of Traditional Souqs: The Case of Souq Mutrah, Oman.'

Table 6.1 The attributes and heritage values of Mutrah old market

Site Attributes		1	2	3	4	5	6	7
Values		Traditional Commercial Hub	el-Zakwany House	the Hindi Mosque	Arab American Mission Complex	Historic Houses (al-Khonji Boutique Hotel Project)	al-Lowatya's Enclosure Wall	Mutrah Fort & Tower
1	Historic	x	x	x	x	x	x	x
2	Aesthetic			x		x	x	x
3	Social	x	x	x	x	x	x	
4	Economic	x						
5	Architectural	x	x	x		x	x	x
6	Urban	x			x	x	x	
7	Cultural	x	x	x	x	x	x	x
8	Religious			x	x		x	

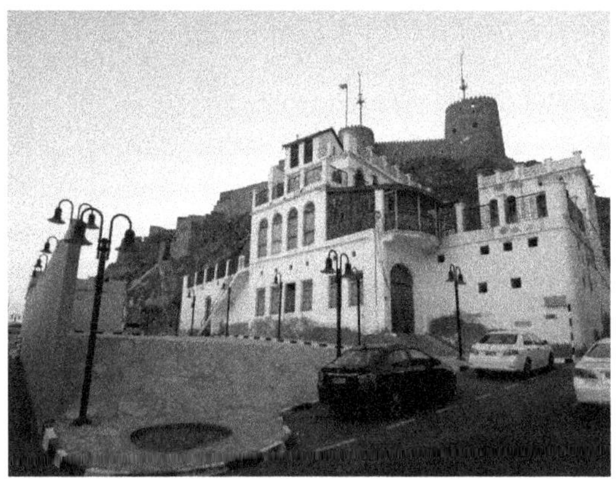

Fig. 6.1 El-Zakwany House, Mutrah Fort and Historic Enclosure Wall. Author's photograph, 2018, CC BY-NC-ND.

Historic value

Mutrah, as a coastal commercial hub with one of the oldest permanent markets in the Arab world, was founded during the historical period of the Magan civilization. However, the transmitted form of Mutrah Old

Market was founded as a historical consequence of the construction of the Portuguese Mutrah fort in the sixteenth century in the centre of the old city of Muscat.[18] Mutrah old market stands as a testament to diverse historical and cultural phases, boasting an urban fabric marked by the Omani tribes as well as Portuguese and British foreign forces in later centuries.

Urban-architectural value

The architectural significance of public markets has played a major role in preserving the identity of heritage cities in the long term.[19] The spatial features of Mutrah old market include both the street markets located in urban districts and the roadside markets situated in rural villages. It is a covered market with 'small-scale retail shops associated with urban market areas'.[20] Thus, the historic buildings, spatial allocation and social interaction are important to consider, especially in redevelopment projects enhancing the traditional context of the market.[21]

As a historic market, the settlements and old market of Mutrah followed a common traditional architecture in Oman. It was formerly constructed of clay and palm leaves, which were a suitable material given the high temperatures and harsh environment of Oman. With the occupation of Mutrah by Portuguese forces in 1507, the continuity of the traditional architectural material and design of the old market was interrupted. The Portuguese influence in Oman manifested in the use of a regular-shaped stone-brick.

On the other hand, the old market has also a unique urban traditional characteristic. Remarking on the convergence of the Omani traditional architecture and the Portuguese architecture of Mutrah Fort, Al-Maimani described Mutrah as 'enclosed by [a] wall, or houses built on the wall,

18 Manuela Gutberlet, 'Searching for an Oriental Paradise? Imaginaries, Tourist Experiences and Socio-Cultural Impacts of Mega-Cruise Tourism in the Sultanate of Oman' (Doctoral thesis, University of Aachen, 2017).

19 Gentry, 'A Sustaining Heritage.'

20 Md. Mustafizur Rahman, Shahidul Islam, and Mohammad Tanvir Hasan, 'A Redevelopment Approach to a Historical Market in Sylhet City of Bangladesh,' *Civil Engineering and Architecture*, 4:3 (2016), 127–138.

21 Al-Maimani, Salama, and Fadli, 'Exploring Socio-Spatial Aspects of Traditional Souqs'.

with four towers in the corners, one gate in the southwest and one gate in the northeast facing the Corniche. There is a high probability that it was built inside one of the Portuguese forts'.[22]

Mutrah old market was Y-shaped around two hundred years ago. It is still on the same layout, functions and the sold traditional products up to now. It consists of two parts - Suq Saghir ('the market of darkness') on the one hand and the large market for wholesale goods on the other—which were connected by numerous pathways and alleyways. According to an urban profile from 1970, Suq Saghir extended from the Prophet Mosque or Lawatiya Mosque to Khawr Bimbah. There, as a part of Omani local identity, most textiles and fabrics, foodstuffs, cosmetics, plastic jewellery, fragrances and pharmaceuticals are sold.

Enhancing the urban-architectural values, the objectives of the Mutrah Redevelopment Master Plan (MRMP) (2005) and the market's redevelopment project (2012, which were provided by Deloitte Touch Tohmatsu India Private Limited (DTTIPL) [23] aimed to preserve the character of the place as 'a public market' for Omani and international visitors and to enhance the thrift shops, arts and crafts, and other socio-economic activities, guaranteeing the market's main functionality.[24] The Muscat municipality renovated Mutrah old market during the regeneration project (2004–2005) and added some decorative motifs from Omani and Islamic architecture to the market's architecture. To maintain its distinctive character, special emphasis was placed on the market's ornamentation following the traditional Omani model. In addition, the market's roads and alleys were paved for the comfort of citizens, residents, visitors and shoppers.[25]

---

22 Ibid.

23 Deloitte Touch Tohmatsu India Private Limited, *Pre-Feasibility Study for Re-development of K R Market: Final Report, Sector Specific Inventory and Institutional Strengthening for Private-Public Partnership Mainstreaming for Bruhat Bengaluru Mahanagara Palike* (*BBMP*) (2012).

24 Al-Maimani, 'Socio-Spatial Study of Traditional Souqs in the Arabian Peninsula the Decline of Traditional Souqs'.

25 Ibid.

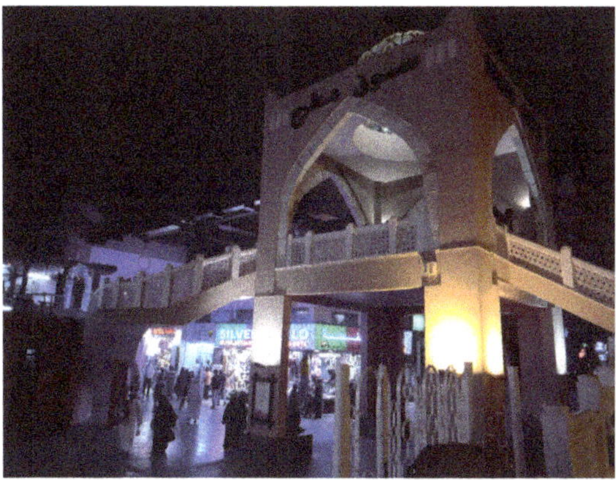

Fig. 6.2 Changes of traditional material (including new building material and design). Development project 2004–2005. Author's photograph, 2018, CC BY-NC-ND.

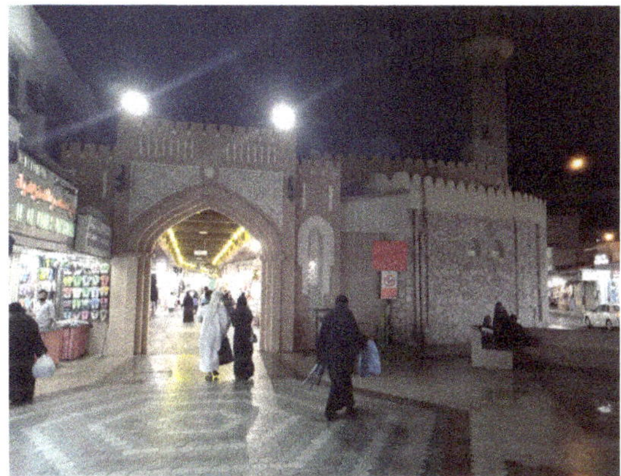

Fig. 6.3 Mutrah Market Old Gate after the development project that took place in 2004–2005. Author's photograph, 2018, CC BY-NC-ND.

Socio-cultural value

Beginning in the sixteenth century, Mutrah was inhabited by the Khoja community, who worked as craftsmen in carpentry, weaving, shipbuilding and so on. They later became involved in trade and the governance of Mutrah village.[26] In addition, it, as a costal public market, has been a space

26 Fred Scholz, *Muscat—Then and Now: Geographical Sketch of a Unique Arab Town* (Berlin: Schiler Hans Verlag, 2014).

for exchanging social and cultural manifestations 'within their respective communities, and [...] integrated into local economic and social life.'[27] Mutrah market was a social focal point for creating a strong relationship between the commercial tribe and local residents.

Mutrah old market is a unique example of a traditional historic market with socio-cultural value throughout its functional continuity, responding to the needs of the local community and the cultural diversity.[28] As a historic, culturally mixed commercial hub, Mutrah attracted people of various ethnicities from Arab regions, Africa (specifically, Zanzibar), Baluchistan, Iran and India. The built context of the historical market hosts their crafts and craftsmanship, traditional products and customs. Thus, the market embodies the local history and cultural identity of the Omani community and its evolution.

Socio-economic value

Embaby emphasises the socio-cultural importance of conserving and developing the economic identity of historical markets, which 'are considered one of the most important cultural memories of the past communities [and] the old lifestyle with its customs, goods and traditions, and the traditional commerce that were famous locally and regionally'.[29]

Historically and recently, the most common products sold in Mutrah old market are traditional Omani male clothes (*Dishdasha*), male embroidered caps (*Kumah*), the bamboo stick (*Khayaran*), headdresses (*Massar*), framed daggers (*Khanjar*), frankincense (*Luban*), incense, palm-made braziers, Arabian perfumes, Omani spices and Omani sweets (*Halwa*). These products contribute to preserving Omani citizens' transmitted traditional lifestyle and cultural identity and pausing the impacts of modernization.[30]

27 John Daniel Gentry, 'A Sustaining Heritage: Historic Markets, Public Space, and Community Revitalization' (Master's thesis, University of Maryland, College Park, 2013).

28 Embaby; Saudi Commission for Tourism and Antiquities, *The Program of Rehabilitation and Development of the Vernacular Markets in K.S.A* (Riyadh: Saudi Commission for Tourism and Antiquities, 2010).

29 Mohga E. Embaby, 'Sustainable Urban Rehabilitation of Historic Markets 'Comparative Analysis,' *International Journal of Engineering Research & Technology (IJERT)*, 3:4 (2014), 1017–31.

30 Al-Maimani, 'Socio-Spatial Study of Traditional Souqs in the Arabian Peninsula, the Decline of Traditional Souqs'.

Additionally, some Omani *Halwa* makers had workshops and shops. There was also a silver market, which was considered the most important part of Suq Saghir on account of its unique products.[31]

> Focusing on the authentic socio-economic value of Mutrah old market the dates-based commercial activities were developed as the main Omani economic sector while preserving the social practices that were emerged as a result of cultural diversity. Scholz identifies dates as a primary 'source of exchanging' and dynamic economic domain in Oman up to the 1960s. Dates were important in agriculture and other indirect manufacturing activities. As Scholz notes, 'cultivated in the oases of inner Oman and the Batinah coast, dates—packaged in woven sacks—were traded in Mutrah and exported via the port of Muscat. [...] The organizers of the export of dates were primarily Hindu merchants in Mutrah. [...] the Khojas involved in the date trade concentrated their activities on the collection and distribution of dates inside Oman'.[32]

SWOT analysis of Mutrah old market

	Strengths	Weaknesses
Internal	(1) Authentic value/heritage significance	(1) Lack of accessibility and limited carrying capacity
	(2) Multi-functionality	(2) Lack of heritage interpretation
	(3) Stable boundaries	(3) Lack of security
	(4) Well-known attraction	(4) Lack of effective cooperation among administrative authorities and key stakeholders
		(5) Demographic decline of Omani inhabitants
		(6)Lack of conservation & infrastructure

31 Al-Maimani, 'Socio-Spatial Study of Traditional Souqs in the Arabian Peninsula, the Decline of Traditional Souqs'; Scholz, *Muscat—Then and Now*.

32 Scholz, *Muscat—Then and Now*.

	Opportunities	Threats
External	(1) Financing prospects (2) Possibility of partnership in GCC (3) Suitable venue for traditional Omani festivals and events	(1) Tourism (2) Rapid urban development, (3) Surrounding development projects, & (4) Modernisation
	Positive	**Negative**

Strengths

1. Authentic value/heritage significance:

As aforementioned assessing the heritage values, Mutrah old market is authentic and unique, consisting of historical layers that provide links with various civilisations of the past, especially those in the Middle East and Europe. Moreover, it has a collection of various buildings that are a harmonised example of architectural heritage. In contrast, the local urban fabric contributes indirectly to preserving the authentic value of the market and maximising the visiting experience.

2. Multi-functionality

Mutrah has a unique interactivity. It hovers between being a commercial space and a residential district and represents diverse socio-economic groups. As a picnic and tourist attraction, it is a suitable place for Omani residents and visitors to hike[33] and enjoy leisure time with their families and friends.

3. Stable boundaries

The layout and borders of Mutrah old market have remained relatively unchanged. Recently, it has clear borders, facing Sultan Qaboos Port to the north, Mutrah Fort to the east, al-Lawatya walled enclosure and mosque to the west and Mutrah Police Station to the south. This

33 Oman Ministry of Tourism, *Trekking Path to Mutrah or Riyam* (Destinationomen.com, 2005), www.destinationoman.com/pdf/trekking+routs2.pdf

connection with the Sultan Qaboos Port ensures that its boundaries cannot be altered in the future, preserving the layout without adding new urban extensions.

4. Well-known and promoted attraction

The old market is considered a landmark for both Omani residents and international visitors. Moreover, it is so near to the most common tourism facilities and services e.g. restaurants, cafes, hotels, local museums and so on.

Weaknesses

1. Lack of accessibility and limited capacity

According to direct observation (2018–2019), the traditional urban fabric of Mutrah old market has narrow subsidiary lanes, decreasing the number of local customers and international visitors that can access some shops. In addition, el-Bahari Road and the corniche separate traditional commercial activities from the oceanfront.

2. Lack of heritage interpretation

Unfortunately, Mutrah old market has insufficient interpretation tools, such as signage, banners, concise historical knowledge and guidance arrows which would allow visitors to better navigate and understand their historic surroundings.

3. Lack of security

Although there is an evacuation plan at the main entrance, the market generally lacks security for visitors, residents and goods.

4. Lack of effective cooperation among administrative authorities

Mutrah old market is administrated by various governmental bodies such as Mutrah *Wali*, Muscat governorate, the Ministry of Tourism and Heritage, and the Ministry of Defence. According to some conversations with local investors, there is insufficient coordination among them to the site's management and development planning. Al-Maimani *et al.* have noted,

> There is subsequent inadequate coordination of investment and management which has consequently a great impact on managing the resources of this traditional market. Mutrah municipality, Mutrah ruler *Walli* and other local authorities do not play an effective role in preserving this old market.[34]
>
> As a result, there has been a 'poor evaluation of the higher tourism potential of cultural heritage that could enrich the socio-cultural experience'.[35]

In addition, regarding the direct observation of the author, he noted a lack of community involvement in the development of cultural heritage, as local strategic partners and a business canvas for adaptive reuse. Subsequently, it might negatively affect the development of societal and cultural values in the future.

5. The demographic decline of Omani inhabitants

In 2019, Gutbertlet observed, 'the majority of the vendors in Mutrah are expatriates [...] from India, Pakistan or Bangladesh. Most of them live and work within walking distance.[36] If Omani cultural policy is adapted to these foreign residents, 'this movement away from the traditional fabric can lead to loss of identity'.[37] In addition, Scholz has observed that:

> The developments in Suq Saghir after 1974 have been outlined [...] increasing numbers of customers who were Asian guest workers and by the decline in Mutrah of the wealthier and more discerning Omani categories of customers. They had emigrated to the new residential districts of the Capital Area or stayed away from this shopping district due to its inaccessibility by car.[38]

---

34 Al-Maimani, Salama, and Fadli, 'Exploring Socio-Spatial Aspects of Traditional Souqs: The Case of Souq Mutrah, Oman'; Al-Maimani, 'Socio-Spatial Study of Traditional Souqs in the Arabian Peninsula, the Decline of Traditional Souqs: The Case of Souq Mutrah, Muscat, Oman.'

35 Al-Maimani, 'Socio-Spatial Study of Traditional Souqs in the Arabian Peninsula, the Decline of Traditional Souqs: The Case of Souq Mutrah, Muscat, Oman.'

36 Gutberlet, 'Searching for an Oriental Paradise? Imaginaries, Tourist Experiences and Socio-Cultural Impacts of Mega-Cruise Tourism in the Sultanate of Oman.'

37 Al-Maimani, 'Socio-Spatial Study of Traditional Souqs in the Arabian Peninsula, the Decline of Traditional Souqs'.

38 Scholz, *Muscat - Then and Now.*

6. Lack of conservation and infrastructure[39]

In the 1950s, Mutrah was incorporated as a part of a capital rather than an independent province. Subsequently, according to the Omani national development plan, Mutrah market and its cultural assets become associated with the Sultan Qaboos Port. This action impacted renovation projects, resulting in new facilities and amenities to accommodate the needs of international visitors and the introduction of modern materials and designs in the maintenance of Mutrah Fort and its towers. In 1970, the designation of Muscat as the Omani political capital likewise contributed to changes in certain traditional elements of the Mutrah old market, such as the clay buildings.[40]

Although 'physical improvements could encourage [new globalised] businesses to open, and especially higher profile ones'[41], these external investments and developments have led to the degradation of some cultural assets because of pressures related to customization and profitability.

Furthermore, the infrastructure does not adequately account for the frequency of heavy rain and high tides. Al-Maimani observed in 2013 that Mutrah exhibits visible physical deterioration. This deterioration has occurred because of a lack of planning, a lack of maintenance policies and a lack of heritage conservation criteria to address the destruction of historic buildings and their valuable heritage. Unfortunately, because of these environmental factors, these buildings are subject to intensive renovation and 'the demolition of such valuable heritage buildings which in turn can lead to a loss of the traditional urban pattern. Each type of physical deterioration affects the socio-cultural and economic conditions of the resident community.[42]

---

39 'The concept of conservation has expanded from archaeological and heritage conservation to sites of cultural values conservation, also the conservation policies developed from heritage building adaptation to comprehensive urban context rehabilitation'. Mohga E. Embaby, 'Sustainable Urban Rehabilitation of Historic Markets Comparative Analysis,' *International Journal of Engineering Research & Technology* (*IJERT*), 3:4 (2014), 1017–31.

40 Al-Maimani, Salama, and Fadli, 'Exploring Socio-Spatial Aspects of Traditional Souqs'.

41 Al-Maimani, 'Socio-Spatial Study of Traditional Souqs in the Arabian Peninsula, the Decline of Traditional Souqs'.

42 Ibid.

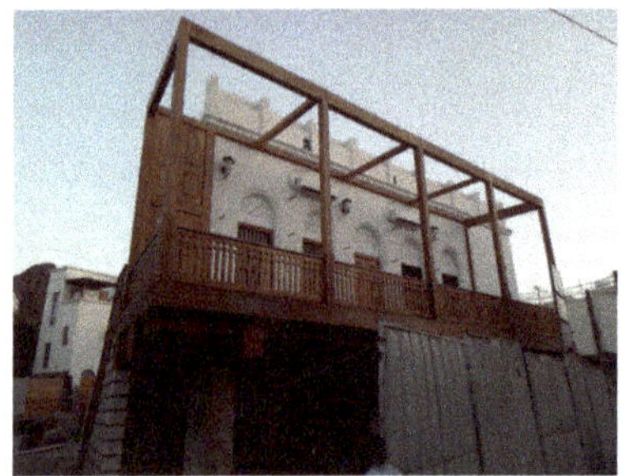

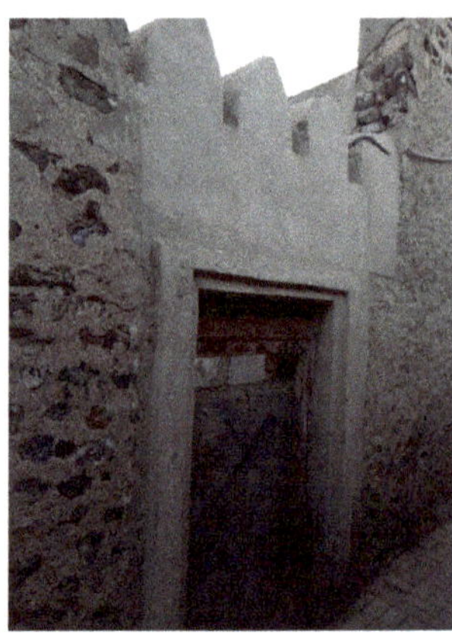

Fig. 6.4 and Fig. 6.5 Lack of conservation criteria in Mutrah. Al Khonji House, al Khonji Boutique Hotels Project (Al-Khonji Real Estate and Development LLC). Author's photograph, 2018, CC BY-NC-ND.

Opportunities

1. Possibility of partnership with local, provincial and federal agencies to preserve the traditional markets in the Gulf Cooperation Council (GCC) countries

Based on the heritage values and the aforementioned strengths, Mutrah can be not only a market or a traditional commercial centre but also a corporate entity emancipating the community involvement as a kind of people-public-private partnership. It has great potential to attract international funds to preserve Omani heritage, especially these kinds of traditional markets. Moreover, the characteristics of Mutrah old market may be suitable to enable partnerships with other provincial and international agencies for assessing and preserving traditional markets, as well as restoring, conserving and managing the old buildings, such as Al-Khonji Real Estate and Development $_{\text{LLC}}$. This step could integrate the market's cultural and traditional commercial agenda with that of other Gulf Cooperation Council (GCC) countries and their neighbour states in the Middle East.

2. Suitable venue for traditional Omani festivals and events

Based on its historic activities, the market's cultural identity has a great effect on Oman's appeal to tourists. Thus, it might encourage the local craftsmen to establish a training centre to pass down these heritage skills to future Omani generations so that this appeal can be maintained. Moreover, al-Khonji settlements might host events representing the tangible and intangible cultural heritage as well as the traditional social practices of the Omani community.

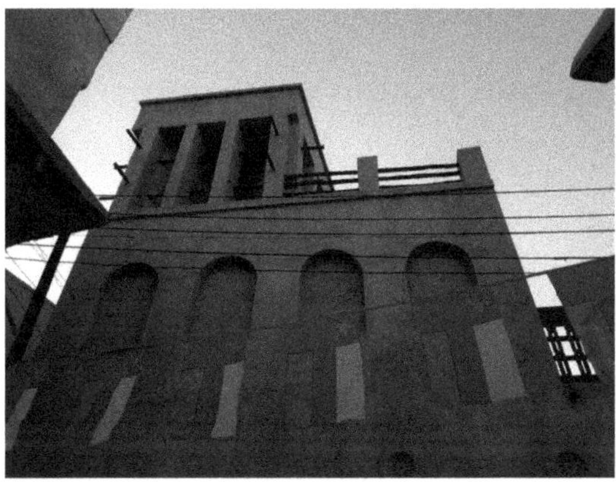

Fig. 6.6 Old house after development; al Khonji Boutique Hotels Project (Al-Khonji Real Estate and Development LLC). Author's photograph, 2018, CC BY-NC-ND.

Threats

1. Impacts of Over-tourism

Because of its location in front of Sultan Qabus Port, Mutrah old market usually receives higher numbers of international visitors during the winter as compared to the summer season. Thus, regarding the fragile carrying capacity of the market, those visitors may materially affect the conservation mandate of the market. Realizing the dimensions of glocalization and its impacts on cultural identity, this over-tourism might socially affect the Omani community's traditional values and demographic structure, behaviour, lifestyle, and living standards.[43]

43 Gutberlet, 'Searching for an Oriental Paradise?'; C. Michael Hall and Alan A. Lew, *Understanding and Managing Tourism Impacts: An Integrated Approach* (London: Routledge, 2009).

2. Rapid urban development

As a result of the increasing number of Bangladeshi and Pakistani employees[44] in the Mutrah market, irregular regenerated constructions have been built in recent decades which do not correspond to the traditional Omani style of the surroundings. Thus, there may be a push to completely reconstruct this historical market to make it more interactive realizing the cultural diversity and to provide a more efficient shopping environment.[45] This could alter the features of the social spaces,[46] as well as negatively affect the cultural identity and traditional urban fabric in Mutrah. Furthermore, the unorganised or visually unappealing buildings may generate visual pollution over the years.

3. Surrounding development projects

Due to previous rehabilitation and development projects, Mutrah, as a historical space, has lost most of its unique aesthetic potential, which stemmed from its picturesque qualities. According to an interview with Badriya al-Siyabi in 2018,[47] a group of investment projects in Sultan Qaboos Port and al-Inshirah district includes restaurants, shopping malls and tourism and recreational facilities. The valorisation of these new branded investments will lead Mutrah old market to competition rather than collaboration which could result in endangering the intangible cultural heritage expressions and authentic cultural knowledge. Consequently, it might affect its socio-economic environment and its conservation in the short or long term.

---

44 Bangladeshi and Pakistani people represent around 70% of the Mutrah market's residents. Badriya Al-Siyabi, *Impact of Sultan Qaboos Port Development Project on Mutrah Old Market*, December 17, 2018.

45 Rahman, Islam, and Hasan, 'A Redevelopment Approach to a Historical Market in Sylhet City of Bangladesh.'

46 Al-Maimani, 'Socio-Spatial Study of Traditional Souqs in the Arabian Peninsula, the Decline of Traditional Souqs'; Andres Duany, Elizabeth Plater-Zyberk, and Jeff Speck, *Suburban Nation: The Rise of Sprawl and the Decline of the American Dream* (Macmillan: North Point Press, 2000).

47 Ms. Badriya al-Siyabi - CSR Manager, Muttrah Tourism Development Company LLC at Sultan Qaboos Port [company was developed by DAMAC (Private Sector) and Omran (Public Business Sector)], 2018.

4. Modernisation

In 1970, Mutrah was faced with rapid economic and infrastructural development and modernised urbanisation which especially impacted the urban fabric of Muscat as the political capital of Oman. New supermarkets and shopping malls were constructed, precipitating a confrontation between traditional Omani crafts and modern manufacturing. This has led to the loss of the cultural significance of traditional markets in the Omani community.[48] Thus, the traditional socio-cultural identity of Mutrah faces a great modernisation-related risk to its significance and survival within a transformed context where 'the most dynamic urban economic activities and high-income households abandoned many historic commercial centres, which often led to further deterioration and obsolescence of buildings and public spaces'.[49]

Conclusion

Mutrah old market has great cultural significance as one of the most well-conserved traditional markets in the GCC region. This historical landmark is one of the few remaining locations in Oman where it is still possible to discern local traditional architecture, both in terms of materials and design. As a traditional commercial space, it is a prime example of sustainability at the local level, transmitting the traditional knowledge and practices of the community.

Given its outstanding values, Mutrah has considerable potential to emerge as a key pillar of a successful sustainable development process.[50] Successful historic markets create jobs both in their rehabilitation and operation, and the profits often stay in the community.[51] Historically,

48 Marica Dorr and Neil Richardson, 'Beyond Tradition,' in *The Craft Heritage of Oman*, vol. 2, ed. by His Highness Seyyid Shihab bin Tariq Al Said (Dubai: Motivate Publishing for the Omani Craft Heritage Documentation Project, 2003), pp. 512–23; Gutberlet, 'Searching for an Oriental Paradise?'.

49 Alessandra Quartesan and Monica Romis, *The Sustainability of Urban Heritage Preservation: The Case of Oaxaca de Juarez* (Washington DC: Inter-American Development Bank, Institutional Capacity and Finance Sector, 2010).

50 Embaby, 'Sustainable Urban Rehabilitation of Historic Markets 'Comparative Analysis.'

51 Theodore M. Spitzer and Hilary Baum, *Public Markets and Community Revitalization* (Washington DC: Urban Land Institute and the Project for Public Spaces, 1995).

Mutrah old market has been an economic engine connecting rural and urban residents. As Bryan Rich has pointed out, 'the old market attracts customers from all economic backgrounds',[52] and it may support partnerships between non-profit entities and other organisations. These partnerships might encourage a financial balance between conservation and management activities and other profitable public goals.[53]

After reviewing the heritage values of Mutrah old market, it is apparent that the market requires a special urban rehabilitation policy. For instance, al-Khonji's reuse project seeks to convert some historic houses into a boutique hotel. Such projects have significant potential to strengthen heritage contexts from a socio-economic perspective, including preserving the local cultural identity and bolstering urban infrastructure. However, they often counteract the aims of conservation by altering the inherited urban fabric.

Consequently, there is a need to unify the priorities and interests of the various stakeholders. Such hybridization or partnership would enable the development of an effective master plan including an overarching set of strategies and policies which reflects the collaboration of the local community, or investors, governmental bodies and public institutions, civic societies and the private sector.

To mitigate the negative effects of customization, the owners, especially local investors, should alter their marketing perspective, upgrading the quality of services, facilities and amenities, and adopting new social, economic, technological, and cultural policies.[54] Hence, a visitor or consumer would be able to find imported modern products alongside traditional Omani products, aligning with the evolving requirements and the customized nature of the modern market in the face of direct and indirect competition.

Using cultural mapping as a heritage interpretation method to sustain a living heritage context, key stakeholders should collaborate to generate a range of creative cultural tourism activities, investments and entrepreneurial projects, rehabilitating and adaptively reusing the

52 Bryan W. Rich, 'Structure, Hierarchy and Kin. An Ethnography of the Old Market in Puerto Princesa, Palawan, Philippines,' *Open Journal of Social Sciences*, 5 (2017), 113–24.

53 Gentry, 'A Sustaining Heritage'.

54 Rahman, Islam, and Hasan, 'A Redevelopment Approach to a Historical Market in Sylhet City of Bangladesh.'

market as an engine for socio-economic development. This joint effort can interact with transmitted values, lessening the rapid modifications of cultural assets and preserving their significance.

Bibliography

Al-Maimani, Ahood Abdullah, *Socio-Spatial Study of Traditional Souqs in the Arabian Peninsula, the Decline of Traditional Souqs: the Case of Souq Mutrah, Muscat, Oman* (MSc in Arts, Doha, Qatar University, 2014).

Al-Maimani, Ahood, Salama, Ashraf M., and Fadli, Fodil, 'Exploring Socio-Spatial Aspects of Traditional Souqs: the Case of Souq Mutrah, Oman', *International Journal of Architectural Research* (*Archnet-IJAR*), 8:1 (2014), 50–65.

Baram, Uzi, 'Marketing Heritage', in *Encyclopaedia of Global Archaeology*, ed. by Claire Smith (New York: Springer, 2014).

Caballero, Gabriel Victor, 'Crossing Boundaries: Linking Intangible Heritage, Cultural Landscapes, and Identity', in *the Proceedings of Pagtib-Ong: UP Visayas International Conference on Intangible Heritage* (UP Visayas International Conference on Intangible Heritage, Iloilo City, Philippines, 2017).

Court, Sarah and Wijesuriya, Gamini, *People-Centred Approaches to the Conservation of Cultural Heritage: Living Heritage* (Rome: ICCROM, 2015).

Cranshaw, Justin B., Luther, Kurt, Kelley, Patrick Gage, and Sadeh, Norman, 'Curated City: Capturing Individual City Guides through Social Curation, in *CHI '14- Proceedings of the SIGCHI Conference on Human Factors in Computing Systems* (Toronto: Association for Computing Machinery, 2014), 3249–58.

Deloitte Touch Tohmatsu India Private Limited, 'Pre-feasibility Study for Re-development of KR Market', in *Final Report, Sector Specific Inventory and Institutional Strengthening for Private-Public Partnership Mainstreaming for Bruhat Bengaluru Mahanagara Palike* (*BBMP*) (2012).

Dorr, Marica and Richardson, Neil, 'Beyond Tradition', in *The Craft Heritage of Oman*, vol. 2, ed. by His Highness Seyyid Shihab bin Tariq Al Said (Dubai: Motivate Publishing for the Omani Craft Heritage Documentation Project, 2003), 512–23.

Duany, Andres, Plater-Zyberk, Elizabeth, and Speck, Jeff, *Suburban Nation: the Rise of Sprawl and the Decline of the American Dream* (Macmillan: North Point Press, 2000).

Embaby, Mohga E., 'Sustainable Urban Rehabilitation of Historic Markets Comparative Analysis', *International Journal of Engineering Research & Technology* (*IJERT*), 3:4 (2014), 1017–31.

Gentry, John Daniel, *A Sustaining Heritage: Historic Markets, Public Space, and Community Revitalization* (MA thesis, University of Maryland, 2013).

Gutberlet, Manuela, *Searching for an Oriental Paradise? Imaginaries, Tourist Experiences and Socio-Cultural Impacts of Mega-Cruise Tourism in the Sultanate of Oman* (PhD thesis, University of Aachen, 2017).

Hall, C. Michael and Lew, Alan A., *Understanding and Managing Tourism Impacts: An Integrated Approach* (London: Routledge, 2009).

Hosagrahar, Jyoti, Soule, Jeffrey, Girard, Luigi Fusco, and Potts, Andrew, 'Cultural Heritage, the UN Sustainable Development Goals, and the New Urban Agenda', in *ICOMOS Concept Note for the United Nations Agenda 2030 and the Third United Nations Conference on Housing and Sustainable Urban Development (HABITAT III)* (Quito, Ecuador: International Council on Monuments and Sites (ICOMOS), February 15, 2016).

ICCROM, 'Background Paper Prepared for the First Strategy Meeting of ICCROM's Living Heritage Sites Programme', in *The ICCROM's Living Heritage Sites Programme First Strategy Meeting* (Rome: ICCROM, 2003).

Lynch, Kevin, *The Image of the City* (Cambridge: Massachusetts Institute of Technology, 1960).

Mason, Rhiannon, 'Heritage and Identity: What Makes Us Who We Are? ', *The Heritage Alliance*, 5 November 2014.

Misiura, Shashi, *Heritage Marketing*, 1st ed. (London: Routledge, 2006).

Miura, Keiko, 'Conservation of a 'Living Heritage Site' a Contradiction in Terms? a Case Study of Angkor World Heritage Site', *Conservation and Management of Archaeological Sites*, 7:1 (2005), 3–18.

Oman Ministry of Tourism, *Trekking Path to Mutrah or Riyam* (Destinationomen. com, 2005), www.destinationoman.com/pdf/trekking+routs2.pdf

Poulios, Ioannis, 'Discussing Strategy in Heritage Conservation: Living Heritage Approach as an Example of Strategic Innovation', *Journal of Cultural Heritage Management and Sustainable Development*, 4:1 (2014), 16–34.

Quartesan, Alessandra and Romis, Monica, *The Sustainability of Urban Heritage Preservation: the Case of Oaxaca de Juarez* (Washington DC: Inter-American Development Bank, Institutional Capacity and Finance Sector, 2010).

Rahman, Md. Mustafizur, Islam, Shahidul, and Hasan, Mohammad Tanvir, 'A Redevelopment Approach to a Historical Market in Sylhet City of Bangladesh', *Civil Engineering and Architecture*, 4:3 (2016), 127–138.

Santoro, Roberta Cauchi, 'Mapping Community Identity: Safeguarding the Memories of a City's Downtown Core', *City, Culture and Society*, 7 (2016), 43–54.

Saudi Commission for Tourism and Antiquities, *The Program of Rehabilitation and Development of the Vernacular Markets in K.S.A* (Riyadh: Saudi Commission for Tourism and Antiquities, 2010).

Scholz, Fred, *Muscat—Then and Now: Geographical Sketch of a Unique Arab Town* (Berlin: Schiler Hans Verlag, 2014).

Smith, Laurajane, 'Theorizing Museum and Heritage Visiting', in *The International Handbooks of Museum Studies: Museum Theory*, 1st ed, vol. 1, ed. by Andrea Witcomb and Kylie Message (Chichester: John Wiley & Sons, Ltd, 2015).

Smith, Laurajane, *The Uses of Heritage* (London: Routledge, 2006).

UNESCO, *Culture: Urban Future. Global Report on Culture for Sustainable Urban Development* (Paris: UNESCO, 2016).

UNESCO, *Operational Guideline for the Implementation of the World Heritage Convention* (Paris: UNESCO World Heritage Centre, 2013).

UNESCO, *Policy Document for the Integration of a Sustainable Development Perspective into the Processes of the World Heritage Convention* (Paris: UNESCO, 2015).

UNESCO, *The Hangzhou Declaration: Placing Culture at the Heart of Sustainable Development Policies* (Paris: UNESCO, 2013).

7. Study on the Visual Perception of Historical Streetscapes Using Kansei Engineering: Cherchell City, Algeria

Lemya Kacha and Mouenes Abd Elrrahmane Bouakar

Introduction

The largest country on the African continent, in the Arab world and the Mediterranean basin, with a rich natural heritage and a wealth of historical and archaeological treasures, Algeria remains largely untouched by mass tourism. This is despite its immense diversity, including panoramic views, exceptional landscapes and a history that bears witness to the passage of several civilisations; the nation has managed to preserve its unique allure. While the tourism potential is evident, the approach to heritage conservation in Algerian cities plays a crucial role in shaping the visitor experience.

Cities in Algeria are distinguished by the legacy of urban forms and local planning authorities actively engage in heritage conservation for various reasons. However, the manner in which this is approached can vary significantly from one location to another, influenced by distinct local political and economic aspirations. Thus, while heritage tourism may be a chosen strategy in certain areas, with the aim of increasing tourist footfall, different destinations tend to focus on themes specific

 https://doi.org/10.11647/OBP.0388.07

to their culture and location.[1] Algerian policies towards both tangible and intangible heritage are laid out clearly in Law No. 98-04 of 15 June 1998 on the protection of cultural heritage, which explains: 'Immovable cultural property includes: historical monuments, archaeological sites and urban or rural settlements' (Article 8) and:

> Urban or rural real estate settlements such as the Kasbah, Medinas, Ksours, villages and traditional agglomerations characterised by their predominance as residential areas, and which, by their homogeneity and their architectural and aesthetic unity, present historical, architectural, artistic or traditional interest such as to justify their protection, restoration, rehabilitation and development, are classified as protected areas (Article 41).

Despite the clear and precise formulation of heritage policies, the urban and architectural heritage in most of Algeria's historic centres is deteriorating. This is a result of various problems related to degradation and destruction, urbanisation, land speculation, demographic changes, and the complex challenges associated with economic and social imbalance.[2] The economic disparities, including uneven development and resource distribution, contribute to the deterioration of heritage. Social imbalances, such as disparities in education and employment opportunities, further exacerbate the challenges faced by these historic centres. Additionally, the loss of identity is manifested through factors like cultural erosion, neglect of traditional values, and the impact of rapid modernization, all of which collectively contribute to the decline of the rich heritage in these areas.

Cherchell is located on the coastal strip about 100 km west of Algiers. As a Roman city, the former capital of Mauritania, it was called Caesarea, and in the Phoenician era, it was called Iol.[3] Today, Cherchell's tangible

1 Tou Chuang Chang, Simon Milne, Dale Fallon and Corinne Pohlmann, 'Urban Heritage Tourism', *Annals of Tourism Research*, 23 (1996), 284–305 (p. 287); Richards Greg, *Cultural Attractions and European Tourism* (Wallingford: CABI Publ., 2006).

2 Nassira Bouanane, *Le patrimoine et sa place dans les politiques urbaines Algériennes* (Master's thesis, University of Constantine, 2008).

3 Youcef Chennaoui, 'Notes sur le modèle urbanistique des villes portuaires de fondation andalouse au Maghreb, après 1492: La médina de Cherchell (Algérie), Le rôle des villes littorales du Maghreb dans l'histoire, RM2E', *Revue de la Méditerranée édition électronique*, 3:1 (2016), 153–168 (p. 154).

heritage is undergoing steadily accelerating degradation[4] despite its immense potential as a site for cultural and heritage tourism. To evaluate the degree of attractiveness of this heritage to tourists, the authors applied the Kansei Engineering method to understand the viewers' subjective impressions of the attractiveness of historical streetscapes. These impressions were then given measurable value using the semantic differential method.

The aim of the present study is the semantic evaluation of the visual attributes of a dataset composed of ten historical streetscape images. It focuses on the emotional impressions of the participants who evaluated the visual richness and attractiveness of the dataset using virtual reality. The study has the following specific objectives: (1) to analyse tourists' emotional responses towards historical streetscapes; (2) to study the semantic differences between three different architectural styles in Cherchell city; and (3) to explain the importance of the valorisation of the historical heritage.

Literature review

The conservative approach to protecting cultural heritage has historically focused mainly on tangible heritage, whereas intangible heritage—manifested in different art forms, popular traditions, languages, religions and so on—was part of a different plan of conservation. Insufficient state funding for the conservation and maintenance of cultural heritage often leads to its neglect, and, consequently, irreversible losses spanning the four fundamental areas of cultural heritage—namely, social, scientific, political and economic heritage.[5]

The growing need to promote local identity in the age of globalisation has prompted a debate among researchers as to the developmental

4 Bachira Ben Ali and Seddik Hammache, 'Cherchell: Aspects Urbanistiques de L'archéologie Urbaine', *Villes En Parallèle*, 36 (2003), 196–209.

5 Mark P. Hampton, 'Heritage, Local Communities and Economic Development', *Annals of Tourism Research*, 32 (2005), 735–59; Dallen J. Timothy, *Cultural Heritage and Tourism in the Developing World a Regional Perspective* (London: Routledge, 2010); Šcitaroci Mladen Obad, Šćitaroci Bojana Bojanić Obad and Ana Mrđa, *Cultural Urban Heritage: Development, Learning and Landscape Strategies* (Cham: Springer International Publishing, 2019).

use, mainly of tangible but also of intangible cultural heritage.[6] The present literature review revealed multiple approaches to studying the symbiotic relationship between historic heritage and tourism, which has the potential to make streetscapes more attractive.[7] The characteristics and quality of the natural and cultural environment are generally what attracts tourists to a given location, and heritage remains one of the major motivations for travel. Patrimonial, cultural and historical richness play an important role in tourist attraction. As long as tourism is a producer of images, generating visual representations or impressions that influence how a particular destination is perceived, it offers the presentation of heritage in its human, historical and cultural contexts.[8]

According to Vuk Tvrtko Opačić, the valorisation of cultural heritage that the tourist industry promotes includes the act of the conversion of heritage into a tourist product. This process includes four main steps, which are as follows: (a) the identification of cultural heritage suitable for conversion into tourism attractions; (b) the evaluation of the attractiveness of cultural heritage to tourists; (c) the determination of the spatial distribution of cultural heritage; and (d) the application of an appropriate model for the valorisation of cultural heritage by the tourist industry.[9] This study focuses primarily on the second stage as it evaluates perceptions of historic streetscapes in the city of Cherchell.

---

6 Hyung Yu Park, *Heritage Tourism* (London: Routledge, Taylor & Francis Group, 2014); Bob McKercher and Hilary Du Cros, *Cultural Tourism: The Partnership between Tourism and Cultural Heritage Management* (New York: Routledge, 2015); Melanie K. Smith, *Issues in Cultural Tourism Studies* (London: Routledge, 2016).

7 Greg Richards, *Cultural Attractions and European Tourism* (Wallingford: CABI Publ., 2006); Claire Smith, 'Urban Heritage', in *Encyclopedia of Global Archaeology* (New York: Springer Reference, 2014); Nicholas Wise and Jimura Takamitsu, *Tourism, Cultural Heritage and Urban Regeneration Changing Spaces in Historical Places* (Cham: Springer, 2020).

8 Dean Maccannell, 'Staged Authenticity: Arrangements of Social Space in Tourist Settings', *American Journal of Sociology*, 79 (1973), 589–603; Alan A. Lew, 'A Framework of Tourist Attraction Research', *Annals of Tourism Research*, 14 (1987), 553–575; Neil Leiper, 'Tourist Attraction Systems', *Annals of Tourism Research*, 17 (1990), 367–84; Nathalie Fabry, 'Clusters de tourisme, compétitivité des acteurs Et attractivité des territoires', *Revue Internationale D'intelligence Économique*, 1 (2009), 55–66 (p. 58).

9 Vuk Tvrtko Opačić, Tourism Valorisation of Cultural Heritage in *Cultural Urban Heritage: Development, Learning and Landscape Strategies* ed. by Šcitaroci Mladen Obad, Šćitaroci Bojana Bojanić Obad, and Ana Mrđa (Cham: Springer International Publishing, 2019), pp. 181–196 (p. 184).

Kansei Engineering is one of the approaches used to quantify visual perception. According to the Japanese dictionary *Shin Meikai*, Kansei is the intuitive mental action of a person who feels some sort of impression from an external stimulus. Intersecting with psychology, the Kansei Engineering method thus endeavours to understand and quantify a person's immediate mental impressions upon being confronted with a certain product or image.[10] The creator of the methodology, Mitsuo Nagamachi, explains this concept by articulating that Kansei is an individual's subjective impression of a certain artefact, environment or situation.[11] Nagamachi has developed various methods of measurement that focus on participants' behaviour, words (semantic differential method), facial expressions, body language and physiological responses (e.g., heart rate, electromyography and electroencephalography). Usually, Kansei Engineering includes an evaluation experiment followed by statistical analysis of the obtained data. The most common process involves three main steps, which are as follows: (a) the selection of Kansei words, (b) a Kansei evaluation experiment using a questionnaire and (c) multivariate analyses of the data issued from the evaluation experiment (e.g., factor analysis; see Fig. 7.1).

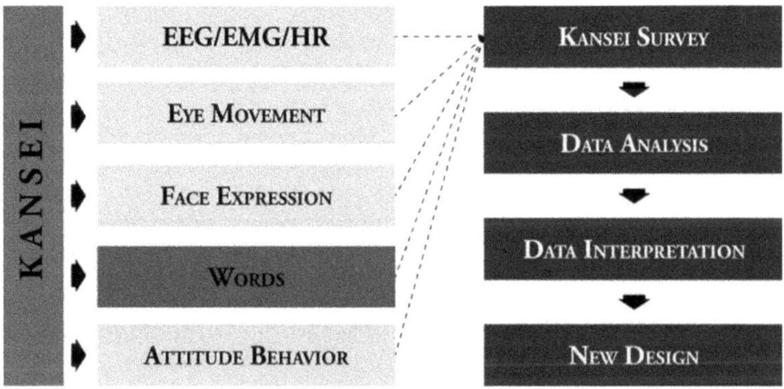

Fig. 7.1 Routes to reach Kansei. Author's diagram, CC BY-NC-ND.

10 Mitsuo Nagamachi, *Kansei/Affective Engineering* (Boca Raton, USA: CRC Press, 2011), p. 2.

11 Mitsuo Nagamachi, *Workshop 2 on Kansei Engineering*, Proceedings of the International Conference on Affective Human Factors Design: 27–29 June 2001 (London: ASEAN Academic Press, 2001).

In Kansei Engineering studies related to affective attributes influencing streetscapes evaluations, notable research examples include the work of Donald Appleyard, Carmen Llinares, and Takumi Nakama. Appleyard, utilizing Kansei Engineering, categorized streets into four principal types based on residents' perceptions—sanctuary, child-rearing, accessibility, and neighbourhood identity.[12] Llinares applied Kansei Engineering to analyse how individuals select their living places within a city based on their perception of urban landscapes,[13] while Nakama used the approach to study the impression of the historic streetscapes of Kyoto city.[14] Other significant applications include Yuichiro Kinoshita's introduction of a Kansei stroll map.[15] Toshio Tsuchiya has used Kansei Engineering to analyse people's subjective responses towards a streetscape plan with a historical townscape.[16] Lemya Kacha has used Kansei Engineering to analyse participants' emotional responses towards the different compositions of streetscapes.[17] In 2021, Tomomi Hatano et al studied the attractiveness of Japanese heritage based on the value structure of Kansei.[18]

Semantic differential, a Kansei Engineering tool used mostly in streetscape studies, was first developed by Charles Osgood in 1951.[19] It is a type of rating scale designed for observing and measuring the

12 Donald Appleyard, M. Sue Gerson and Mark Lintell, *Livable Streets* (Berkeley: University of California Press, 1981).

13 Carmen Llinares and F. Page Alvaro, 'Differential Semantics as a Kansei Engineering Tool for Analysing the Emotional Impressions Which: The Case of Valencia, Spain', *Landscape and Urban Planning*, 87 (2008), 247–257.

14 Takumi Nakama and Yuichiro Kinoshita, 'A Kansei Analysis of the Streetscape in Kyoto: An Application of the Kansei Structure Visualization Technique', *International Conference on Kansei Engineering and Emotion Research* (2010), 314–323.

15 Yuichiro Kinoshita, Tsukanaka Satoshi and Nakama Takumi, 'Kansei Stroll Map: Walking around a City Using Visualized Impressions of Streetscapes', *Interacting with Information* (2011), 211–20.

16 Toshio Tsuchiya, 'Kansei Engineering Study for Streetscape Zoning Using Self Organizing Maps', *International Journal of Affective Engineering*, 12 (2013), 365–373.

17 Lemya Kacha, Naoji Matsumoto and Ahmed Mansouri, 'Study on the Evaluation of Impression in Streetscapes in Algeria and Japan Using Kansei Engineering', *Journal of Architecture and Planning*, 80 (2015), 1357–1363.

18 Tomomi Hatano, Tomomi Takezawa, Masashi Sugimoto, Xu Kuangzhe,Takashi Morikawa, Yasuhiro Azuma, Kazuo Shibuta and Noriko Nagata, 'Visualization of Visit Motivation Based on Kansei Value Structure and Attractiveness of Tourism Resource: Toward Attracting Inbound Visitors Based on Ako Salt, a Japan Heritage', *IEICE Tech. Rep.*, 121 (2021), 13–18.

19 Charles E. Osgood, Percy H. Tannenbaum and George J. Suci, *The Measurement of Meaning* (Urbana, Il.: University of Illinois Press, 1978).

psychological meanings of concepts on a scale between two bipolar words or adjectives. It has proven to be a flexible and reliable instrument for measuring attitudes towards a wide range of stimuli. The semantic differential method was used in this research to grasp the emotional impressions of twenty participants regarding different visual attributes, using virtual reality, in a dataset of three different styles of historical heritage in Cherchell—that is to say, Roman, Arab-Andalusian and colonial streetscapes.

Area of the study

Cherchell occupies the site of the Caesarea Mauretaniae, which was one of the most important cities of North Africa in Roman antiquity. It is located a hundred kilometres west of Algiers. From its geographical position, it offers pleasant panoramic views of both sea and forest.

Cherchell reflects the transition of several civilisations from the Prehistoric to the Egyptian, Phoenician, Berber, Roman, Ottoman, Arab-Andalusian and French colonial periods.[20] In terms of its architecture, the Islamic residential buildings of Cherchell are austere and devoid of decorative elements, especially on the exterior. The only decoration that enriches the city's streetscape is the arch, which appears in different variants (i.e., the semi-circular arch, horseshoe arch and Cherchell arch, which has the shape of a basket handle that ends in a triangular brace).[21] The French colonial buildings are more ornate and intricate, featuring many decorative elements of different varieties (arches, triangles, rectangles, ornaments, etc.; see Fig. 7.2).

---

20 Henri Marchand, 'Cherchell Préhistorique', *Bulletin De La Société Préhistorique De France*, 29 (1932), 474–480; François Lenormant, *Manuel d'histoire Ancienne de L'orient Jusqu'aux Guerres Médiques* (Paris, 1869), p. 247; Jean Joseph Francois Poujoulat, *Histoire De Saint Augustin* (Tours: Alfred Mame, 1885); Phillippe Leveau, *Ceasarea de Maurétanie, uneville romaine et sescampagnes* (Ecole française de Rome, 1984); Bruno Baudoin, Véronique Blanc-Bijon and Stéphanie Satre, 'La Documentation Sur Césarée De Maurétanie Au Centre Camille-Jullian. De L'Inventaire À Une Base De Données Épigraphique', *Les Nouvelles De L'archéologie* (2016), 37–41.

21 Abdelkader Behiri and Naima Chabbi-Chemrouk, 'Cherchell: An Algerian Mediterranean Historical City With A Rich Islamic Heritage Housing', *Journal of Islamic Architecture*, 3 (2015), 127–134 (p. 132).

The historic centre of Cherchell is becoming a tourist location as it is increasingly recognized for its rich natural, historical and cultural heritage. It represents the central core of the whole city and the main place of exchange. It is characterised by a strong concentration of commercial, administrative, cultural and educational activities. Based on data availability and relevant previous experience, the authors of this study selected the historic centre of Cherchell city as the main focus of their research.

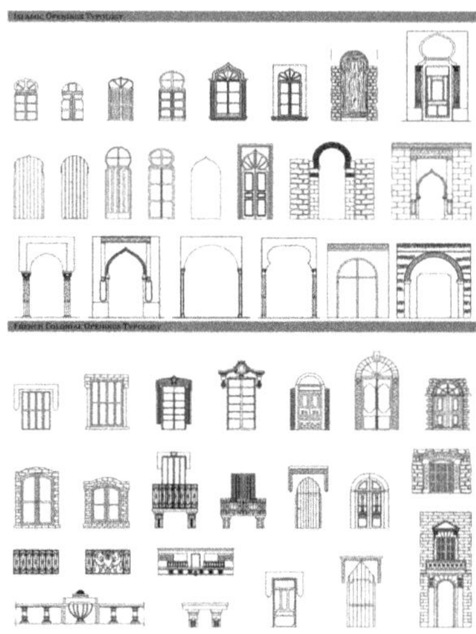

Fig. 7.2 A typology of openings from the Islamic and French colonial periods. Author's illustration, CC BY-NC-ND.

Research design

The purpose of this study was to carry out the first phase of Kansei Engineering to analyse tourists' emotional responses towards the state of historical streetscapes. To achieve this objective, we used the Kansei procedure, following the standard process established by Nagamachi (2011), which includes an evaluation experiment followed by statistical analysis of the obtained data. Twenty participants were asked to evaluate ten 360° panoramic pictures using a virtual reality headset. The questionnaire was composed of ten bipolar adjectives related to different visual attributes using a seven-point scale (see Fig. 7.3).

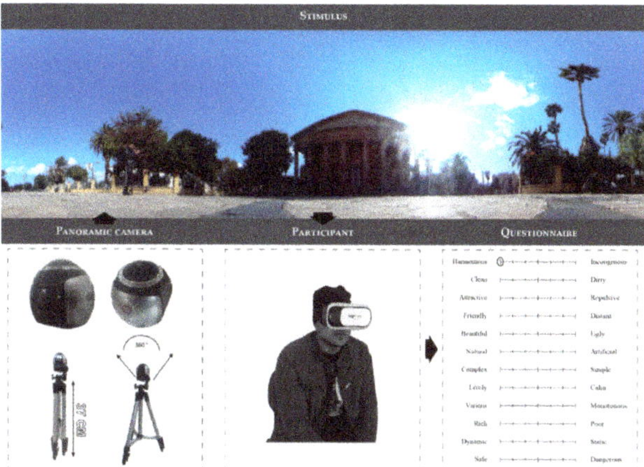

Fig. 7.3 Procedure of the experiment. Author's photograph, 2020,

Data collection

The dataset used in this study was composed of ten streetscape images. Two images were shot at the Roman site within the historic centre. Three images were shot in Ainksiba streets (examples of Islamic heritage). The other five images were taken in French colonial streets. All images were taken in the daytime, on a sunny winter day, using a panoramic digital camera (2448P, 30 fps, 16MP, 360° H, 220° V, fisheye lens). The camera was fixed on a tripod to avoid artefacts caused by the camera shaking (see Fig. 7.3).

Experiment

Participants

This study involved twenty domestic tourist participants,[22] all of whom were Algerian students in the Department of Architecture at the University of Batna.[23] In order to ensure that participants fully grasped

22 Domestic tourism includes the activities of a visitor residing within the boundaries of the reference country.

23 The distance between the cities of Batna and Cherchell is about 376 km as the crow flies.

the content of the experiment, the majority of those selected to participate in the study were master's students in the Architecture program with an average age of twenty-three years old. The sample included fourteen female participants and six male participants (74% and 26%, respectively), as it was not possible to ensure equal representation of each gender.

Procedure

Images in the dataset were presented to participants using a virtual reality headset (see Fig. 7.3), and each participant was given ample time to evaluate the dataset in its entirety.

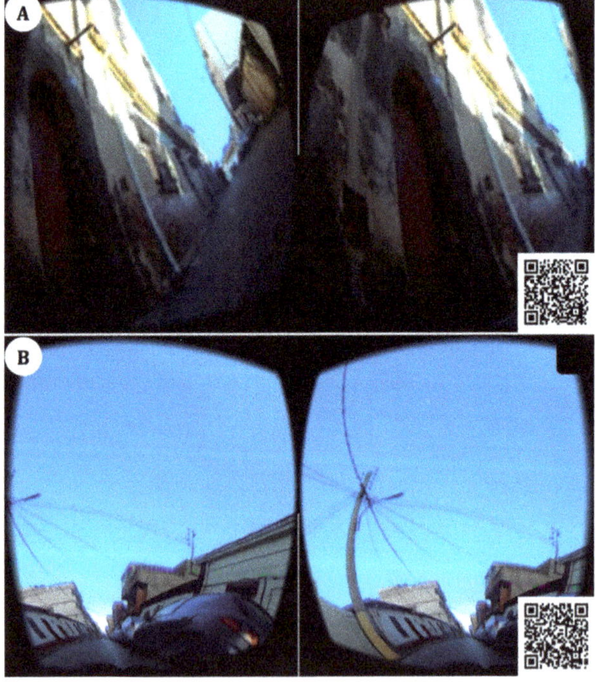

Fig. 7.4 Example of the experiment using the virtual reality headset: (A) Ainksiba, (B) French colonial. Author's photograph, 2020, CC BY-NC-ND.

The authors explained the aim of the experiment and asked each participant to evaluate the visual attributes of each streetscape image. Participants were confronted with stimulus material and marked the seven-point scale between a polar pair of adjectives, in accordance with their subjective reaction towards the stimulus material.[24] Figure 7.4 shows an example of what participants saw during the experiment.

Questionnaire

Participants completed a questionnaire comprising ten bipolar adjective pairs. These bipolar adjectives were selected after conducting a preliminary inquiry about commonly used adjectives to describe preference and attractiveness in the study of streetscapes.[25] The adjectives were presented in French on account of the educational background of the Algerian participants.

Results and discussion

Descriptive statistics of the dataset

Standard deviation shows the amount of variation from the mean. The standard deviation of the evaluation of all participants indicates that the distribution tended to be high, showing that the values were spread out over the maximum range (between 1 and 7).

Factor analysis

Principal axis factoring with varimax rotation was the method selected to analyse the factorial structure of the semantic scoring related to the cognitive appraisal. The resulting factor scoring was classified into different clusters using cluster analysis (the Ward method). The results showed that the perception of the collected streetscapes could be expressed through three independent factors, which explained 89.17% of the variance in the sampled perception (see Table 7.1). These three semantic axes represent concepts related to the following attributes: (1) attractiveness, (2) complexity and (3) security. Table 7.1 shows the designation of factorial axes.

24 Mitsuo Nagamachi, *Innovations of Kansei Engineering* (Boca Raton, USA: CRC Press, 2017), p. 54.

25 Henry Sanoff, *Visual Research Methods in Design* (London: Routledge, 2018), p. 83.

We can observe that the Roman heritage was considered more attractive for its originality, defined by the materials and techniques that preserved its identity and testify to a certain amount of knowledge; Arab-Andalusian heritage was viewed as monotonous because of its simplicity (blind facades), its physical conditions (lack of maintenance) and the changes it has undergone through time; colonial heritage was considered ordinary because the participants were familiar with this style of architecture and because it has been modified by its users. Moreover, the fact that these buildings have rich and complex features with many openings produced a sense of security.

Table 7.1 Results of factor analysis including cognitive clustering of adjectives and streetscapes using the Ward method. Author's illustration, 2020, CC BY-NC-ND.

Axes	*Label*	*Bipolar Adjectives*			*Factor 1*	*Factor 2*	*Factor 3*
1st Axis	Attractiveness	Harmonious	—	Incongruous	**0.972**	0.093	0.011
		Clean	—	Dirty	**0.901**	0.138	0.187
		Attractive	—	Repulsive	**0.898**	0.243	0.334
		Friendly	—	Distant	**0.898**	0.243	0.334
		Beautiful	—	Ugly	**0.883**	0.342	0.178
		Natural	—	Artificial	**0.688**	-0.584	-0.350
		Complex	—	Simple	**0.598**	0.534	-0.440
2nd Axis	Complexity	Lively	—	Calm	-0.044	**0.923**	0.051
		Various	—	Monotonous	0.348	**0.795**	-0.141
		Rich	—	Poor	0.308	**0.793**	0.113
		Dynamic	—	Static	0.219	**0.720**	0.596
3rd Axis	Security	Safe	—	Dangerous	0.474	0.005	**0.846**
Eignvalue					5.470	3.520	1.711
Contribution Ratio (%)					45.582	29.332	14.254
Cumulative Contribution Ratio (%)					45.582	74.914	89.168

Extraction Method: Principal Axis Factoring
Rotation Method: Varimaxwith Kaiser Normalization.

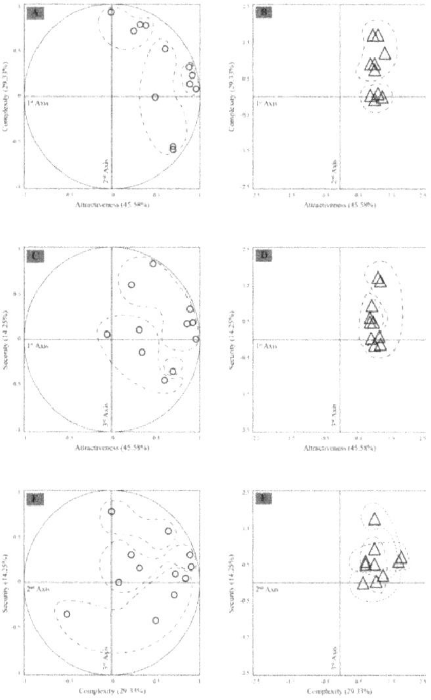

Analysis of semantic differential evaluation

The semantic differential diagram shows that Roman heritage was viewed as presenting positive characteristics (between 1 and 4), whereas the Arab-Andalusian heritage was assigned negative characteristics (between 4 and 7). The French colonial heritage was considered to possess more or less ordinary characteristics (tendency towards 4).

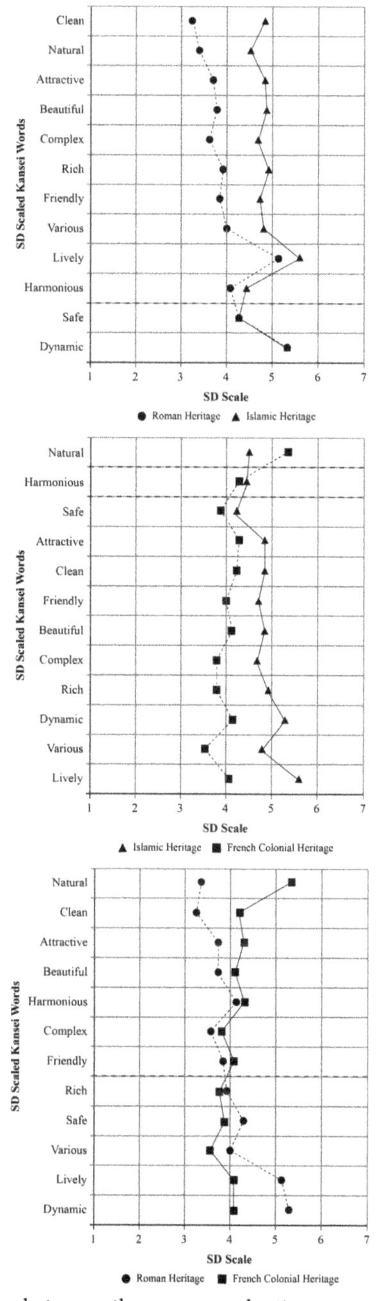

Fig. 7.5 Comparison between the mean evaluation scores of three different heritages. Author's graphs, CC BY-NC-ND. (A) Roman vs. Islamic, (B) Islamic vs. French colonial, (C) Roman vs. French colonial.

Roman heritage was ascribed positive meanings—namely, it is attractive, beautiful, rich and clean because of its originality, its unique materials and antique architecture.

Arab-Andalusian heritage has undergone many changes during the transitions between different civilisations throughout history, and the Arab-Andalusian buildings have lost their originality primarily due to inadequate maintenance. The two diagrams converge on two points—specifically, they are not very static and not very secure. This is due to the lack of distinctive architectural elements on the Arab-Andalusian buildings, particularly evident in the prevalence of blind facades with minimal openings (see Fig. 7.5a).

The French colonial heritage was deemed less natural than the Arab-Andalusian heritage, whereas the Arab-Andalusian heritage was assigned fewer positive characteristics than the colonial heritage. This is due to the degraded physical conditions of buildings, exemplified by noticeable decay, the various modifications these structures have undergone, such as alterations to façades or structural changes, and the diverse functions that wholly or partially alter their original form, illustrated by repurposing buildings for commercial use or conversion into residences (facades; see Fig. 7.5b).

The results show that participants have cognitive preferences towards Roman heritage rather than colonial heritage. The latter is considered less beautiful, natural, clean and harmonious but more varied, dynamic and rich (see Fig. 7.5c). This can be attributed to the way users occupy this tangible heritage and how they treat it.

Conclusion

This study set out to explain the importance of the valorisation of historical heritage by evaluating the visual attributes assigned to a dataset composed of ten historical streetscape images collected from three different architectural heritages—Roman, Arab-Andalusian and French colonial. The semantic differential method was applied as a Kansei Engineering tool to grasp the subjective impressions of attractiveness in the dataset, as evaluated by twenty domestic tourists.

The findings of this research identified three main factorial axes that summarise the semantic attributes of the selected streetscapes and explain 89.17% of the variance. These axes covered attractiveness, complexity and security. The semantic attributes of Roman heritage covered more positive characteristics, such as attractiveness, beauty, naturalness, cleanliness and richness, whereas the semantic attributes of Arab-Andalusian heritage reflected more negative characteristics—that is to say, monotonous, static, simple, poor and repulsive. The semantic attributes of French colonial heritage covered ordinary characteristics.

The results of this study confirm that the originality of the materials and the unique construction techniques that allow the preservation of identity are important elements for the attractiveness of architectural heritage. Our investigation primarily focused on the impact of physical alterations and changes, such as modern renovations, structural modifications and shifts in land use. We found that degradation and lack of maintenance are key factors that have led to the loss of heritage value. The findings also suggest that physical changes, particularly those that alter the original character and historical significance, result in heritage being perceived as more ordinary over time, thereby decreasing its real value. Finally, this study indicates that buildings with elaborate features and numerous openings evoke a heightened sense of security.

The methodology and findings of this research have the potential to positively inform future renovation projects in Cherchell by pinpointing existing problems and suggesting strategies to increase the appeal of urban heritage and conserve the city's image. In turn, these processes are likely to contribute to enhancing both cultural and urban tourism in the long term.

Bibliography

Appleyard, Donald, Gerson, M. Sue and Lintell, Mark, *Livable Streets* (Berkeley: University of California Press, 1981).

Baudoin, Bruno, Blanc-Bijon, Véronique and Satre, Stéphanie, 'La Documentation Sur Césarée De Maurétanie au Centre Camille-Jullian. De L'Inventaire À Une Base De Données Épigraphique', *Les Nouvelles De L'archéologie*, 2016, 37–41, https://doi.org/10.4000/nda.3804.

Behiri, Abdelkader and Chabbi-Chemrouk, Naima, 'Cherchell: An Algerian Mediterranean Historical City with A Rich Islamic Heritage Housing', *Journal of Islamic Architecture*, 3 (2015), 127–134, https://doi.org/10.18860/jia.v3i3.2745.

Ben Ali, Bachira and Hammache, Seddik, 'Cherchell: Aspects Urbanistiques de L'archéologie Urbaine', *Villes En Parallèle*, 36 (2003), 196–209, https://doi.org/10.3406/VILPA.2003.1397.

Bouanane, Nassira, *Le patrimoine et sa place dans les politiques urbaines Algériennes* (Master's thesis, University of Constantine, 2008).

Chang, Tou Chuang, Milne, Simon, Fallon, Dale and Pohlmann, Corinne, 'Urban Heritage Tourism', *Annals of Tourism Research*, 23 (1996), 284–305.

Chennaoui, Youcef, 'Notes sur le modèle urbanistique des villes portuaires de fondation andalouse au Maghreb, après 1492: La médina de Cherchell (Algérie), Le rôle des villes littorales du Maghreb dans l'histoire, RM2E', *Revue de la Méditerranée édition électronique*, 3:1 (2016), 153–168.

Fabry, Nathalie, 'Clusters de tourisme, compétitivité des acteurs Et attractivité des territoires', *Revue Internationale D'intelligence Économique*, 1 (2009), 55–66, https://dx.doi.org/10.3166/r2ie.1.55-66.

Greg, Richards, *Cultural Attractions and European Tourism* (Wallingford: CABI Publishing, 2006).

Hampton, Mark P., 'Heritage, Local Communities and Economic Development', *Annals of Tourism Research*, 32 (2005), 735–59, http://dx.doi.org/10.1016/j.annals.2004.10.010.

Hatano, Tomomi, Takezawa, Tomomi, Sugimoto, Masashi, Kuangzhe, Xu, Morikawa, Takashi, Azuma, Yasuhiro, Shibuta, Kazuo and Nagata, Noriko, 'Visualization of Visit Motivation Based on Kansei Value Structure and Attractiveness of Tourism Resource: Toward Attracting Inbound Visitors Based on Ako Salt, a Japan Heritage', *IEICE Tech. Rep.*, 121 (2021), 13–18.

Kacha, Lemya, Matsumoto, Naoji and Mansouri, Ahmed, 'Study on the Evaluation of Impression in Streetscapes in Algeria and Japan Using Kansei Engineering', *Journal of Architecture and Planning*, 80 (2015), 1357–1363, https://doi.org/10.3130/AIJA.80.1357.

Kinoshita, Yuichiro, Satoshi, Tsukanaka and Takumi, Nakama, 'Kansei Stroll Map: Walking around a City Using Visualized Impressions of Streetscapes', *Interacting with Information* (2011), 211–20, http://dx.doi.org/10.1177/1365480217717530.

Leiper, Neil, 'Tourist Attraction Systems', *Annals of Tourism Research*, 17 (1990), 367–84, https://doi.org/10.1016/0160-7383(90)90004-B.

Lenormant, François, *Manuel d'histoire Ancienne de L'orient Jusqu'aux Guerres Médiques* (Paris, 1869).

Leveau, Phillippe, *Ceasarea de Maurétanie, uneville romaine et sescampagnes* (Ecole française de Rome, 1984).

Lew, Alan A., 'A Framework of Tourist Attraction Research', *Annals of Tourism Research*, 14 (1987), 553–575.

Llinares, Carmen and Alvaro, F. Page, 'Differential Semantics as a Kansei Engineering Tool for Analysing the Emotional Impressions Which: The Case of Valencia, Spain', *Landscape and Urban Planning*, 87 (2008), 247–257, https://doi.org/10.1016/j.landurbplan.2008.06.006.

Maccannell, Dean, 'Staged Authenticity: Arrangements of Social Space in Tourist Settings', *American Journal of Sociology*, 79 (1973), 589–603, https://doi.org/10.1086/225585.

Marchand, Henri, 'Cherchell Préhistorique', *Bulletin De La Société Préhistorique De France*, 29 (1932), 474–480, http://doi.org/10.3406/bspf.1932.5652.

McKercher, Bob and Du Cros, Hilary, *Cultural Tourism: The Partnership between Tourism and Cultural Heritage Management* (New York: Routledge, 2015).

Mladen Obad, Šcitaroci, Bojanić Obad, Šćitaroci Bojana and Mrđa, Ana, *Cultural Urban Heritage: Development, Learning and Landscape Strategies* (Cham: Springer International Publishing, 2019).

Nagamachi, Mitsuo, *Innovations of Kansei Engineering* (Boca Raton, USA: CRC Press, 2017).

Nagamachi, Mitsuo, *Kansei/Affective Engineering* (Boca Raton, USA: CRC Press, 2011), https://doi.org/10.1201/b16799.

Nagamachi, Mitsuo, *Workshop 2 on Kansei Engineering*, Proceedings of the International Conference on Affective Human Factors Design: 27–29 June 2001 (London: ASEAN Academic Press, 2001).

Nakama, Takumi and Kinoshita, Yuichiro, 'A Kansei Analysis of the Streetscape in Kyoto: An Application of the Kansei Structure Visualization Technique', *International Conference on Kansei Engineering and Emotion Research* (2010), 314–323, https://doi.org/10.1007/978-3-642-21793-7_25.

Opačić, Vuk Tvrtko, *Tourism Valorisation of Cultural Heritage in Cultural Urban Heritage: Development, Learning and Landscape Strategies*, ed. by Mladen Obad, Šcitaroci, Šćitaroci Bojana Bojanić Obad, and Mrđa Ana (Cham: Springer International Publishing, 2019), pp. 181–196, https://doi.org/10.1007/978-3-030-10612-6.

Osgood, Charles E., Tannenbaum, Percy H. and Suci, George J., *The Measurement of Meaning* (Urbana, Il.: University of Illinois Press, 1978).

Poujoulat, Jean Joseph Francois, *Histoire De Saint Augustin* (Tours: Alfred Mame, 1885).

Richards, Greg, *Cultural Attractions and European Tourism* (Wallingford: CABI Publ., 2006).

Sanoff, Henry, *Visual Research Methods in Design* (London: Routledge, 2018), https://doi.org/10.4324/9781315541822.

Smith, Claire, 'Urban Heritage', in *Encyclopedia of Global Archaeology* (New York: Springer Reference, 2014), https://doi.org/10.1007/978-1-4419-0465-2_1137.

Smith, Melanie K., *Issues in Cultural Tourism Studies* (London: Routledge, 2016).

Timothy, Dallen J., *Cultural Heritage and Tourism in the Developing World a Regional Perspective* (London: Routledge, 2010).

Tsuchiya, Toshio, 'Kansei Engineering Study for Streetscape Zoning Using Self Organizing Maps', *International Journal of Affective Engineering*, 12 (2013), 365–373, https://doi.org/10.5057/ijae.12.365.

Wise, Nicholas and Takamitsu, Jimura, *Tourism, Cultural Heritage and Urban Regeneration Changing Spaces in Historical Places* (Cham: Springer, 2020), https://doi.org/10.1007/978-3-030-41905-9.

Yu Park, Hyung, *Heritage Tourism* (London: Routledge, 2014).

8. Western Churches in Nagasaki and Amakusa as Sites of Memory

Joanes Rocha

Introduction

Our interest in *lieux de mémoire*, those places where memory crystallizes and secretes itself, has occurred at a particular historical moment. It is a turning point where our consciousness of a break with the past is bound up with the sense that our collective memory has been ruptured—but ruptured in such a way as to pose the problem of the embodiment of memory in certain sites where a sense of historical continuity persists.[1]

In his classic *Les lieux de mémoire* (1997), Pierre Nora defines the term 'site of memory' in an expansive way. His definition encompasses not only tangible heritage items, such as buildings, structures, archives and memorials, but also intangible cultural heritage which expresses a community's identity, such as practices, representations, expressions and knowledge.[2] In other words, for Nora, a site of memory is a place with architectural, archaeological or cultural features deeply related to a specific memory that needs to be revisited.[3]

Although Nora's study has been criticised in the field of French history for his strong desire to achieve an ultimate sense of French nationhood

1 Pierre Nora, 'Between Memory and History: Les Lieux de Mémoire', *Representations*, 26 (1989), 7–24 (p. 7).

2 *Les lieux de mémoire*, ed. by Pierre Nora (Paris: Gallimard, 1997), pp. 23–43.

3 This chapter incorporates the idea of sites of memory as a conceptual tool, following Nora's notion that sites of memory are not independent of outside events or influences.

 https://doi.org/10.11647/OBP.0388.08

and inflexible opposition between 'history' and 'memory', his ideas can be expanded to bring new approaches to other research fields, such as heritage studies, as demonstrated by Maurice Halbwachs[4] and Frances Yates.[5] In this way, the 'site of memory' conceptual approach can enable us to better understand the relationship between tangible and intangible heritage in determining local, or even national, senses of belonging.

Currently, the most prominent World Heritage Sites (WHS) recognised as Sites of Memory are linked to painful memories. Examples of these sites include the Hiroshima Peace Memorial (*Genbaku Dome*) and the former Auschwitz Concentration Camp, both of which are widely known for the horrors of war which transpired there.

Inscribed as a World Heritage Site in 2018, the 'Hidden Christian Sites in the Nagasaki Region' also shares a painful past that needs to be revisited,[6] which is precisely the topic of this chapter. Moreover, since sites of memory are usually connected with sensitive issues, it is crucial to use consistent ethical approaches and appropriate methods to conserve the interpretative process and ensure that all stakeholders are heard.[7]

Thus, heritage professionals, such as historians, archaeologists, anthropologists and architects, play a significant role in evaluating and preserving those sites. Yet, the process of identifying sites of memory is often not initiated by heritage professionals but by communities, which indicates the local willingness to preserve the history and memory of these sites. Nagasaki and Amakusa are no exceptions to this.

From tangible to intangible heritage

Yamanaka Hiroshi states that the process for the recognition of Hidden Christian Sites in the Nagasaki Region as a World Heritage Site

---

4 Maurice Halbwachs, *On Collective Memory* (Chicago; London: Chicago University Press, 1992).

5 Frances Yates, *The Art of Memory* (London; New York: Routledge, 1999).

6 Fukami Satoshi and Sim Ji-Hyun, 'World Heritage and Dark Tourism: A Case Study of "Hidden Christian Sites in the Nagasaki Region Japan', *Academia Journal of Environmental Science*, 6 (2018), 11–19.

7 UNESCO World Heritage Centre, *Managing Cultural World Heritage and Managing Natural World Heritage* (Whc.unesco.org, 2013), https://whc.unesco.org/en/managing-cultural-world-heritage

started in 2001, when a group of volunteers called the Association for Declaring the Nagasaki Church Group a World Heritage Site sought to protect Catholic churches located in Nagasaki's remote villages on the Kyūshū Islands of the Japanese Archipelago.[8] Initially, the Japanese government was reluctant to agree. However, following the inclusion of several Nagasaki churches and Christian sites on the United Nations Educational, Scientific and Cultural Organization (UNESCO) World Heritage Tentative List in 2007, the government shifted its stance and began making efforts to promptly recognise these places as World Heritage Sites. This included supporting the Nagasaki World Heritage Scholarly Committee project, along with the International Council on Monuments and Sites (ICOMOS) Japan and Nagasaki Prefecture.

During the conferences to decide the scope of the nomination, fourteen historic sites were listed, and, in 2015, a proposal entitled *Churches and Christian Sites in Nagasaki* was presented to the World Heritage Committee. However, in 2016, an interim report prepared jointly by UNESCO and ICOMOS clarified that the submission would not be successfully approved as it was presented.

The Japanese government withdrew the proposal during the ICOMOS Evaluation Process in 2016, and three months later, at the government's invitation, an ICOMOS advisory mission helped local authorities in the drafting of a new proposal.[9] In the end, the advisory mission maintained the advisory panel's suggestions.

Among the proposed changes, the most significant was changing the nomination from tangible to intangible heritage. As the title indicates, the *Churches and Christian Sites in Nagasaki* focused on the local churches, the earliest of which was built in 1864; however, in response to UNESCO and ICOMOS suggestions, it later incorporated several anthropological, ethnographic and intangible characteristics of the Hidden Christian communities, which had covertly preserved their religious beliefs during persecutions that lasted for at least 250 years.

Thus, in 2017, Japan submitted a new proposal entitled *Hidden Christian Sites in the Nagasaki Region* with the following explanation:

---

8 Yamanaka Hiroshi, 'Nagasaki Katorikku kyōkai-gun to tsūrizumu', *Studies in Philosophy*, 33 (2007), 155–176.

9 UNESCO World Heritage Center, *Hidden Christian Sites in the Nagasaki Region* (Whc.unesco.org, n.d.), https://whc.unesco.org/en/list/1495/

> The nominated property bears unique testimony to the history of people and their communities who secretly transmitted their faith in Christianity during the time of prohibition spanning more than two centuries in Japan, from the seventeenth to the nineteenth centuries.[10] [...] Hidden Christians gave rise to a distinctive religious tradition that was seemingly vernacular, yet which maintained the essence of Christianity, and they survived continuing their faith over the ensuing two centuries.[11]

We must emphasise that this shift from tangible heritage (churches) to intangible heritage (Hidden Christian traditions and cultural landscape) influenced not only the proposal for recognition as a World Heritage Site, but also the Japanese Catholic community's perception of its past. Moreover, the history of Christianity in Japan had to be rewritten due to this change.

The first proposal focused on the churches meant to be inscribed under Criteria (ii), (iii) and (iv) of Outstanding Universal Value (OUV).[12] However, at the end of the nomination process, the Hidden Christian Sites in the Nagasaki region were recognised solely under Criterion (iii): 'to bear a unique or at least exceptional testimony to a cultural tradition or to a civilization which is living or which has disappeared'.[13]

The official description of the *Hidden Christian Sites in the Nagasaki Region* explicitly states that the principal subjects are the *Senpuku kirishitan* communities, which encompass Japanese Christians persecuted under the Tokugawa shogunate from the sixteenth to the nineteenth centuries. Yet, because Criterion (iii) mentions both 'living or disappeared' cultures, some visitors, and even professionals, are confused about how much of the nomination is about the 'disappeared' *Senpuku kirishitan*

10 Agency for Cultural Affairs (ACA), *Main Document: Hidden Christian Sites in the Nagasaki Region* (Tōkyō: ACA, 2017a), p. 209.

11 Ibid., p. 241.

12 *Criteria (ii)* 'To exhibit an important interchange of human values, over a span of time or within a cultural area of the world, on developments in architecture or technology, monumental arts, town-planning or landscape design.'
Criteria (iv) 'to be an outstanding example of a type of building, architectural or technological ensemble or landscape which illustrates (a) significant stage(s) in human history.' UNESCO, *Criteria for Selection*, Operational Guidelines for the Implementation of the World Heritage Convention (Whc.unesco.org, 2021), https://whc.unesco.org/en/criteria/

13 Ibid.

and how much of it is about their 'living' descendants that maintain their tradition, today called *Kakure kirishitan*.

Things become even more complicated in languages other than Japanese, such as English, as the word 'hidden' often represents both *Senpuku* and *Kakure*, complicating the recognition of the target group. Consequently, we must take a brief look at the history of Christianity in Japan to better grasp which elements are 'remembered', why these churches can be identified as sites of memory and their contributions to bringing together tangible and intangible heritage perspectives.

Revisiting the past

The first encounter between Japan and Europe occurred in September 1543, with the arrival of two Portuguese merchants on a Chinese vessel in Tanegashima.[14] However, the Catholic Church's missionary work only began in 1549 when the Jesuit Francis Xavier arrived in Kagoshima.[15]

Christianity soon began to spread among the local lords. Some later converted to Catholicism and became prominent supporters of missionaries in Japan, providing financial and political aid to build churches and seminaries, arguably to profit from overseeing trade.[16] Meanwhile, many plebeians converted to Christianity because of missionaries' efforts or demands from these Christian lords, also known as *Kirishitan daimyō* (from the Portuguese word *cristão*).[17]

However, the late sixteenth and early seventeenth centuries witnessed a series of anti-Christianity edicts. In 1587, Toyotomi Hideyoshi was the first to issue an edict against the practice of Christianity. He went on to banish Catholic missionaries from specific areas in Japan and

14 Olof G. Lidin, *Tanegashima: The Arrival of Europe in Japan* (Copenhagen: NIAS Press, 2004), p. 3.

15 Thomas Worcester, *The Cambridge Encyclopedia of the Jesuits* (Cambridge: Cambridge University Press, 2017); Jurgis Elisonas (George Elison), 'Christianity and the daimyō', in *The Cambridge History of Japan*, IV Early Modern Japan, ed. by John W. Hall (Cambridge: Cambridge University Press, 2006), pp. 368–372.

16 Miki Seiichirō, *Teppō to sono jidai* (Tōkyō: Yoshikawa kōbunkan, 2012), pp. 25–28.

17 Some famous *Kirishitan daimyō* were Amakusa Hisatane, Hasekura Tsunenaga, Ōmura Sumitada (Dom Bartolomeu), Arima Harunobu (Don Protasio), Takayama Ukon (Takayama Justus) e Ōtomo Yoshishige (Ōtomo Sōrin or Don Francisco, also named King of Bungo).

consolidate his rule over the Kyūshū region that served as the gateway to the Lusitanian trade of Japanese silver and Chinese silk via Macao.

After the death of Hideyoshi, Tokugawa Ieyasu gained military control over the region. At first, Tokugawa was willing to establish commercial relationships with Portugal and Spain through the Philippines. However, in 1614, the Tokugawa shogunate enacted laws that banned the practice of Christianity, leading to the prosecution of Christian followers, the demolition of churches and the deportation of missionaries and Christians.

In the years to come, especially under the reigns of Tokugawa Hidetada and Tokugawa Iemitsu, the oppression of Christianity was further intensified by two specific policies:

1. *Sakoku* (Japanese for 'closed country'), the isolationist foreign policy under which relations and trade between Japan and other countries were limited;[18] and
2. Finding and punishing Japanese nationals who were followers of Christianity and forcing Christian communities to register in a Buddhist temple (*shumon aratamecho*). Furthermore, the Japanese government used *fumi-e* (Japanese for 'stepping on a picture') to reveal Catholics and Catholic sympathisers. In brief, those who were suspected of being Christian were forced to step on the images of the Virgin Mary and Jesus.[19]

After the martyrdom of the last missionary, Mancio Konishi, in 1644, the remaining Japanese followers of Christianity had to practice their religious ceremonies in secret. Scholars of Japanese history state that, in addition to seventy-five missionaries who were executed publicly, more than a thousand faced death during the intense persecution between 1617 and 1644.

The prohibition of the Christian faith and other oppressive measures taken by the Japanese authorities forced the remaining Christians into

18 Nearly all foreign nationals were prohibited from entering Japan, with the exception of a few Chinese traders and the Dutch trading post in Dejima, Nagasaki.

19 These events provided the background for Shūsaku Endō's novel *Chinmoku* (Silence, 1966), which was later adapted into movies directed by Masahiro Shinoda (1971) and Martin Scorsese (2016).

hiding, which led to the coinage of the term *Senpuku kirishitan* (translated in this chapter as Hidden Christians following the document *Hidden Christian Sites in the Nagasaki Region*).

To conceal themselves and maintain their Christian faith, these communities had to join temples and shrines to hide their religious affiliation. For example, in the villages on Kuroshima Island, communities secretly worshipped a Buddhist statue as if it was a statue of the Virgin Mary (Maria Kannon). In Sakitsu Village in Amakusa, they used statues of the traditional Japanese divine beings Daikokuten and Ebisu—which are considered two of the Seven Gods of Fortune (*Shichifukujin*)—and worshipped them as Christian *Deusu* (the Japanese pronunciation of the Portuguese word *Deus*, meaning God in English).

Those living in the villages of Shitsu and Ono, located in Sotome, used to sing prayers called *orasho* (derived from the Latin word *oratio*) consisting of Japanese, Latin and Portuguese verses; today, this is considered one of the most remarkable features of the oral tradition of Hidden Christianity among the living descendants.

It is important to stress that even before the ban on Christianity was imposed in the late sixteenth century, the Catholic communities in Japan had already established *confrarias* (the Portuguese word for 'brotherhoods'; translated as *kumi* in Japanese) in different regions under the guidance of the Jesuits. During the Tokugawa shogunate, however, only in the Nagasaki and Amakusa regions could these *confrarias* survive. According to scholars such as Kentarō Miyazaki,[20] Roger Munsi,[21] Gonoi Takashi[22] and Stephen Turnbull,[23] this can be explained in terms of several unique factors, which include:

- The solidity of the religious group (*confrarias*) in the Kyūshū region before the prohibition, as this region was the centre of the trade with Europe in the sixteenth and seventeenth centuries;

20 Kentarō Miyazaki, *Kakure Kirishitan: Orasho Tamashii no Tsusoteion* (Nagasaki: Nagasaki Shinbunsha, 2001); Kentarō Miyazaki, *Kakure Kirishitan no jitsuzo: Nihonjin no kirisuto kyorikai to juyō* (Tōkyō: Yoshikawa Kōbunkan, 2014).

21 Roger Vanzila Munsi, 'Kakure Kirishitan in Urban Contexts: An Ethnographic Analysis of the Survival Strategies', *The Japan Mission Journal*, 68:1 (2014), 39–57.

22 Gonoi Takashi, *Nihon Kirisutokyo-shi* (Tōkyō: Yoshikawa Kōbunkan, 1990).

23 Stephen Turnbull, *The Kakure Kirishitan of Japan: A Study of Their Development, Beliefs and Rituals to the Present Day* (Abingdon: Routledge, 2016).

- The persistent efforts of local religious leaders of those religious groups, such as *mizukata* and *chōkata*, who performed Christian rituals and helped others learn about the catechism during the ban on Christianity from late sixteenth century until 1873;[24]
- Cooperation with Buddhist and Shintoist communities;
- Local authorities turned a blind eye to the activities of Hidden Christians as long they did not cause any problems.

Japan's tensions with the outside world became domestic issues in the late eighteenth century. Thus, the Tokugawa shogunate decided to reopen several docks to Western countries in 1854, including the Nagasaki port.[25] The missionaries from the *Société des Missions étrangères de Paris* (Society of Foreign Missions of Paris, MEP) undertook to build churches to observe Sunday Mass once they arrived in Japan. One of these churches was the *Ōura Tenshudō*, or Ōura Cathedral, which gained popularity as the stage for the so-called *Shinto hakken*, when a Japanese group from Urakami Village visited Father Petitjean in 1865 and confessed their faith by saying, 'We are of one heart with you'.[26]

Although the French missionaries of the nineteenth century were aware of the Portuguese and Spanish missionaries' work during the sixteenth and seventeenth centuries, they were astounded to come across Christian communities after two and a half centuries of isolation. Nevertheless, soon after the *Shinto hakken*, other secret Christian groups began to seek help from missionaries both within and outside Japan.[27]

---

24 The person who carried out baptisms in the absence of missionaries was called a *mizukata*, literally the 'person with water'. The person responsible for keeping the liturgical calendar was called a *chōkata*, literally the 'person with the notebook'. During the ban on Christianity, these *chōkata* used a copied calendar from 1634, the last calendar compiled by a missionary they had access. Usually, it was a patriarchal linage, but it was constated that in Nokubi Village, women rather than men served as leaders of the Hidden Christian communities because male householders had to take part in the Okinokojima Shrine rituals (ACA, *Main Document: Hidden Christian Sites in the Nagasaki Region*, p. 124).

25 As mentioned above, Nagasaki was one of the few places open for foreign trade during the Edo seclusion.

26 Francisque Marnas, *Nihon Kirisutokyō fukkatsushi* (Tōkyō: Misuzu Shobo, 1985).

27 Martin Nogueira Ramos, *La foi des ancêtres. Chrétiens cachés et catholiques dans la société villageoise japonaise* (Paris: CNRS Editions, 2019).

Despite the decision to gradually open Japan to the outside world and allow foreigners to perform their religious duties, the Tokugawa shogunate still took severe measures against the native Japanese Christians. Hidden Christians in the Nagasaki village of Urakami Village were arrested in 1867 during the fourth persecution of Urakami Christians (*Urakami yoban kuzure*).

Moreover, the Meiji government continued to implement the policy of systemic oppression from the 1860s. This government exiled more than 3,000 Christians to other regions and tortured many others, in an effort to force them to convert. Harassment of Christians continued until 1873 when the prohibition on Christianity was lifted, and new churches were erected by those who reconciled with the Holy See. Those are the Churches listed in the first proposal entitled *Churches and Christian Sites in Nagasaki.*

Interpreting sites of memory: Churches in Nagasaki and Amakusa as a case study

The Hidden Christian Sites in the Nagasaki and Amakusa regions is a serial nomination with twelve components—eleven sites and one monument—that bear witness to the traditions of the Hidden Christian communities. Some of these sites date back to the sixteenth century, when the first contact with European missionaries occurred. Hirado Island, where Francis Xavier taught Catholicism in 1550, and Shitsu and Ono villages,[28] where Jesuit missionaries introduced Catholicism in 1571, host the most ancient of these Hidden Christian communities.

Isolation from the Vatican for more than 250 years resulted in a unique blend of Christian rituals with Buddhist and Shinto customs among Hidden Christians. Thus, following Japan's reopening, this new contact with the Holy See led to uncertainty among Christian communities about their Christian identity and raised the missionaries' concerns about the legitimacy of the baptisms carried out by the *Senpuku kirishitan* in their absence.

The communities ended up splitting into different groups: Some accepted reconciliation with the Vatican (called *katorikku* in Japanese),

28 In 1571, Ono Village was under a *Kirishitan daimyō* as part of the Ōmura Domain.

some renounced Christianity and self-declared as Buddhists and/or Shintoists, some continued their religious practices (today called *Kakure kirishitan*) and some declined to be affiliated with any religion.

According to Keir Reeves, '[S]uch sites of memory are important to historians because they represent the enduring physical places where the past is remembered, commemorated, and constructed in the present day'.[29] This phenomenon can also be observed among churches erected in places associated with historical events by those who reconciled with the Holy See in the 1880s,[30] such as the former and current churches in Sakitsu, Amakusa.

According to the UNESCO website and documentation,[31] the nomination is called in English 'Hidden Christian Sites in the Nagasaki Region', clearly focusing on the Nagasaki prefecture. However, official documents and literature written in the Japanese language reveal another name, 'Hidden Christian Sites in the Nagasaki and Amakusa Regions'[32], as the nomination also includes Sakitsu village in Amakusa, the present Kumamoto prefecture.

Therefore, since Nagasaki's heritage sites—both city and prefecture—are relatively well known, I shall redirect our attention to the equally fascinating fishing village of Sakitsu, which was selected as an Important Cultural Landscape by the Japanese government in 2012.[33]

The first Christian communities in Amakusa were established in 1569 due to Jesuit Luis de Almeida's missionary work. During the ban, as previously mentioned, they had to be officially registered in a Buddhist temple. Simultaneously, they were outwardly affiliated with the Sakitsu Suwa Shrine and behaved like Shinto practitioners to camouflage their

29 Keir Reeves, 'Sites of Memory', in *History, Memory and Public Life: The Past in the Present*, ed. by Anna Maerker, Simon Sleight, Adam Sutcliffe (Abingdon: Routledge, 2018), pp. 65–79 (p. 65).

30 ACA, *Main Document: Hidden Christian Sites in the Nagasaki Region*, p. 149.

31 UNESCO, *Hidden Christian Sites*.

32 長崎と天草地方の潜伏キリシタン関連遺産 (*Nagasaki to Amakusa-chihō no senpuku kirishitan kanren'isan*).

33 The first designation as Important Cultural Landscape was on 7 February 2011 (Ministry of Education, Culture, Sports, Science and Technology of Japan, MEXT, official notice no. 22). However, with some additions in the following year, it became the current 'Cultural Landscape of Sakitsu and Imatomi in Amakusa' on 19 September 2012 (MEXT, official notice no. 158).

Catholic faith.[34] In the fishing village of Sakitsu, 'the local community found its way to venerate Christian symbols using the shells of abalone and fan-mussel clams with their mother-of-pearl patterns to the image of the Virgin Mary, and also making medals from shells of the white-lipped pearl oyster'.[35]

The first Sakitsu Church was built in 1888 at a site offered by a Catholic who had served as a *mizukata* during the ban on Christianity. This site was also adjacent to the Sakitsu Suwa Shrine, where *oratio* prayers were performed secretly during the prohibition. However, the Church's location was changed in 1934 due to the ageing of the structure.[36] The new and present location of the Church was once the dwelling of the former village headmen from the Yoshida family, where the Hidden Christians were forced to step on Christian images.

Not only in Sakitsu but also across Kyūshū, the new churches reveal the local desire to reconnect with the Roman Curia without losing their community identity. Several churches were built in the neo-Gothic style using Western-style materials and methods. For example, the Ono Church was built with bricks and stones, and the Kuroshima Church has porcelain around the altar. The effects of European architecture on the churches built in distant regions of Japan testify to the local Catholic community's desire to have a 'Western Catholic church', such as those designed by Tetsukawa Yosuke (1879–1976).[37]

However, local elements that call to mind the period of persecution can still be found in these structures. Instead of the European floral ornaments commonly seen in Catholic churches and graveyards,[38] the

34 When some villagers were exposed as Hidden Christians during the *Amakusa Kuzure*, or crackdown, in 1805, they were required to hand over their devotional items to the Sakitsu Suwa Shrine. However, no further persecution occurred.

35 ACA, *Main Document: Hidden Christian Sites in the Nagasaki Region*, p. 78.

36 Ibid., pp. 78–79.

37 Tetsukawa was a local Japanese architect from Kamigoto who learned Western-style architecture from Father de Rotz and Father Pelu and became famous for his church's architectural designs. Although Yosuke's family specialised in building Buddhist Temples and Shinto Shires, and even if he was a Buddhist himself, he reflected the Catholic aesthetic sense in all the churches he designed (Katsuhiko Kimura, *Nagasaki ni okeru Katorikku kyōkai junrei to tsūrizumu* [Pilgrimage to Roman Catholic Churches and Tourism in Nagasaki], *Nagasaki kokusaidaigaku ronsō*, 7 (2007), 123–133).

38 Concerning the Hidden Christian graveyards, they were identical to Buddhist graveyards in their outward appearance, however the bodies interred there were positioned in a distinctive manner. While Buddhists laid the bodies of the deceased

Japanese camellia (native to the island of Gotō) was carved on the churches as a symbol of the Virgin Mary, keeping a tradition that had started among the *Senpuku kirishitan* during the ban.

As we saw at the opening of this chapter, Pierre Nora defines the term 'site of memory' as a place encompassing tangible and intangible heritage that expresses a community's identity. Thus, the local Japanese community chose to build in the neo-Gothic style while preserving local symbolisms, such as the Japanese camellia. Moreover, when the second Church was erected at the same dwelling where the Hidden Christians used to be forced to step on Christian images, the local catholic communities were reinterpreting the space.

In sum, they were transforming those spaces from places of sorrow into sites of memory with a strong message of resilience and hope and giving those locations a new significance, as they are now freely praying in the same places where their ancestors were tormented because of their faith.

***

Now we turn from Amakusa to the city of Nagasaki, the Japanese gate to the outside world for the past five centuries. During a field study in 2018—just a few months after the World Heritage Site designation—flags and messages of congratulations could be observed everywhere around the city, most of which were placed by the Nagasaki prefecture and secretary of tourism. However, going deeper into the city, there were also fascinating handwritten posters praising the designation, presumably made by citizens.

Nowadays, several public places, such as museums and churches, host artefacts imported to Japan in the mid-seventeenth century or produced by the Hidden Christians during the late seventeenth and eighteenth centuries. However, many others are still preserved by the

---

in the coffin in a sitting position (*zakan*), Hidden Christians bent the knees of the deceased, laying their bodies on the side, with their heads toward the south (ACA, *Main Document: Hidden Christian Sites in the Nagasaki Region*, p. 88. Also vide, Bebio Vieira Amaro, *Minato-shi Nagasaki ni okeru kirishitan shisetsu ni kansuru kenkyū*, PhD thesis, Graduate School of Engineering, University of Tokyo (2016), pp. 101–102; and Carla Tronu, 'Jesuit Accommodation Method in 16th & 17th Century Japan', in *Los Jesuitas, religión, política y educación (s.XVI-XVIII)*, ed. by José Martínez Millán et. al. (Madrid: Universidad Pontificia Comillas, 2012), pp. 1617–1642.

Kakure kirishitan communities in their houses or private collections. Some are still used for familiar ceremonies—and along with oral history—and these artefacts represent the Hidden Christians' customs, practices and traditions, giving us insight into the *Senpuku kirishitan*'s cultural heritage.

In anticipation of international visitors after becoming a World Heritage Site, the Japanese Agency for Cultural Affairs (ACA)—the principal agency for preserving Japanese culture—started training local volunteers as guides, and established museums, souvenir shops, restrooms and similar facilities in selected churches.

The local volunteers, including Catholics and non-Catholics, are given responsibilities, such as managing the number of visitors and providing them with information about the churches and historical sites.[39] This strategy aims to moderate the effect of tourism on the local lifestyle, as the houses of *Kakure kirishitan* must be considered private spaces.

Although this study has focused on the Catholic churches, the fascinating *Kakure kirishitan* communities should not be undervalued. They are significant for our understanding of home-grown history and are engaged in preserving local traditions. It is vital to remember that sites of memory require extensive research on tangible and intangible heritage features to ensure that different stakeholders and narratives are heard, including *Kakure kirishitan* communities. Thus, according to the ACA, those communities are expected to benefit from sustainable tourism and pilgrimage around the churches, which can generate profits without interfering with religious rituals.[40]

Despite this, a report prepared by the Nagasaki prefecture emphasises that younger people are migrating to bigger cities searching for academic and professional opportunities, causing the interruption

---

39 Agency for Cultural Affairs (ACA), *Supplementary Material on the Nomination of Hidden Christian Sites in the Nagasaki Region* (Japan: ACA, 2017b); International Council on Monuments and Sites (ICOMOS), *Preparing World Heritage Nominations*, 2nd ed. (Paris: UNESCO World, 2011).

40 Today, the most important legislation concerning heritage in Japan is the 'Law for the Protection of Cultural Properties' (enacted in 1950 and revisited in 2004). However, it is also a necessary survey on the Ancient Shrines and Temples Preservation Law (1897); Law for the Preservation of Historic Sites, Places of Scenic Beauty and Natural Monuments (1919); National Treasures Preservation Law (1929), and Natural Parks Act (1957).

and extinction of traditional practices and rituals among both *Kakure kirishitan* and reunified Catholics.[41]

In order to prevent this extinction, the Nagasaki and Amakusa prefectures, with the support of the Japanese national government and international communities, are not only creating new job opportunities through sustainable tourism, but also incorporating educational programmes that can help reaffirm a sense of identity among young people. As Sara McDowell argues, 'without memory, a sense of self, identity, culture, and heritage is lost'.[42]

Conclusion

The author had the opportunity to visit Nagasaki and Amakusa several times before and after the nomination, and what that field research revealed can be expressed in the words of Michael Rothberg, a scholar of memory studies, who said, 'Sites of memory do not remember by themselves; they require the active agency of individuals and publics.'[43]

Thus, using the churches in Nagasaki and Amakusa as a case study—particularly those in Amakusa, which are commonly forgotten by Western scholars—and using relevant sources written in Japanese and Western languages, this chapter calls attention to the fact that even if the churches lost their primacy when the project shifted from tangible heritage (churches) to intangible heritage (the Hidden Christian traditions) in 2017, these churches are still playing a vital role in the local heritage preservation strategy, as this change influenced not only the necessary documentation for recognition as a World Heritage Site but also reformed the Japanese Catholic community's perception of its past.

This can be observed via the architectural features of the modern churches—erected from the 1880s—comprising Japanese regional and Western symbols, such as the Japanese camellia (native to the island of

41 See Agency for Cultural Affairs (ACA), *Comprehensive Preservation and Management Plan. Hidden Christian Sites in the Nagasaki Region* (Japan: ACA, 2017c).

42 Sara McDowell, 'Heritage, Memory and Identity', in *The Ashgate Research Companion to Heritage and Identity*, ed. by Brian Graham and Peter Howard (Abingdon: Routledge, 2016), p. 42.

43 Michael Rothberg, 'Introduction: Between Memory and Memory', *Yale French Studies*, 118 (2010), p. 8.

Gotō), used instead of European neo-gothic floral ornaments commonly seen in Catholic churches and graveyards at the time. The Japanese camellia was carved on the churches as a symbol of the Virgin Mary, keeping a tradition that had started among the *Senpuku kirishitan* during the persecution (1614–1873); they evince the local people's desire to reconnect with the Holy See without losing their Japanese identity. Historical churches now welcome current Japanese Catholics who now pray in the same places where their ancestors were martyred. In sum, this chapter has described how such history strengthens a sense of identity rooted in both tangible and intangible heritage, as befitting a site of memory.

Bibliography

Agency for Cultural Affairs, *Main Document: Hidden Christian Sites in the Nagasaki Region* (Tōkyō: The Agency for Cultural Affairs (ACA), 2017).

Elisonas, Jurgis, 'Christianity and the daimyō', in *The Cambridge History of Japan*, IV Early Modern Japan, ed. by John W. Hall (Cambridge: Cambridge University Press, 2006), pp. 368–372.

Endo, Shusaku, *Chinmoku* [Silence] (Tōkyō: Shinchosha, 1966).

Fukami, Satoshi and Sim, Ji-Hyun, 'World Heritage and Dark Tourism: A Case Study of "Hidden Christian Sites in the Nagasaki Region Japan', *Academia Journal of Environmental Science*, 6 (2018), 11–19.

Gonoi, Takashi, *Nihon Kirisutokyo-shi* [History of Japanese Christianity] (Tōkyō: Yoshikawa Kōbunkan, 1990).

Halbwachs, Maurice, *On Collective Memory* (Chicago: Chicago University Press, 1992).

Keir Reeves, 'Sites of Memory', in *History, Memory and Public Life: The Past in the Present*, ed. by Anna Maerker, Simon Sleight, Adam Sutcliffe (Abingdon: Routledge, 2018), pp. 65–79.

Kimura, Katsuhiko, 'Nagasaki ni okeru Katorikku kyōkai junrei to tsūrizumu' [Pilgrimage to Roman Catholic Churches and Tourism in Nagasaki], *Nagasaki kokusaidaigaku ronsō*, 7 (2007), 123–133.

Lidin, Olof G., *Tanegashima: The Arrival of Europe in Japan* (Copenhagen: NIAS Press, 2004).

Marnas, Francisque, *Nihon Kirisutokyō fukkatsushi* [History of Japanese Christian Revival] (Tōkyō: Misuzu Shobo, 1985).

McDowell, Sara, 'Heritage, Memory and Identity', in *The Ashgate Research Companion to Heritage and Identity*, ed. by Brian Graham and Peter Howard (Abingdon: Routledge, 2016).

Miki, Seiichiro, *Teppō to sono jidai* [Teppō and its time] (Tōkyō: Yoshikawa kōbunkan, 2012).

Miyazaki, Kentaro, *Kakure Kirishitan no jitsuzo: Nihonjin no kirisuto kyorikai to juyō* [The Reality of Kakure Kirishitan: Japanese Understanding and Acceptance of Christianity] (Tōkyō: Yoshikawa Kōbunkan, 2014).

Miyazaki, Kentaro, *Kakure Kirishitan: Orasho Tamashii no Tsusoteion* [Kakure kirishitan: Oratio—The Quiet Voices of Soul] (Nagasaki: Nagasaki Shinbunsha, 2001).

Munsi, Roger V., 'Kakure Kirishitan in Urban Contexts: An Ethnographic Analysis of the Survival Strategies', *The Japan Mission Journal*, 68:1 (2014), 39–57.

Nora, Pierre, ed., *Les lieux de mémoire* (Paris: Gallimard, 1997).

Nora, Pierre, 'Between Memory and History: Les Lieux de Mémoire', *Representations*, 26 (1989), 7–24.

Ramos, Martin N., *La foi des ancêtres. Chrétiens cachés et catholiques dans la société villageoise japonaise* (Paris: CNRS Editions, 2019).

Rothberg, Michael, 'Introduction: Between Memory and Memory', *Yale French Studies*, 118 (2010).

Tronu, Carla, 'Jesuit Accommodation Method in 16th & 17th Century Japan', in *Los Jesuitas, religión, política y educación* (s.XVI-XVIII), ed. by José Martínez Millán et. al. (Madrid: Universidad Pontificia Comillas, 2012), pp. 1617–1642.

Turnbull, Stephen, *The Kakure Kirishitan of Japan: A Study of Their Development, Beliefs and Rituals to the Present Day* (Abingdon: Routledge, 2016).

Vieira Amaro, Bebio, *Minato-shi Nagasaki ni okeru kirishitan shisetsu ni kansuru kenkyū* [Research on Christian Facilities in the Port Nagasaki], PhD thesis, Graduate School of Engineering, University of Tokyo (2016).

Worcester, Thomas, *The Cambridge Encyclopedia of the Jesuits* (Cambridge: Cambridge University Press, 2017).

Yamanaka, Hiroshi, 'Nagasaki Katorikku kyōkai-gun to tsūrizumu' [Nagasaki Catholic Church Group and Tourism], *Studies in Philosophy*, 33 (2007), 155–176.

Yates, Frances, *The Art of Memory* (London; New York: Routledge, 1999).

IV. HERITAGE SITES AND PRESERVATION CHALLENGES

9. Tradition Versus Modernity in Heritage Preservation Discourse in Postcolonial Morocco: Jemaa el-Fna Plaza, Marrakesh

Assia Lamzah

Introduction

Postcolonial theory is a valuable tool in architecture and heritage management discourse to understand and challenge the relationship between the coloniser and the colonised in the French protectorate. This relationship and its impacts still shape postcolonial heritage management in Morocco. This chapter shows how Orientalism and colonialism explain the ways in which dominant perceptions of the world are organised according to hierarchical false dualities, such as tradition/modernity, West/non-West and centre/periphery. It analyses colonialism and the representation of the self and the other in the context of Orientalism, as defined by Said,[1] Bhabha,[2] Aijaz,[3] Spivak,[4]

1 Edward Said, *Orientalism* (New York: Vintage Books, 1978).

2 Homi Bhabha, *The Location of Culture* (London and New York: Routledge, 1994).

3 Ahmad Aijaz, *In Theory: Classes, Nations, Literatures* (London and New York: Verso, 1992).

4 Gayatri C. Spivak, 'Interview with Gayatri C. Spivak' in *A Review of International English Literature*, by Kock de Leon (New Nation Writers Conference: South Africa, 1992), 23:3, 29–47. See also Gayatri C. Spivak, *A Critique of Postcolonial Reason: Toward a History of the Vanishing Present* (Cambridge: Harvard University Press, 1999).

 https://doi.org/10.11647/OBP.0388.09

and Young.[5] In addition to analysing how the tradition/modernity duality has been constructed and normalised, this chapter questions it and the ideological assumptions that underpin its construction. In relation to postcolonial heritage management discourse in Morocco, this duality is a useful theoretical tool to deconstruct the Orientalist mechanisms through which Moroccan medinas have been constructed and reconstructed and the way these mechanisms still may be working to shape the postcolonial context.

This chapter is organised into three main parts. The first focuses on the relationship between space, Orientalism and colonialism. The second analyses the false dichotomy between modernity and tradition as a result of the Orientalist hegemonic discourse. The third part is a case study of the Jemaa el-Fna Plaza in terms of these concepts and their false dichotomy and how they contribute to constructing and reconstructing the urban identity and social practice of the plaza. The analysis of issues of Orientalism, modernity, tradition and postcolonialism is not an anthropological interpretation of these concepts or phenomena; rather, it is an attempt to establish their utility in relation to the specific historical, political and social contexts of the Marrakesh medina in general and Jemaa el-Fna Plaza in particular. Since Orientalism and the debate about modernity and traditionalism still apply to the context of architectural and urban heritage in Morocco, I analyse them not to reproduce their initial meanings but to verify them and hopefully develop them.

1. Orientalism, colonialism and space

Orientalism, as defined by Said[6] and later criticised by other scholars,[7] is still relevant in the postcolonial understanding of colonial cities and societies. It helps deconstruct the mechanism through which dominant societies have constructed their 'other'—thereby creating an image of themselves.[8;9]

5 J. C. Robert Young, *Postcolonialism: An Historical Introduction* (New York and London: Blackwell, 2001).

6 Said, 1978.

7 Aijaz, 1992; Bhabha, 1994; Spivak, 1999; and Young, 2001.

8 Michel Foucault, *The Archaeology of Knowledge* (New York: Pantheon, 1972).

9 Said, 1978.

Said explores the impact of Orientalism on the 'Oriental' and argues that Orientalist discourse is so powerful that it creates a double consciousness in the 'Oriental' mind. Said cites the work of Gramsci, who developed the concept of hegemony at the end of the nineteenth century based on the idea that people in the working class identified their good with the good of the bourgeoisie and contributed to maintaining the existing social order instead of revolting. He developed a theory that emphasised the importance and role of the superstructure in maintaining or fracturing the relations to the base. Said applied Gramsci's polemic against hegemonic culture to colonialism and Orientalism. In these contexts, the concept of hegemony is used to illustrate how the 'colonised' or the 'oppressed' come to see themselves and their interests through their colonisers' and oppressors' eyes, helping to maintain the social order and even to foster the hegemonic culture instead of a revolution that could help the colonised avoid the vicious circle of oppression and self-degradation. In this context, 'Orientals' become unable to see themselves outside of the frame constructed by the 'West', or the coloniser.

Said's work was revolutionary for its understanding of the power relations between the coloniser and the colonised, but it is not unproblematic. Many postcolonial thinkers have criticised Said's approach for its oversimplification of the relationship between 'East' and 'West' as one of passive versus active. They also criticised it for its unidimensional conception of colonialism and static model of colonial power relations. They agree that the colonial discourse, as defined by Said, does not leave space for agency, resistance or negotiation on the part of the colonised and for a change in the relationship between the coloniser and the colonised.

In the mid-nineteenth century, with the rise of capitalism, European powers competed to expand their economic dominance to newly colonised regions. They sought out new territories that could provide materials for industry and constitute new markets for goods and services. Colonialism allowed the conquest and domination of those new territories in a literal sense, as well as allowing Europeans, differently and at different levels, to show and exercise their power and 'superiority' over the 'other'. Colonialism had tremendous economic, social and cultural impacts on both the coloniser and the colonised. As a result of this European colonial expansion, the 'West' was constructed as the centre of the discourse of civilisation and 'modernity', while in contrast, the 'other'—the dark side—represented those peoples locked in the past, repressed and undeveloped. As King[10] explains, under the colonial paradigm, the world was divided into two kinds of peoples and two types of societies—'powerful, administratively advanced, racially Caucasoid, nominally Christian, mainly European, dominant nations, and powerless, organizationally backward, "traditionally" rooted, dominated societies'.[11] However, was the separation that sharp? Was this duality true? Or was this duality itself a creation of Eurocentrism and Orientalism?

The work of Orientalism has been extended to architecture and urban planning to see how Orientalists used space and the built environment to stress false dichotomies between modern/traditional, East/West and coloniser/colonised, thereby justifying their colonial actions as a civilising mission. Indeed, such scholars as Marcais, Le Tourneau and Massignon[12] have adopted an Orientalist approach to North African architectural and urban space, especially medinas. In their effort to understand the structure, functions and organisation of their urban territory, they have constructed the so-called 'Islamic city' as a theoretical model. They based this model on the presence of a central mosque, a souq that developed between the centre and the city gates, a division of the neighbourhoods according to an ethnic basis and the absence of any municipal organisation. They argued for the Islamic city's lack of regularity, constructing it as a non-city, a non-urbanism, in opposition to European cities.

Two main Orientalist approaches are identified in the study of the Islamic city. The first one, by British and German scholars, explained the structure of the city according to social and religious factors. The second, proposed by French scholars, aimed at a detailed understanding of the

10 Anthony D. King, *Urbanism, Colonialism and the World Economy* (London and New York: Routledge, 1990).

11 Anthony D. King, 'Global Norms and Urban Forms in the Age of Tourism: Manufacturing Heritage, Consuming Tradition', in *Consuming Tradition, Manufacturing Heritage: Global Norms and Urban Forms in the Age of Tourism*, ed. by Nizar al-Sayyad (London, New York: Routledge, 2001), p. 5.

12 Georges Marçais, 'L'urbanisme Musulman' in *5ème congrès de la Fédération des Sociétés Savantes de l'Afrique du Nord* (Tunis, 6–8 April 1939). See also Georges Marcais, 'La conception des villes en Islam', in *Revue d'Alger*, 2 (1945), 517–33.

city's structure on the physical and morphological levels in order to control it. Both approaches constructed the Islamic city as a theoretical model rather than an actual urban form that resulted from a historical, political and social context. They also generalised this model to apply to the rest of the Islamic world. Such an Orientalist approach has been applied by French architects and planners to Moroccan medinas. Indeed, the Marrakesh medina is one of the most significant examples to study how colonialism in Morocco used architecture and planning to impose its ideology.[13]

Contemporary urban studies of cities in the Islamic world have demonstrated the limitations and biases of this Orientalist approach. Abu-Lughod,[14] Celik[15] and Wright[16] are among the scholars who have related part of their research to a critique of the Orientalist approach to North Africa. On the one hand, they demonstrated the impossibility of constructing one unified model of the Islamic city. On the other, they contributed to shifting the focus from constructing a theoretical unified model that would be applied to the whole Islamic world, to a different approach that looked at specific regions. More importantly, they revealed the importance of the link between the physical layout and morphology of the city and its specific geographical and socio-political contexts.

In the Marrakesh medina, to explore the structural complexities and the social meanings of the city as an urban organism, the work of Orientalism—re-examined in relation to the new challenges posed by contemporary urban and postcolonial studies—reveals how ambivalent the colonial discourse was and how diverse the city is in relation to multiple group interests and social realities.[17] The case of Jemaa el-Fna Plaza is illustrative of this, as is discussed below.

---

13 Assia Lamzah, 'Urban Design and Architecture in the Service of Colonialism in Morocco', *International Journal of Global Environmental Issues*, 13:2–4 (2014), 326–38.

14 Janet Abu-Lughod, 'What is Islamic about a City?' in *Urbanism in Islam*, Proceedings of the International Conference on Urbanism in Islam (ICUIT) I (1987), Oct. 22–28, Tokyo, 193–218.

15 Zeynep Celik, *Urban Forms and Colonial Confrontations: Algiers Under French Occupation* (Berkeley, Los Angeles, London: University of California Press, 1992).

16 Gwendolyn Wright, *The Politics of Design in French Colonial Urbanism* (Chicago: Chicago University Press, 1991).

17 Assia Lamzah, *Colonialism, Architecture and Cultural Heritage: Marrakesh, Morocco* (Berlin: PAF Edition, 2018).

The built environment is more than a mere representation or reflection of social order, or an environment in which socialisation takes place. Rather, physical and spatial urban forms constitute and represent much of social and cultural existence; society is to a large extent constituted through the very buildings and spaces it creates. Therefore, the analysis of the built environment can explain how colonialism, by shaping cities, consciously transformed their social structure. The same relationship between the representation of a supposedly pre-existing entity and its construction operates in contemporary societies and environments in previously colonised cities.

Under colonialism, political and economic forces shaped cities and changed the cultural, racial and ethnic composition of local populations. Due to colonialism, the physical landscape was drastically altered and radically changed. While these changes employed the most current structural technologies, building types and planning ideals, they ignored local needs, and more importantly, they introduced a new aesthetic and visual order.[18] Socially, this had—and still has—consequences for local people's self-definition, identity and space. Moreover, the central social fact of the colonial process was segregation: Segregated cities created segregated societies and vice versa.

2. Tradition versus modernity: A false dichotomy

The constructed opposition between tradition and modernity is relevant to understanding the Moroccan context and the impact of colonialism on it. This dichotomy is too blunt, and the evolutionism underlying it is naïvely optimistic. Thus, it is highly contested. Numerous scholars have shown that social systems are not as simple and homogeneous as these false dichotomies suggest. Traditional values are still persistent in spite of social, economic and political changes.

During the colonial period, zoning was adopted when planning Moroccan cities, in order to isolate the locals, in their walled, precolonial medinas, from the Europeans living in the *ville nouvelle* (new city). This physical separation created a segregation that has changed the social meaning of the medina space and the relationship people had with it.[19]

18 al-Sayyad, 1991.
19 Lamzah, 2014.

The binary opposition between 'tradition' and 'modernity' is one of the main direct impacts on spatial production and perception in Moroccan medinas, and this still prevails in the urban and architectural discourses of contemporary Moroccan cities.

Modernity and tradition should not be approached as a binary opposition but rather as a 'vibrant couplet'[20] in which each defines the other and continuously shapes it. Historians and space theorists have assumed that modernity has transformed how people relate to their built environments and dwellings, and that it has broken the traditional relationship people had with their everyday cultural and physical environments. This traditional relationship was supposed to be natural. Giddens[21] argues that in pre-modern contexts, people lived under a closed system of religious beliefs that created space inscribed within its sacred authority, and therefore, people never approached the space rationally. Modernity, he argues, freed people from this system of beliefs and caused them to approach their space rationally. Under these conditions, tradition was redefined in a modern way, which made it lose its 'authenticity'. Thus, he concludes that tradition no longer exists.

The problem here is that Giddens presents modernity and tradition in a binary opposition, and for him, nothing can be conceived outside of modernist thinking. This can be compared with Hobsbawm and Ranger's[22] 'Invented Traditions', where the authors argue that in the contemporary modern world, all traditions are invented, and 'authentic' ones no longer exist. However, this is predicated on the idea that somewhere, at some time, a 'true,' 'real' tradition formerly existed, and the contemporary one is fake and an ideological malformation.[23] Jacobs argues that modernity and tradition should both be seen as existing in the present, as a vibrant couplet where each part defines the other in a tension that is continuous and where meaning is always contested and changing. This is what makes tradition dynamic rather than static, and this is what allows it to change, alter, grow and develop.

---

20 Jane Jacobs, 'Tradition is (not) Modern: Deterritorializing Globalization', in *The End of Tradition*, ed. by Nizar al-Sayyad (New York: Routledge, 2004).

21 Anthony Giddens, *The Consequences of Modernity* (Stanford: Stanford University Press, 1990).

22 *The Invention of Tradition*, ed. by Eric Hobsbawn and Terence Ranger (London: Cambridge University Press, 1983).

23 Jacobs, 2004.

Several scholars have challenged the apparent stasis of this theoretical structure. In her article on 'Disappearing Dichotomies', Abu-Lughod argues against dichotomies between modernity and tradition. Instead, she proposes a re-conceptualisation of the term 'tradition' by focusing on process—what she calls 'traditioning'—rather than on tradition or the traditional.

Upton[24] also argues that looking for the pure or the 'authentic' can be both risky and unproductive. In his view, we should look for the contested, the multiple and the ambiguous. Al-Sayyad[25] argues that traditions must not be interpreted as static legacy of the past, as has been done by the Orientalist and modernist project, but rather as dynamic reinterpretations of the present.

Walsh argues that one of the key features of modem thinking is the philosophy of progress. He explains,

> An essential proposition of modem thought is an idea of progress, a belief which developed as a constituent part of Enlightenment thinking, and provided modem thinkers with a faith in the ability of humankind to manipulate and exploit their environments for the benefits of society. Such a society could escape from the debilitating elements of the past and could move forward to new horizons. If modernity has a particular essence, it is a belief in rational advancement through increments of perpetual improvement.[26]

This idea of progress emerged in the context of utopian beliefs about modernisation. This context associated the modem with the rational, the functional and the practical, in opposition to the pre-modem, which was supposedly irrational and random.

Buns and Kahn[27] argue that tradition is not frozen but always living, even if only minutely changing; people negotiate their lived spaces and contexts in terms of how traditional and modern they are. For instance, apparently modern space can be made traditional by human

24 Dell Upton, 'Authentic Anxieties' in *Consuming Tradition, Manufacturing Heritage*, ed. by Nezar al-Sayyad (New York: Routledge, 2001).

25 al-Sayyad, 2001.

26 Kevin Walsh, *The Representation of the Past: Museums and Heritage in the Post-modern World* (New York: Routledge, 1992), p. 5.

27 Carol J. Burns and Kahn Andrea, *Site Matters: Design Concepts, Histories, and Strategies* (New York: Routledge, 2005).

action and vice versa. Jemaa el-Fna Plaza is a good example to illustrate this argument, where it occurs in urban space. In Jemaa el-Fna Plaza, performers and workers dress in a typical precolonial dress that may be perceived as 'traditional clothing' or being 'traditional', but they live a modern life and use smartphones and smart devices.

Modernity is not a phenomenon that belongs to the 'West'. Nor is it perceived or experienced evenly all over the world. There are multiple 'modernities', and Morocco's modernity is different from that of other countries. Each one should be defined and understood in relation to its specific social and historical contexts.

3. Jemaa el-Fna Plaza: An illustrative case

Jemaa el-Fna Plaza is widely considered the most important symbolic landscape of Morocco. Since its foundation in the eleventh century by the Almoravid dynasty, it has been the most important part of the Marrakesh medina and one of its canonical sites. The origin and meaning of its name are unclear. In Arabic, *Jemaa* means congregation or mosque, and *el-Fna* means either death or a courtyard in front of a building. The plaza is a square and marketplace where local inhabitants and tourists gather to shop, eat or observe the various shows taking place. Inscribed on the United Nations Educational, Scientific and Cultural Organization (UNESCO) World Heritage List in 2001, it was presented and described in the official tourist narratives as a symbol of Moroccan life and emblematic of its traditions, it is also—ironically—presented as unique. The tourist brochures describe the site as mysterious, as a place where time has stopped, where tourists can get closer to the 'real Morocco' to be able to understand its culture and traditions. One such brochure proclaims, 'It is the ideal choice for all those enamoured of exoticism; for all incurable romantic dreamers'.[28]

Moroccan authorities and intellectuals see Jemaa el-Fna as an important component of national historical and cultural heritage. The rhetoric that constructs this site has its roots in the colonial period, as discussed above, and it is on such narratives that tourist brochures are based now. As a result of French colonial imaginary, Marrakesh

28 Alpitour tourist guide, edition 2005, p. 259.

in general, and Jemaa el-Fna specifically, has been presented by the Moroccan government and private tourism agencies as a land of myths.[29]

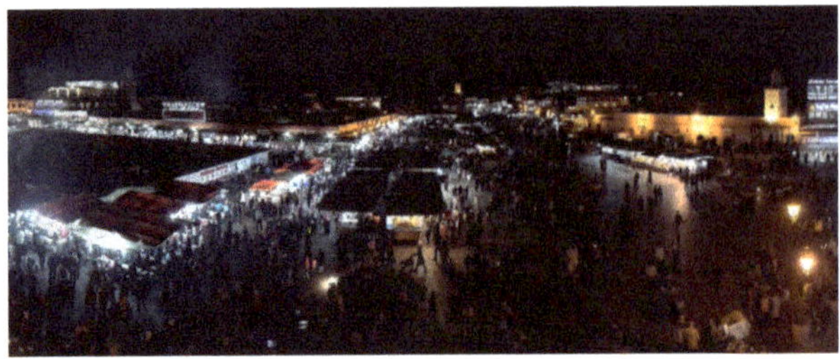

Fig. 9.1 Overview of Jemaa el-Fna Plaza. Author's photograph, 2021, CC BY-NC-ND.

Colonial narratives are used to construct and answer nostalgic questions by contemporary tourists, while presenting the heritage preservation discourses as anti-colonial. An illustrative example is the Francorosso Tours Guide, a major Italian operator. It states:

> No stay in Morocco is complete without a visit to Marrakesh, without immersing yourself in the magical atmosphere of its medina, the tortuous alleys of its countless souqs and its religious monuments [...]. The real soul of Marrakesh, the 'Red City,' can be found in the Jamaa el Fna [...] an open-air stage where every day an endless procession of storytellers, gymnasts, musicians, sellers, fire-eaters and snake charmers perform from morning to nightfall.[30]

Most international tourists faithfully follow the steps described in the guides used for their exploration of the medina. In Jemaa el-Fna, most prefer to sit in French-style cafes and gaze on the plaza from the higher point of view of the terraces. The reason for this, as explained by some international tourists, is twofold. Firstly, the terrace is the best place for a panoptic view of the plaza. Secondly, the encompassing vista allows the tourist to observe without being physically involved with the locals and their activities. Most use cameras to take pictures from the terraces, to freeze the plaza, to capture the square and 'immortalise' the Jemaa

29 *L'Appel du Maroc*, ed. by Daniel Rondeau (Paris: Flammarion, 1999).

30 Francorosso Tours Guide, 2005, p. 33.

el-Fna experience. Minca[31] states: 'The tourist-photographers are clearly very aware of their "appropriately" dominant position, of their choice of the right framing, the right perspective, at the right time of day'. Minca goes on to argue that this presents a landscape paradox in the plaza:

> On the one hand the tourists have to consciously position themselves atop a building in order to 'enjoy' the landscape and to frame it in appropriate fashion, in a clear effort at the 'manufacture' of a cultural product. On the other hand, however, with this gesture and with their photographs, they implicitly treat the landscape as an object, an object that can materially be found in Marrakesh, and captured/ reproduced in an infinity of ways.[32]

Thus, tourists are always creating and re-creating the landscape of the plaza. French-style cafes with terraces are sites built with the specific and explicit intent of allowing tourists to gaze upon the square and its spectacles, photographing and capturing it. These sites help establish a specific relation of power between the tourists and the square and therefore between the tourist and the locals. At the same time, cafes are part of Jemaa el-Fna's built environment and landscape. This is significant in the sense that they become part of essentialised site, reflecting the interplay and ambivalence of Jemaa el-Fna between a space that is supposedly purely Moroccan and a space consumed by tourists (and previously colonialists). This ambivalence contributes to the constituting and re-constituting of the identity of the square as landscape.

The colonial legacy is embodied in Jemaa el-Fna both by the European tourist, looking for a glorious Orientalised and exotic past, and by the Moroccan authorities, who try to construct national heritage and justify its preservation via the square.[33]

The locals and tourists experience and conceive the plaza in relation to specific places and spaces—imagined and real geographies—by mobilising a spatial theory of Self and Other relationships. The snake charmers, monkey dressers, storytellers, women who tattoo with

31 Claudio Minca, 'The Tourist Paradox', *Social and Cultural Geography*, 8:3 (2007), 443–453 (p. 444).

32 Ibid., p. 443.

33 Amina Touzani, *La Culture et la Politique Culturelle* (Casablanca: Croisée des chemins, 2003).

henna, dancers and others all work as professional performers at the plaza. In trying to attract tourists, they consciously use an Orientalist repertoire of activities and actions. Some of these play on the cultural differences between the performer and audience. They all consciously present themselves as the 'Oriental subject' for the tourist gaze, with an underlying economic motivation.

Most tourists let themselves enjoy the spectacle, possibly to make their experience of Jemaa el-Fna more richly exotic. However, this 'encounter' does not last long, and shortly after, it takes the form of a 'commercial transaction'.[34] The service has a price and demands payment. Minca comments on this moment of encounter, confirming that maybe 'sometimes in that instant, a doubt seizes both subjects; who is the colonizer and who is the colonized?'[35] This encounter allows both local performers and tourists to define themselves and the other in that specific place at that specific time. The ambivalence of the relationship between the locals and the tourists is crucial in shaping the way in which both of them experience the medina and its landscape in continuously changing and challenging ways.

Jemaa el-Fna is both traditional and modern, but it is a Moroccan modernity, not an imported, imposed modernity. It is the appropriation of the space and its intercalation with the users' cultural and social background, rather than only its physical and aesthetic features, that determines its meaning. Therefore, modernity cannot be approached as a style or conglomeration of physical features alone but must also be considered as a mode of living and of interacting with one's space, a landscape or built environment.

Conclusion

Under colonial rule, space and cultural heritage were used as means of power and domination. After independence, post (neo)-colonial space has always been contested and continuously reshaped. The problematic arising from an examination of such space consists of the means by which it is continuously negotiated. The question is whether

34 Minca, 2007.
35 Ibid., p. 444.

these neo-colonial spaces are constituted essentially by the binary opposition between the colonised and the coloniser, between tradition and modernity, or by a relationship that is more complex. This chapter has argued that modernity and tradition should not be approached as a binary opposition but rather as a vibrant couplet in which each defines the other and continuously shapes it.

In the case of Moroccan cities, it has been assumed that modernity or modernisation was the sole result of French colonial intervention. However, this cannot be true because the local notables and the local elites also contributed to this process of modernisation. They endeavoured to transform the body of the medina to better suit the European notion of progress. Jemaa el-Fna Plaza, in the Marrakesh medina, constitutes an interesting example to illustrate how an intangible heritage is at the same time a reflection of a tradition of pre-colonial conception and a construction of urban space on the one hand, and a fully contemporary public space that answers contemporary needs on the other. The old romantic image of Jemaa el-Fna Plaza now jars with the contemporary reality of a society continuously under construction.

Bibliography

Abu-Lughod, Janet, 'What is Islamic about a City?', *Urbanism in Islam*, Proceedings of the International Conference on Urbanism in Islam (ICUIT) I (1987), Oct. 22–28, Tokyo, 193–218.

Aijaz, Ahmad, *In Theory: Classes, Nations, Literatures* (London and New York: Verso, 1992).

Bhabha, Homi, *The Location of Culture* (London and New York, Routledge, 1994).

Burns, Carol J. and Andrea, Kahn, *Site Matters: Design Concepts, Histories, and Strategies* (New York: Routledge, 2005).

Celik, Zeynep, *Urban Forms and Colonial Confrontations: Algiers Under French Occupation* (Berkeley, Los Angeles, London: University of California Press, 1992).

Foucault, Michel, *The Archaeology of Knowledge* (New York: Pantheon, 1972).

Giddens, Anthony, *The Consequences of Modernity* (Stanford: Stanford University Press, 1990).

Hobsbawn, Eric and Ranger, Terence, eds., *The Invention of Tradition* (London: Cambridge University Press, 1983).

Jacobs, Jane, 'Tradition is (not) Modern: Deterritorializing Globalization,' in *The End of Tradition*. ed. by Nizar al-Sayyad (New York: Routledge, 2004).

King, Anthony D, *Urbanism, Colonialism and the World Economy* (London and New York: Routledge, 1990)

King, Anthony D, 'Global Norms and Urban Forms in the Age of Tourism: Manufacturing Heritage, Consuming Tradition', In *Consuming Tradition, Manufacturing Heritage: Global Norms and Urban Forms in the Age of Tourism*, ed. By Nizar al-Sayyad (London, New York: Routledge, 2001).

Lamzah, Assia, 'Urban Design and Architecture in the Service of Colonialism in Morocco', *International Journal of Global Environmental Issues, Inderscience Enterprises Ltd*, 13:2–4 (2014), 326–38.

Lamzah, Assia, *Colonialism, Architecture and Cultural Heritage: Marrakesh, Morocco* (Berlin, PAF Edition, 2018).

Marçais, Georges, 'L'urbanisme Musulman', in *5ème congrès de la Fédération des Sociétés Savantes de l'Afrique du Nord* (Tunis, 6–8 April 1939).

Marcais, Georges, 'La conception des villes en Islam', *Revue d'Alger*, 2 (1945), 517–33.

Minca, Claudio, 'The Tourist Paradox', *Social and Cultural Geography*, 8:3 (2007), 443–453.

Rondeau, Daniel, ed., *L'Appel du Maroc* (Paris, Flammarion, 1999).

Said, Edward, *Orientalism* (New York, Vintage Books, 1978).

Spivak, Gayatri C, 'Interview with Gayatri C. Spivak', *A Review of International English Literature*, ed. by Kock de Leon (New Nation Writers Conference: South Africa, 1992), 23:3, 29–47.

Spivak, Gayatri C., *A Critique of Postcolonial Reason: Toward a History of the Vanishing Present* (Cambridge, Mass.: Harvard University Press, 1999).

Touzani, Amina, *La Culture et la Politique Culturelle* (Casablanca, Croisée des chemins, 2003).

Upton, Dell, 'Authentic Anxieties', in *Consuming Tradition, Manufacturing Heritage*, ed. by Nezar al-Sayyad (New York: Routledge, 2001).

Walsh, Kevin, *The Representation of the Past: Museums and Heritage in the Post-modern World* (New York: Routledge, 1992).

Wright, Gwendolyn, *The Politics of Design in French Colonial Urbanism* (Chicago: Chicago University Press, 1991).

Young, C. Robert, *Postcolonialism: An Historical Introduction* (New York and London: Blackwell, 2001).

10. Integrity and Authenticity Humberstone and Santa Laura Saltpeter Works (Chile)[1]

Fabiola Solari Irribarra and
Guillermo Rojas Alfaro

Introduction

The Humberstone and Santa Laura Saltpeter Works were inscribed on the World Heritage List in July 2005 as a single industrial complex, although they operated independently in the past. They were included on the List of World Heritage in Danger simultaneously because of their structures' vulnerability—namely, the integrity threat stemming from extensive damage to metal and wood, accentuated by the harsh desertic environment. UNESCO's decision recognized the need to both safeguard and conceptually reflect on the site's authenticity when undertaking conservation works that might involve the replacement of irredeemably deteriorated materials.[2]

1 The authors thank Agencia Nacional de Investigación y Desarrollo (ANID) Magister Becas Chile 2019/73200337, ANID Doctorado Becas Chile 2019/72200044 Scholarships and the Master of Urban and Cultural Heritage program at the University of Melbourne. The authors also thank Dr. Stuart King for his comments and support, as well as Diego Ramírez, Juan Vásquez Trigo, María Pilar Matute, Servicio Nacional del Patrimonio Cultural (Chile) and Corporación Museo del Salitre for their generosity in sharing information and photographs.

2 UNESCO World Heritage Centre, *Humberstone and Santa Laura Saltpeter Works* (Whc.unesco.org, n.d.), https://whc.unesco.org/en/list/1178/

 https://doi.org/10.11647/OBP.0388.10

Moreover, the aim to conserve original material traces, as evidence and sources for an understanding of the past, is particularly challenging in mining complexes, where the infrastructure usually responded to the needs and life cycle of the extracting process and its materials were not designed to last.

This chapter discusses the concept of authenticity theoretically, and its relationship with original material integrity in the context of world heritage, to evaluate the conservation works undertaken in Humberstone and Santa Laura which brought it into compliance with the Desired State of Conservation for the Removal (DSOCR) from the List of World Heritage in Danger in 2019. The case study illustrates how integrity and authenticity concerns were approached at a World Heritage Site made up of vulnerable temporary mining structures under extreme environmental conditions.

Authenticity in world heritage

In the heritage field, few topics have been more controversial than authenticity.[3] Lowenthal warns that 'authenticity risks being a risible as well as a futile quest'.[4] Similarly, Page states that architectural authenticity is no more than a 'mirage, and a chimera, something we can only imagine exists'.[5] Page relates authenticity to something original, pristine or unchanged.[6] In defining authenticity by those parameters, it becomes evident that any place that appears perfectly authentic cannot be so because all materials age and change.

Regarding understandings of heritage, Starn argues that the Venice Charter of 1964 was responsible for situating the concept of authenticity at the core of conservation practice.[7] The Venice Charter stated that it

---

3 Marilena Alivizatou, 'Debating Heritage Authenticity: Kastom and Development at the Vanuatu Cultural Centre', *International Journal of Heritage Studies*, 18:2 (2012), 124–43.

4 David Lowenthal, 'Authenticity? The Dogma of Self-Delusion', in *Why Fakes Matter: Essays on Problems of Authenticity*, ed. by Mark Jones (London: British Museum Press, 1993), pp. 184–92 (p. 189).

5 Max Page, *Why Preservation Matters* (New Haven: Yale University Press, 2016), p. 33.

6 Ibid.

7 Randolph Starn, 'Authenticity and Historic Preservation: Towards an Authentic History', *History of the Human Sciences*, 15:1 (2002), 1–16.

is our duty to safeguard and handle historic monuments 'in the full richness of their authenticity'.[8] In the Venice Charter, the concept of authenticity translates into honest conservation—that is, replacements should be distinguishable from the original and at the same time integrated harmoniously with the whole; restoration must rely on evidence, not conjecture; and documentation of works must be precise.[9]

The 1972 Convention Concerning the Protection of the World Cultural and Natural Heritage incorporates the concept of Outstanding Universal Value (OUV) as the fundamental condition for inscription as World Heritage,[10] where the definition is specified by the Operational Guidelines for the Implementation of the World Heritage Convention. These guidelines are revised and updated periodically, while the Convention document remains unchanged from its 1972 version. In the 1977 version of the operational guidelines, it states that properties should 'meet the test of authenticity in design, materials, workmanship and setting'[11]to become part of the World Heritage List, along with complying with at least one of the criteria for inclusion.[12]

The definition of authenticity in the Operational Guidelines was expanded in 2005 after the Nara Document on Authenticity (1994) was developed.[13] The Nara Document became part of Annex 4 to the 2005 guidelines to further bolster the concept's interpretation.[14] Both Jones and Starn emphasise the relevance of Article 11 as a turning point from previous notions of authenticity.[15]

---

8 ICOMOS, 'International Charter for the Conservation and Restoration of Monuments and Sites (The Venice Charter 1964)', 1964.

9 Ibid.

10 Jokilehto, Jukka, and ICOMOS, eds., *The World Heritage List - What Is OUV? Defining the Outstanding Universal Value of Cultural World Heritage Properties*, Monuments and Sites, XVI (Berlin: hendrik Bäßler verlag, 2008), p. 47.

11 UNESCO, *Operational Guidelines for the Implementation of the World Heritage Convention*, 1997, p. 3, https://whc.unesco.org/archive/opguide77b.pdf

12 UNESCO, *Operational Guidelines for the Implementation of the World Heritage Convention*, 1977.

13 Jokilehto and ICOMOS, 2008, p. 43.

14 UNESCO, *Operational Guidelines for the Implementation of the World Heritage Convention*, 2005, pp. 91–93, https://whc.unesco.org/en/guidelines/

15 Siân Jones, 'Negotiating Authentic Objects and Authentic Selves: Beyond the Deconstruction of Authenticity', *Journal of Material Culture*, 15:2 (2010), 181–203; Starn, 2002.

> Article 11 of the Nara Document on Authenticity (1994):
>
> All judgements about values attributed to cultural properties as well as the credibility of related information sources may differ from culture to culture, and even within the same culture. It is thus not possible to base judgements of values and authenticity within fixed criteria. On the contrary, the respect due to all cultures requires that heritage properties must be considered and judged within the cultural contexts to which they belong.[16]

The Nara Document relativises the idea of authenticity, acknowledging that it cannot mean the same thing to different cultures because it should be judged within its cultural setting. Nonetheless, the document still relies on the credibility of information sources to determine veracity according to the specific nature of heritage values. After the Nara conference, the International Council on Monuments and Sites (ICOMOS) and National Committees of the Americas met to discuss the concept of authenticity in their specific context, consolidating the Declaration of San Antonio in 1996. The Southern Cone, which includes Chile, prepared the Carta de Brasilia (The Brasilia Charter) in 1995 for the San Antonio assembly, in which it was argued that authenticity is entangled with the idea of identity, and as such, is changeable, adaptable and dynamic. The Charter indicates that identities acquire value; they can also devalue or become valuable again as part of social processes.[17] The Brasilia Charter relates authenticity to the correspondence between an object and its significance; it states, '[*N*]*os hallamos ante un bien auténtico cuando existe una correspondencia entre el objeto material y su significado*' [We face an authentic object when some correspondence exists between the material object and its significance].[18] Therefore, it could be argued that the Brasilia Charter advocates for a notion of authenticity that is self-verifiable in the fulfilment of its values—that is, significance.

The Declaration of San Antonio (1996) states, 'the authenticity of our cultural resources lies in the identification, evaluation and interpretation of their true values as perceived by our ancestors in the

16 ICOMOS, *The Nara Document on Authenticity*, 1994.

17 ICOMOS Argentina and others, *Carta de Brasilia*, 1995, http://www.icomoscr.org/doc/teoria/VARIOS.1995.carta.brasilia.sobre.autenticidad.pdf

18 ICOMOS Argentina and others, 1995, p. 2.

past and by ourselves now as an evolving and diverse community'.[19] It also emphasises the importance of values being true. Almost ten years later, in the Declaration of San Miguel de Allende of 2005, as part of the *New Views on Authenticity and Integrity in the World Heritage of the Americas*, 'it is noted that the concepts of authenticity and integrity need to be fully integrated into field practices in all its facets'.[20] It is interesting to compare the statement of the declaration with the specific section on *La Autenticidad e integridad en las polítcas de patrimonio mundial de Chile* [Authenticity and integrity in world heritage policies of Chile], where Ángel Cabeza, former head of the institution responsible for the protection of national cultural heritage, the National Monuments Council of Chile, endorses the view that authenticity and integrity are the axes of the identification, management and use of heritage conservation.[21] However, he also states, '[*L*]*a comunidad debe tener claros los valores que se deben conservar, y su respaldo a la autenticidad se dará por añadidura*' [The community must understand the values that need to be conserved, and with their support authenticity will come naturally].[22]

From the revision of charters and conventions, two dimensions emerge for determining authenticity. One refers to the truthfulness of significance or values, the judgment of which should be contextually defined and expressed by their attributes ('including form and design; materials and substance; use and function; traditions, techniques and management systems; location and setting; language, and other forms of intangible heritage; spirit and feeling; and other internal and external

19 ICOMOS National Committees of the Americas, *The Declaration of San Antonio (1996)*, ICOMOS, https://www.icomos.org/en/charters-and-texts/179-articles-en-francais/ressources/charters-and-standards/188-the-declaration-of-san-antonio.

20 ICOMOS, *Nuevas Miradas sobre la Autenticidad e Integridad en el Patrimonio Mundial de las Américas | New Views on Authenticity and Integrity in the World Heritage of the Americas*, ed. by Francisco Javier López Morales, 2nd ed. (México: Instituto Nacional de Antropología e Historia, 2017), p. 22.

21 Ángel Cabeza Monteira, 'La Autenticidad e Integridad En Las Políticas de Patrimonio Mundial En Chile', in *Nuevas Miradas sobre la Autenticidad e Integridad en el Patrimonio Mundial de las Américas | New Views on Authenticity and Integrity in the World Heritage of the Americas*, by ICOMOS, ed. by Francisco Javier López Morales, 2nd ed. (México: Instituto Nacional de Antropología e Historia, 2017), pp. 147–55.

22 Cabeza Monteira, 2017, p. 155.

factors').[23] The other dimension relates to the veracious transmission of significance by practice and/or interpretation.

Although the conventions appear to relate authenticity to truthfulness, there is yet another understanding of authenticity that is of interest. In Jones' article titled 'Negotiating Authentic Objects and Authentic Selves: Beyond the Deconstruction of Authenticity', she states that a problematic dichotomy characterises our understanding of authenticity. On one hand, there is the constructivist perspective that understands authenticity as a cultural construction, while on the other, there is the materialist approach that assumes authenticity is an integral part of objects. Jones proposes that authenticity should be considered as neither culturally constructed nor integral to objects, but instead described as 'a product of the relationships between people and things'.[24] Hence, heritage objects embody networks of authentic relationships.[25] Although Smith's work relates to the constructivist approach, as authenticity may be understood as a product of the Authorised Heritage Discourse, it is interesting to note that in *Uses of Heritage*, Smith mentions that 'authenticity of heritage lies ultimately in the meanings people construct for it in their daily lives'.[26] Therefore, Jones' understanding of authenticity relates to Smith's statement, viewing it as something neither foreign nor inherent in objects but something in between that emerges in the relation between people and places. Both Jones and Smith see authenticity as dynamic rather than stable and not inherent, but relational.

How authenticity is understood may qualify what is expected of conservation works, conditioning whether interventions are considered appropriate. When judging authenticity through the lens of the UNESCO Operational Guidelines, many outcomes are possible. One could conclude that material and substance contribute to a site's authenticity, and thus that ageing and patina are befitting of a heritage site, being the proper condition of original material, which needs to be safeguarded. Opposingly, following the same guidelines, authenticity can be related

23 UNESCO, *Operational Guidelines for the Implementation of the World Heritage Convention*, 2019, p. 27, https://whc.unesco.org/en/guidelines/.

24 Jones, 2010, p. 200.

25 Ibid.

26 Laurajane Smith, *Uses of Heritage* (Abingdon, Oxon, New York: Routledge, 2006), p. 6.

to use and function. Therefore, a derelict condition could be considered a sign of neglect that makes the history of the site less legible, threatening its authenticity by making its use difficult to interpret. In this sense, 'tampering with the past is inescapable, its outcome neither true nor false, right nor wrong, but a matter of choice and chance'.[27]

The Humberstone and Santa Laura Saltpeter Works as World Heritage

World Cultural Heritage is defined in Article 1 of the World Heritage Convention Concerning the Protection of the World Cultural and Natural Heritage as monuments, groups of buildings or sites of OUV.[28] According to the 2005 Operational Guidelines, the World Heritage Committee considers a site as having OUV when it meets at least one of ten criteria, complies with conditions of integrity and/or authenticity and has adequate protection and management. All properties must satisfy the integrity condition, whereas only properties nominated under Criteria (i) to (vi) must meet the authenticity condition. Criteria (i) to (vi) refer to cultural heritage, whereas Criteria (vii) to (x) characterise natural heritage.[29]

Fulfilling the integrity and authenticity aspects can be especially challenging for mining complexes. These industries are usually located in extreme environmental conditions with materials likely to be vulnerable, because they were not designed for endurance but rather to provide a temporary settlement for the duration of extraction processes. The Humberstone and Santa Laura Saltpeter Works exemplify this dilemma. Both its integrity and authenticity were considered endangered—either because of the damaged condition of its fabric or the potential replacement of its original materials for conservation purposes.

The Humberstone and Santa Laura Saltpeter Works were inscribed as cultural heritage under Criteria (ii), (iii) and (iv). These criteria

27 David Lowenthal, 'Authenticities Past and Present', *CRM: The Journal of Heritage Stewardship*, 5:1 (2008), 6–17 (p. 14).

28 UNESCO, *Convention Concerning the Protection of the World Cultural and Natural Heritage*, 1972, http://whc.unesco.org/archive/convention-en.pdf.

29 UNESCO, *Operational Guidelines for the Implementation of the World Heritage Convention*, 2005, pp. 19–23.

refer to the interchange of human values, manifested in the exchange between people of South America and Europe, the testimony of a cultural tradition revealed in the distinct culture of the inhabitants of the area—the *pampinos*—and the illustration of a significant stage in human history, as the saltpeter mines in the north of Chile transformed the Pampa[30] and agricultural lands that benefited from nitrate as fertiliser. How the site complies with the three cultural criteria is specified in the Decisions of the 29th session of the World Heritage Committee as follows:

> Criterion (ii): The development of the saltpeter industry reflects the combined knowledge, skills, technology, and financial investment of a diverse community of people who were brought together from around South America, and from Europe. The saltpeter industry became a huge cultural exchange complex where ideas were quickly absorbed and exploited. The two works represent this process.
>
> Criterion (iii): The saltpeter mines and their associated company towns developed into an extensive and very distinct urban community with its own language, organisation, customs, and creative expressions, as well as displaying technical entrepreneurship. The two nominated works represent this distinctive culture.
>
> Criterion (iv): The saltpeter mines in the north of Chile together became the largest producers of natural saltpeter in the world, transforming the Pampa and indirectly the agricultural lands that benefited from the fertilisers the works produced. The two works represent this transformation process'[31].

Along with these criteria, in order to be considered to have OUV, the Humberstone and Santa Laura Saltpeter Works had to comply with an integrity and authenticity condition. The authenticity description of this property on the UNESCO website considers both tangible and intangible dimensions. In terms of the tangible aspect, it states that the remains at the site are 'authentic and original'. Their authenticity is enhanced by their setting in a desertic landscape, evidencing the territory's

30 According to the Royal Academy of the Spanish language, the word Pampa comes from the Quechua language and means plain or prairie; it refers to extending plains of South America without arboreal vegetation.

31 World Heritage Committee, *Decisions of the 29th Session of the World Heritage Committee*, 2005, p. 142, https://whc.unesco.org/archive/2005/whc05-29com-22e.pdf

occupation, and a lack of additions from periods other than the saltpeter era. The Saltpeter Week gathering of saltpeter workers and descendants is mentioned as one of the intangible attributes contributing to the site's authenticity.[32] Saltpeter Week is a festival that takes place every third week of November and gathers people from different *pampinos'* associations to commemorate and celebrate the Pampa culture. Activities have been held in Iquique—the nearest major city—and culminated in Humberstone since 1981.[33]

In terms of integrity, Humberstone and Santa Laura are the most intact vestiges of the 200 saltpeter works that once populated the area of Antofagasta and Tarapacá in Chile. The sites were inscribed together, despite operating independently in the past, because looting and demolition had affected the integrity of both saltpeter works. Nonetheless, when combined, they were deemed to still reflect 'the key manufacturing processes and social structures and ways of life of these company towns'.[34] The industrial equipment is readable in Santa Laura, whereas the urban settlement is distinct in Humberstone (see Fig. 10.1 and Fig. 10.2).

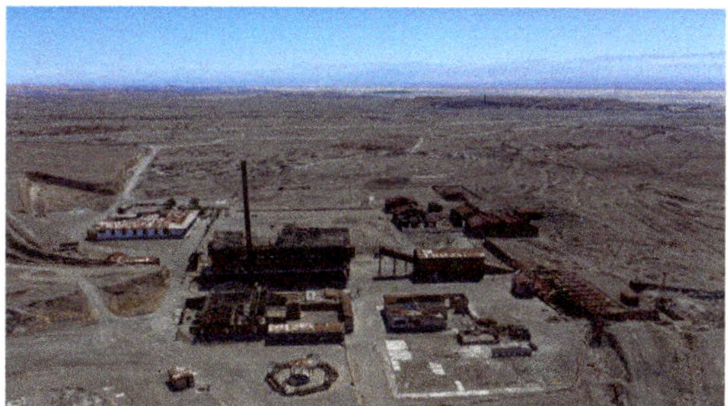

Fig. 10.1 Santa Laura Saltpeter Works. Photograph by Diego Ramírez, 2019, CC BY-NC-ND.

32 UNESCO World Heritage Centre, *Humberstone and Santa Laura Saltpeter Works*.

33 Ministerio de las Culturas, las Artes y el Patrimonio de Chile and UNESCO World Heritage, *Humberstone and Santa Laura Saltpeter Works, Google Arts & Culture*, https://artsandculture.google.com/story/humberstone-and-santa-laura-saltpeter-works/XQVRfkn12rzafA; Republic of Chile, *Humberstone and Santa Laura Saltpeter Works. Nomination for Inclusion on the World Heritage List/UNESCO*, 2003, p. 78; *UNESCO World Heritage Convention*, https://whc.unesco.org/en/list/1178/documents/; *Corporación Museo del Salitre*, http://www.museodelsalitre.cl/

34 UNESCO World Heritage Centre, *Humberstone and Santa Laura Saltpeter Works*.

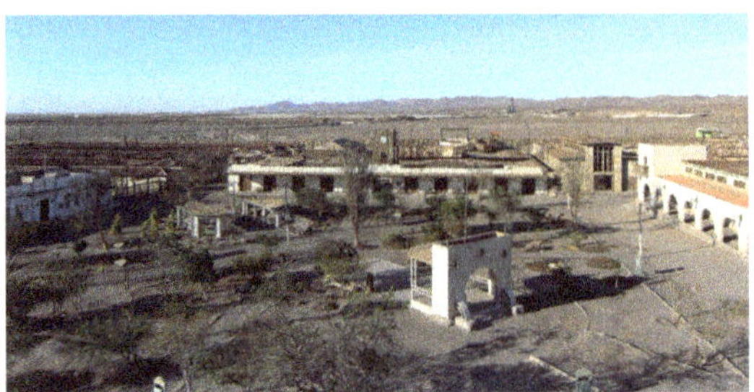

Fig. 10.2 The public heart of Humberstone, with the plaza surrounded by the *pulpería*, the market and the hotel in photograph from the theatre (2012). Photograph by Juan Vásquez Trigo, 2012, CC BY.

Humberstone stands as an example of the many urban camps that existed at the Pampa, and its infrastructure is representative of the urban lifestyle in the saltpeter works. The site comprises living quarters, a tennis court, an administration house, the main square, a theatre, a grocery store, a swimming pool, a chapel, a hospital and a school, among other urban equipment and some of the industrial infrastructure that belonged to the complex (see Fig. 10.3, Fig. 10.4 and Fig. 10.5). In contrast, the Santa Laura remnants mostly comprise the industrial infrastructure necessary to extract the mineral, including the leaching plant, where the water tanks necessary for processing the nitrate were stored. This is the only such structure that survives from all the saltpeter works that once existed at the Pampa (see Fig. 10.6).[35] Both sites conserve their tailing cakes, 'where all the waste from the mine was dumped'.[36]

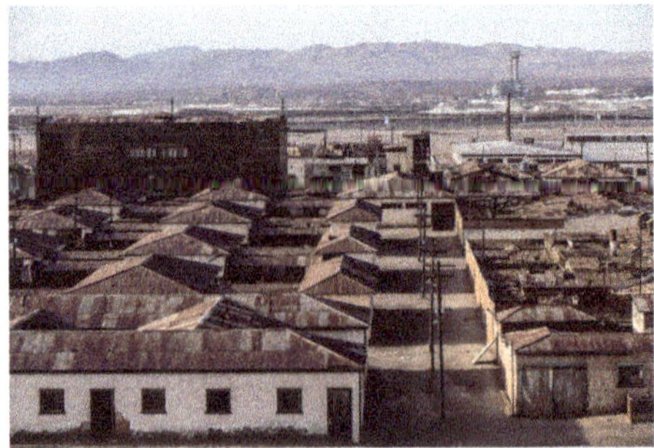

Fig. 10.3 Humberstone theatre and housing. Photograph by Jorge López, 2019, *Servicio Nacional del Patrimonio Cultural*, CC BY-NC-ND.

35 Republic of Chile, 2003, pp. 29–45.

36 Ibid. p. 30.

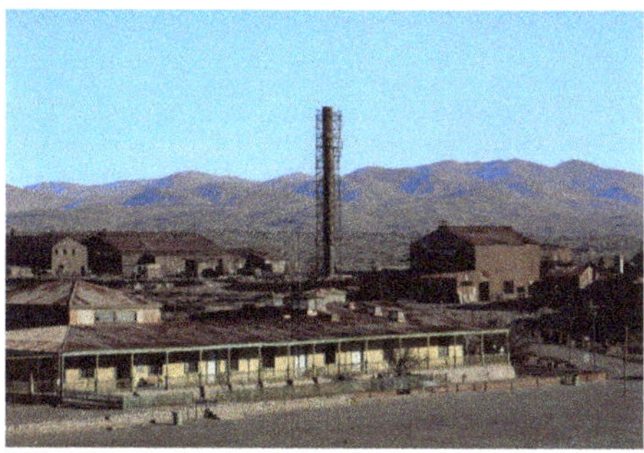

Fig. 10.4 Succession of woods, corrugated zinc plates, caliche grounds and hills to define the view to the northwest of the camp and the industrial sector. Photograph by Juan Vásquez Trigo, 2012, CC BY.

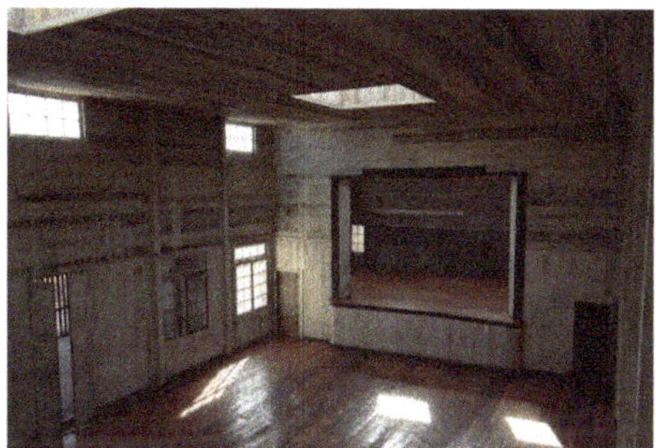

Fig. 10.5 The old theatre of La Palma, transformed into the Boy Scouts headquarters. Photograph by Juan Vásquez Trigo, 2012, CC BY.

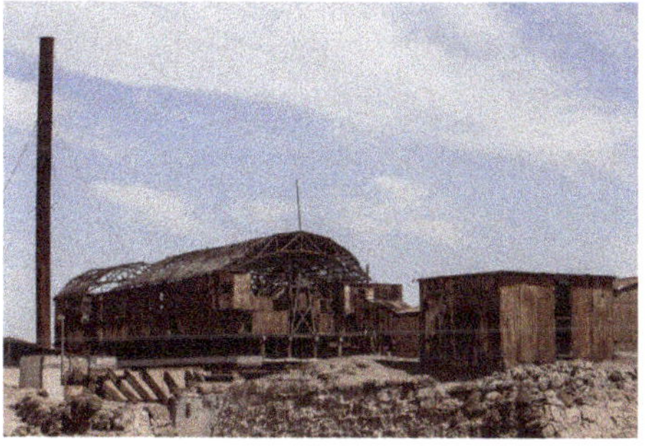

Fig. 10.6 In the picture, Santa Laura's chimney and leaching plant are visible. Photograph by Jorge López (2019), *Servicio Nacional del Patrimonio Cultural*, CC BY-NC-ND.

The Humberstone Saltpeter Works is located approximately 1.5 km northeast of the Santa Laura Saltpeter Works. The nearest town to the World Heritage Site is Pozo Almonte, located 8 km south. Its closest city is the port of Iquique, the Tarapacá Region's capital, located 47 km east of the complex.[37] Both saltpeter works are located in the dry and arid Pampa landscape, where the average annual temperature rises to 30 °C during the day and drops to 2 °C at night.[38] The sites' buildings were constructed mainly of timber and calamine (metal sheets).[39]

The Humberstone Saltpeter Works, formerly La Pampa, was established in 1862, whereas Santa Laura was built in 1872. Both remained up and running during the saltpeter industry rise, boom and crisis, closing their doors in 1960. The saltpeter industry flourished at the Pampa from the first decade of the nineteenth century. Nitrate was processed to be used as fertiliser. It was widely exported to international markets until the production of synthetic fertilisers in the 1920s, which led to the saltpeter crisis, followed by the Great Depression of 1929. As a result, both saltpeter works stopped their production and were bought by the Chilean private company Compañía Salitrera de Tarapacá y Antofagasta (COSATAN). In 1959, COSATAN was shut down, and Humberstone and Santa Laura were auctioned off in 1961 to be dismantled.[40]

The saltpeter works were protected by Chilean law as Historic Monuments in 1970 to avoid their demolition, however, they remained neglected until the 1990s. No management plan was developed until 2002, when the Saltpeter Museum Corporation—a non-profit institution formed in 1997 by the inhabitants and descendants of the various former Pampa saltpeter workers—acquired the site by public auction.[41] The *pampinos* were the ones that pushed the nomination of the site. They submitted the 20,000 signatures that endorsed the nomination to the UNESCO World Heritage Centre.[42]

The lack of maintenance that threatened the site over forty years had repercussions for the evaluation undertaken by ICOMOS for the World Heritage Committee, which emphasised the need to keep the

37 Republic of Chile, 2003, p. 13.
38 Ministerio de las Culturas, las Artes y el Patrimonio de Chile and UNESCO World Heritage.
39 Republic of Chile, 2003, p. 31.
40 Ibid., pp. 54–61.
41 Ibid., pp. 76–80.
42 Ibid., p. 5.

buildings standing and avoid further 'erosion of integrity'.[43] As a result, the saltpeter works were inscribed on the List of World Heritage in Danger, 'considering the ascertained threats to the vulnerable structures forming the property, and in order to support the urgent and necessary consolidation work, as well as to safeguard the authenticity of the property by setting appropriate benchmarks in the conservation plans',[44]

In terms of how the conservation works should manifest, UNESCO states that 'it is necessary to conceptually reflect on authenticity which opens up a space coherently with replacing those pieces and sections that have irredeemably deteriorated, defining a criteria for change associated with that degradation, in order to maintain them for all time'.[45] There appears to be an inherent contradiction in the aim to maintain what was not meant to last for all time. Nonetheless, from an atheoretical standpoint, authenticity does not depend exclusively on the site's material aspect, and conservation works will unescapably modify physical attributes.

World Heritage in danger: Conservation efforts and the inevitability of change in Humberstone and Santa Laura Saltpeter Works

UNESCO based the decision to include Humberstone and Santa Laura in the List of World Heritage in Danger on the urgent need for consolidation work and the safeguarding of authenticity 'by setting appropriate benchmarks in the conservation plans'.[46] To be removed from the Heritage List in Danger, which happened in July 2019,[47] the site had to achieve the DSOCR. The DSOCR included four conservation axes, described as follows:

---

43 ICOMOS, *Humberstone and Santa Laura (Chile) No 1178*, 2005, p. 194.

44 UNESCO World Heritage Centre, *Decision 29 COM 8B.52, Inscription on the List of World Heritage in Danger (Humberstone and Santa Laura Saltpeter Works)* (2005), *UNESCO World Heritage Convention*, https://whc.unesco.org/en/decisions/517/.

45 UNESCO World Heritage Centre, *Humberstone and Santa Laura Saltpeter Works*.

46 UNESCO World Heritage Centre, *Decision 29 COM 8B.52, Inscription on the List of World Heritage in Danger (Humberstone and Santa Laura Saltpeter Works)*.

47 UNESCO World Heritage, *The Humberstone and Santa Laura Saltpeter Works Site (Chile), Removed from the List of World Heritage in Danger* (2019), *UNESCO World Heritage Convention*, https://whc.unesco.org/en/news/1997/

a. Stability, authenticity, integrity, safety, and security: Urban and industrial constructions of the Santa Laura and Humberstone saltpeter works have been stabilised, and their integrity and authenticity are guaranteed, on the basis of an agreed, long-term, comprehensive conservation strategy, and conservation plan. These buildings bear witness to the key historical, industrial, and social processes associated with the Humberstone and Santa Laura saltpeter works,

b. Management system and plan: The management system is fully operational, with adequate funding for operation. The comprehensive management plan, with conservation and management provisions for the property and its buffer zone, is fully enforced and implemented through an interdisciplinary group, with the participation of involved institutions and social stakeholders,

c. Presentation of the Property: The World Heritage property complies with safety and security standards for visitors and workers, and the assets of the property are adequately protected. Its Outstanding Universal Value is reliably conveyed to the public, which facilitates comprehension of the saltpeter era and the mining processes,

d. Buffer Zone: There is a buffer zone that is protected and regulated'[48].

The first axis, focusing on integrity and authenticity, was accomplished by the three following actions: implementing the Priority Interventions Programme (PIP), developing a comprehensive conservation plan and implementing security and protection measures.[49] The Ministry of Public Works, the Saltpeter Museum Corporation and the National Council of Monuments developed the PIP in 2005. Its objective was

48 UNESCO World Heritage Centre, *Decision 37 COM 7A.37 Humberstone and Santa Laura Saltpeter Works (Chile) (C 1178)* (2013), *UNESCO World Heritage Convention*, https://whc.unesco.org/en/decisions/5014/

49 Chilean Government, Ministry of Cultures, Arts and Heritage, 'Being in Danger, an Honest Way to Safeguard. The Case of Humberstone and Santa Laura Saltpeter Works' (presented at the HeRe—Heritage Revivals—Heritage for Peace, Bucharest, Romania, 2019).

to establish which structures should be subject to intervention and when, in order to ensure the site's integrity.[50] The PIP describes four kinds of actions—setting security standards for visitors and workers, cleaning and selecting material, engaging in structural consolidation and establishing new infrastructure works.[51] The programme included intervention on former housing, industrial areas, some public buildings and the extension of water and electrical supply to allow the site's use as a museum.

The site's conservation goals translate into efforts to stabilise and consolidate its structures, allow its feasible management and interpretation, and guarantee the security of the site as well as its visitors. The actions described in the PIP follow the minimum intervention principle, replacing what is beyond salvation using the same materials and construction systems as used in the rest of the site.[52] The consolidation and stabilisation measures relate to the conservation of the tangible assets as 'archaeological evidence', which, according to the Joint ICOMOS–TICCIH Principles for the Conservation of Industrial Heritage Sites, Structures, Areas and Landscapes, may be jeopardised if significant components are destroyed or removed.[53] Nonetheless, as Cosson states, the evidential importance in the archaeological sense is not the only value embodied in industrial places, nor is it necessarily the most important.[54] The site's interpretation may conserve other industrial heritage dimensions when communicating workers' skills, memories and social lives. One of the PIP's actions to this end was establishing an interpretation centre at Humberstone's former grocery store. Through human-scale sculptures as well as various artifacts and documents,

50 Consejo de Monumentos Nacionales, Corporación Museo del Salitre, and Ministerio de Obras Públicas, *Programa de Intervenciones Prioritarias Para Las Oficinas Salitreras Humberstone y Santa Laura, 2005-2006*, 2005, p. 2.

51 Consejo de Monumentos Nacionales, Corporación Museo del Salitre, and Ministerio de Obras Públicas, 2005, pp. 2–3.

52 Ibid.

53 ICOMOS, *Joint ICOMOS–TICCIH Principles for the Conservation of Industrial Heritage Sites, Structures, Areas and Landscapes*, 2011, https://www.icomos.org/Paris2011/GA2011_ICOMOS_TICCIH_joint_principles_EN_FR_final_20120110.pdf

54 Neil Cossons, 'Why Preserve Industrial Heritage', in *Industrial Heritage Re-Tooled: The TICCIH Guide to Industrial Heritage Conservation*, ed. by James Douet (Lancaster, United Kingdom: Carnegie Publishing Limited, 2012), pp. 6–16.

it re-creates how the site was inhabited and offers a comprehensive exhibition of the saltpeter's history.[55]

The interventions that have been undertaken so far in Humberstone and Santa Laura Saltpeter Works can be described as selective and focused on particular security, accessibility and stabilisation issues. Because of the concerns for integrity and authenticity, activities have been largely focused on maintenance and consolidation rather than extensive restoration. For example, the conservation works on the energy house—where electricity was generated—consisted of the cleaning and removal of rubble; the restoration of a beam; the repositioning of metal sheets, windows and doors; and the implementation of security railings. At the same time, the conservation works on the corridor houses for married workers concerned the restoration of ceilings, reinforcements and reparation of cracks, and the installation of doors and windows.[56]

Dereliction prevails in Humberstone and Santa Laura even after the conservation works, which may be a consequence of intervening only to the extent strictly necessary for accessibility, keeping the original material fabric and replacing what is beyond salvation. This policy aligns with an understanding of the fabric on site as a source of valuable information about historical working conditions and economic structures of the saltpeter era, allowing reflections about the use or, perhaps, abuse of natural resources.[57] Comprehension of the site relies on both the acknowledgment of its structures as specimens of a certain type of construction or architecture, and its relationship with its setting or surrounding landscapes, which were 'affected by the industrial processes' and 'often have within their boundaries archaeological evidence spanning a considerable depth of time'.[58] For example,

55 Capture3DChile, *Pulpería de Santiago Humberstone, Corporación Museo del Salitre* (2020), *MPEmbed.*

56 Gobierno de Chile and Servicio Nacional del Patrimonio Cultural, *Programa de Intervenciones Prioritarias 2005-2018. Sitio de Patrimonio Mundial Oficinas Salitreras Humberstone y Santa Laura* (Chile, 2018).

57 Norbert Tempel, 'Post-Industrial Landscapes', in *Industrial Heritage Re-Tooled: The TICCIH Guide to Industrial Heritage Conservation*, ed. by James Douet (Lancaster, United Kingdom: Carnegie Publishing Limited, 2012), pp. 142–49.

58 Iain Stuart, 'Identifying Industrial Landscapes', in *Industrial Heritage Re-Tooled: The TICCIH Guide to Industrial Heritage Conservation*, ed. by James Douet (Lancaster, United Kingdom: Carnegie Publishing Limited, 2012), pp. 48–54.

the site's tailing cakes stand as evidence of the transformation of the surroundings in the course of resource exploitation.

The site's dilapidated appearance following the conservation works does not seem to be problematic to the site's OUV; as the mission report from the ICOMOS visit in 2018 states,

> [T]he property retains the authenticity of the attributes which contribute to its OUV. All the elements that compose the property manifest the different stages and processes through which the history of the place has evolved since its founding in the 19th century, its boom in the early 20th century, and the period of abandonment and partial decommissioning up to its recovery at the beginning of the 21st century.[59]

As the commission mentions, abandonment is one of the site's historical layers that is discernible when visiting. Once the industry's decline is recognised and understood as part of the site's life cycle and constitutive of its authenticity, it is possible to embrace the material decay rather than fight against it. Although the site's decayed state is not explicitly described as a desirable attribute, the lack of additions of elements different from the original is seen as helping to maintain the property's authenticity, making the material decay an integral part of the scene.[60] In her book titled *Curated Decay, Heritage Beyond Saving*, DeSilvey describes 'arrested decay' as the conservation policy used 'when one wishes to maintain the site's structural integrity yet preserve their ruined appearance'.[61]The Humberstone and Santa Laura conservation works seem to have developed in this direction because of the environmental conditions that are likely to keep the site's patina.

Despite the apparent decay, the timber is expected to endure in the future; recent studies of wood structures in the leaching house of Santa Laura have shown that despite wood defibration, the material is mostly healthy and able to withstand a significant seismic event.[62]

59 UNESCO, *Report of the ICOMOS Advisory Mission to Humberstone and Santa Laura Saltpeter Works (Chile) (1178bis)*, 2018, p. 23, https://whc.unesco.org/en/soc/3883.

60 UNESCO World Heritage Centre, *Humberstone and Santa Laura Saltpeter Works*.

61 Caitlin DeSilvey, *Curated Decay: Heritage Beyond Saving* (Minneapolis: University of Minnesota Press, 2017), p. 32.

62 R. Ortiz and others, 'Diagnóstico de la Planta de Lixiviación de la oficina Salitrera Santa Laura en Chile. Patrimonio de la Humanidad', *Informes de la Construcción*, 67:540 (2015), e115.

The structural diagnosis may reinforce the practicality of minimum intervention criteria in the rest of the complex. It seems that the ruined fabric's presence can also allow communities' self-identification with material remains of their stories, which perform important emotional and symbolic functions on a personal level. The wear and tear of machinery, graffiti, and forgotten personal belongings convey the stories of workers and the wider community, whose lives were in the hands of the industry. These elements allow inferences to be made about people, places and purposes.[63] With age, they carry personal significations to their users and enable users' self-identification with them.

DeSilvey explores the relevance of accepting change and creative transformation as productive and positive in heritage contexts. She proposes that 'the disintegration of structural integrity does not necessarily lead to the evacuation of meaning'.[64] She suggests that change needs to be incorporated rather than denied because gradual decay may also provide memory-making engagement and interpretation opportunities in some contexts.[65] As Holtorf argues, '[I]f we want to understand what heritage does and what is done to it in the contemporary world we need to see heritage in terms of persistence and change, persevering in a process of continuous growth and creative transformation'.[66]

Change can take many forms. In industrial sites, decay may reveal the 'culture behind the material' experienced through signs of age.[67] Those sites are 'identified with a value no longer measured in terms of functional performance but in its ability to evoke what is lost'.[68]

The inevitability of change in the Humberstone and Santa Laura Saltpeter Works is evident. It can be argued that the conservation works on the site are responding to this reality and aim to manage it rather than

63 Michael Emmison and Philip Smith, *Researching the Visual: Images, Objects, Contexts and Interactions in Social and Cultural Inquiry* (London: SAGE, 2000).

64 DeSilvey, 2017, p. 5.

65 DeSilvey, 2017, pp. 1–21.

66 Cornelius Holtorf, 'Averting Loss Aversion in Cultural Heritage', *International Journal of Heritage Studies*, 21:4 (2015), 405–21 (p. 418).

67 Thomas Schlereth, 'Material Culture and Cultural Research', in *Material Culture: A Research Guide*, ed. by Thomas Schlereth (Lawrence: University of Kansas Press, 1985), pp. 1–34 (p. 3).

68 Pierre Nora, 'Between Memory and History: Les Lieux de Mémoire', *Representations*, 26 (1989), 7–24 (p. 17).

deny it. The conservation goals are not intended to restore all buildings; rather, they are aimed at making the site accessible and secure, avoiding vandalism and guaranteeing the safety of both people and structures. In this sense, recent surveys that contribute to the site's accessibility align with the conservation efforts undertaken. For example, since May 2020, it has been possible to explore the Saltpeter Interpretation Centre virtually and take guided tours of Santa Laura from home.[69] Indeed, Santa Laura's online tour allows access to the Leaching Plan's first floor, which is not accessible on the site because of security concerns. Humberstone and Santa Laura's recorded guided tour was arranged for the Chilean national *Día del Patrimonio Cultural* (Day of Cultural Heritage), and it is still available online, among other digital resources.[70]

The measures taken at the site are considered to have actively supported people's connection to place while allowing for its feasible management, and each intervention provides specific opportunities for negotiation and challenge. The site depends on diverse stakeholders' agreement, and it is this ongoing local negotiation that will shape its future. Documenting and partially allowing the Humberstone and Santa Laura Saltpeter Works' material detriment seems appropriate when considering the mining heritage material's life cycle as constitutive of the site's character. Nonetheless, the decay of the site will be in tension with the current needs of accessibility and interpretation, and it is this tension that will define its future.

Conclusion

The Humberstone and Santa Laura conservation efforts take into account the periods of abandonment and subsequent recovery in the site's history. The UNESCO and Chilean integrity concerns about the vulnerability of its structures and the possible consequences for its authenticity reveal views about the relationship between these concepts and material conservation, which can be jeopardised by the disappearance or damage

69 Getarq, *Planta de Lixiviacion, Salitrera Santa Laura, Patrimonio Accesible*, https://www.getarq.com/tour360/santa_laura/index.htm

70 *Recorrido por Humberstone | Colores del norte* (2020), *Facebook*, https://www.facebook.com/watch/live/?v=692114534918224&ref=watch_permalink

of fabric. Nevertheless, the conservation works carried out at the site, such as security measures, consolidation and stabilisation work and new infrastructure for interpretation, inevitably change material aspects of the site. However, when authenticity is understood as dynamic and multidimensional in the sense that interpretation, accessibility and reflective actions add to it as it is constantly co-created, change may be a constructive force for the future of heritage.

It is tempting to discard the concept of authenticity as vague and overly fixated on material originality. This line of thought would see our present and future as an uncomfortable and inauthentic disruption of the past. However, authenticity may be useful when we understand heritage not as found authentic places but rather as sites for the constant re-creation of values, significance, and therefore, authenticity.

The difficulties that have emerged from integrity and authenticity concerns in Humberstone and Santa Laura imply negotiations between different stakeholders who, in allowing the conservation, share the common objectives of accessibility, transmission and forging of significance while allowing the educational use of the site. The cautious approach partially accepts decay as a natural part of the site's heritage, while allowing change that works towards its contemporary valorisation.

In Humberstone and Santa Laura, the material decay of temporal mining camps coexists with efforts to keep them standing for their interpretation. The conservation efforts on site shift between enabling the expression of age and keeping the saltpeter era legible. Still, since heritage values are not inherent properties of a place or construction, conservation status or attitudes to conservation cannot be viewed as final. Conversely, they should be adaptive and transient enough to comprehend and enhance the malleable reality of the substance to be conserved and the changeable reality of its beholders.

Bibliography

Alivizatou, Marilena, 'Debating Heritage Authenticity: Kastom and Development at the Vanuatu Cultural Centre', *International Journal of Heritage Studies*, 18:2 (2012), 124–43, https://doi.org/10.1080/13527258.2011.602981.

Cabeza Monteira, Ángel, 'La Autenticidad e Integridad En Las Políticas de Patrimonio Mundial En Chile', in *Nuevas Miradas Sobre La Autenticidad e*

Integridad En El Patrimonio Mundial de Las Américas | New Views on Authenticity and Integrity in the World Heritage of the Americas, by ICOMOS, ed. by Francisco Javier López Morales, 2nd ed. (México: Instituto Nacional de Antropología e Historia, 2017), pp. 147–55.

Capture3DChile, *Pulpería de Santiago Humberstone, Corporación Museo del Salitre* (2020).

Chilean Government, Ministry of Cultures, Arts and Heritage, 'Being in Danger, an Honest Way to Safeguard. The Case of Humberstone and Santa Laura Saltpeter Works' (presented at the HeRe—Heritage Revivals—Heritage for Peace, Bucharest, Romania, 2019).

Consejo de Monumentos Nacionales, Corporación Museo del Salitre, and Ministerio de Obras Públicas, *Programa de Intervenciones Prioritarias Para Las Oficinas Salitreras Humberstone y Santa Laura, 2005-2006*, 2005.

Corporación Museo del Salitre, http://www.museodelsalitre.cl/.

Cossons, Neil, 'Why Preserve Industrial Heritage', in *Industrial Heritage Re-Tooled: The TICCIH Guide to Industrial Heritage Conservation*, ed. by James Douet (Lancaster, United Kingdom: Carnegie Publishing Limited, 2012), pp. 6–16.

DeSilvey, Caitlin, *Curated Decay: Heritage Beyond Saving* (Minneapolis: University of Minnesota Press, 2017).

Emmison, Michael, and Philip Smith, *Researching the Visual: Images, Objects, Contexts and Interactions in Social and Cultural Inquiry* (London: SAGE, 2000).

Getarq, *Planta de Lixiviacion, Salitrera Santa Laura, Patrimonio Accesible*, https://www.getarq.com/tour360/santa_laura/index.htm.

Gobierno de Chile, and Servicio Nacional del Patrimonio Cultural, *Programa de Intervenciones Prioritarias 2005-2018. Sitio de Patrimonio Mundial Oficinas Salitreras Humberstone y Santa Laura* (Chile, 2018).

Holtorf, Cornelius, 'Averting Loss Aversion in Cultural Heritage', *International Journal of Heritage Studies*, 21:4 (2015), 405–21, https://doi.org/10.1080/13527258.2014.938766.

ICOMOS, *Humberstone and Santa Laura (Chile) No 1178*, 2005.

ICOMOS, 'International Charter for the Conservation and Restoration of Monuments and Sites (The Venice Charter)', 1964.

ICOMOS, *Joint ICOMOS–TICCIH Principles for the Conservation of Industrial Heritage Sites, Structures, Areas and Landscapes*, 2011, https://www.icomos.org/Paris2011/GA2011_ICOMOS_TICCIH_joint_principles_EN_FR_final_20120110.pdf.

ICOMOS, *Nuevas Miradas Sobre La Autenticidad e Integridad En El Patrimonio Mundial de Las Américas | New Views on Authenticity and Integrity in the World Heritage of the Americas*, ed. by Francisco Javier López Morales, 2nd ed. (México: Instituto Nacional de Antropología e Historia, 2017).

ICOMOS, *The Nara Document on Authenticity*, 1994, https://www.icomos.org/charters/nara-e.pdf.

ICOMOS Argentina, ICOMOS Brasil, ICOMOS Chile, ICOMOS Paraguay, and ICOMOS Uruguay, *Carta de Brasilia*, 1995, http://www.icomoscr.org/doc/teoria/VARIOS.1995.carta.brasilia.sobre.autenticidad.pdf.

ICOMOS National Committees of the Americas, *The Declaration of San Antonio* (1996), https://www.icomos.org/en/charters-and-texts/179-articles-en-francais/ressources/charters-and-standards/188-the-declaration-of-san-antonio.

Jokilehto, Jukka, and ICOMOS, eds., *The World Heritage List - What Is OUV? Defining the Outstanding Universal Value of Cultural World Heritage Properties*, Monuments and Sites, 16 (Berlin: hendrik Bäßler verlag, 2008).

Jones, Siân, 'Negotiating Authentic Objects and Authentic Selves: Beyond the Deconstruction of Authenticity', *Journal of Material Culture*, 15:2 (2010), 181–203, https://doi.org/10.1177/1359183510364074.

Lowenthal, David, 'Authenticities Past and Present', *CRM: The Journal of Heritage Stewardship*, 5:1 (2008), 6–17.

Lowenthal, David, 'Authenticity? The Dogma of Self-Delusion', in *Why Fakes Matter: Essays on Problems of Authenticity*, ed. by Mark Jones (London: British Museum Press, 1993), pp. 184–92.

Ministerio de las Culturas, las Artes y el Patrimonio de Chile, and UNESCO World Heritage, *Humberstone and Santa Laura Saltpeter Works, Google Arts & Culture*, https://artsandculture.google.com/story/humberstone-and-santa-laura-saltpeter-works/XQVRfkn12rzafA.

Nora, Pierre, 'Between Memory and History: Les Lieux de Mémoire', *Representations*, 26 (1989), 7–24, https://doi.org/10.2307/2928520.

Ortiz, R., A. Jamet, A. Moya, M. González, M. Paz Varela, M. Hernández, and others, 'Diagnóstico de la Planta de Lixiviación de la oficina Salitrera Santa Laura en Chile. Patrimonio de la Humanidad', *Informes de la Construcción*, 67:540 (2015), e115, https://doi.org/10.3989/ic.14.101.

Page, Max, *Why Preservation Matters* (New Haven: Yale University Press, 2016).

Recorrido por Humberstone | Colores del norte (2020), https://www.facebook.com/watch/live/?v=692114534918224&ref=watch_permalink.

Republic of Chile, *Humberstone and Santa Laura Saltpeter Works. Nomination for Inclusion on the World Heritage List/UNESCO*, 2003, https://whc.unesco.org/en/list/1178/documents/.

Schlereth, Thomas, 'Material Culture and Cultural Research', in *Material Culture: A Research Guide*, ed. by Thomas Schlereth (Lawrence: University of Kansas Press, 1985), pp. 1–34.

Smith, Laurajane, *Uses of Heritage* (Abingdon, Oxon.; New York: Routledge, 2006).

Starn, Randolph, 'Authenticity and Historic Preservation: Towards an Authentic History', *History of the Human Sciences*, 15:1 (2002), 1–16, https://doi.org/10.1177/0952695102015001070.

Stuart, Iain, 'Identifying Industrial Landscapes', in *Industrial Heritage Re-Tooled: The TICCIH Guide to Industrial Heritage Conservation*, ed. by James Douet (Lancaster, United Kingdom: Carnegie Publishing Limited, 2012), pp. 48–54.

Tempel, Norbert, 'Post-Industrial Landscapes', in *Industrial Heritage Re-Tooled: The TICCIH Guide to Industrial Heritage Conservation*, ed. by James Douet (Lancaster, United Kingdom: Carnegie Publishing Limited, 2012), pp. 142–49.

UNESCO, *Convention Concerning the Protection of the World Cultural and Natural Heritage*, 1972, http://whc.unesco.org/archive/convention-en.pdf.

UNESCO, *Report of the ICOMOS Advisory Mission to Humberstone and Santa Laura Saltpeter Works (Chile) (1178bis)*, 4 November 2018, https://whc.unesco.org/en/soc/3883.

UNESCO World Heritage, *The Humberstone and Santa Laura Saltpeter Works Site (Chile), Removed from the List of World Heritage in Danger*, 2019, https://whc.unesco.org/en/news/1997/.

UNESCO World Heritage Centre, *Decision 29 COM 8B.52 Inscription on the List of World Heritage in Danger (Humberstone and Santa Laura Saltpeter Works)*, 2005, https://whc.unesco.org/en/decisions/517/.

UNESCO World Heritage Centre, *Decision 37 COM 7A.37 Humberstone and Santa Laura Saltpeter Works (Chile) (C 1178)* (2013), *UNESCO World Heritage Convention*, https://whc.unesco.org/en/decisions/5014/.

UNESCO World Heritage Centre, *Humberstone and Santa Laura Saltpeter Works, UNESCO World Heritage Convention*, https://whc.unesco.org/en/list/1178/.

UNESCO World Heritage Centre, *Operational Guidelines for the Implementation of the World Heritage Convention*, 2005, https://whc.unesco.org/en/guidelines/.

UNESCO World Heritage Centre, *Operational Guidelines for the Implementation of the World Heritage Convention*, 1977, https://whc.unesco.org/archive/opguide77b.pdf.

UNESCO World Heritage Centre, *Operational Guidelines for the Implementation of the World Heritage Convention*, 2019, https://whc.unesco.org/en/guidelines/.

World Heritage Committee, *Decisions of the 29th Session of the World Heritage Committee*, 2005, https://whc.unesco.org/archive/2005/whc05-29com-22e.pdf.

11. (Identity) Politics and the National Museum of Bosnia and Herzegovina[1]

Aliye Fatma Mataracı

Introduction

Zemaljski Muzej, referred to as *Lándesmuseum* in its Austro-Hungarian designation and as the National Museum of Bosnia and Herzegovina (BiH)[2] in its English designation, is one of the country's most significant heritage institutions. It stands alongside the History Museum of Bosnia and Herzegovina on the boulevard that was notoriously known as

1 An initial version of this chapter was presented during the closing conference of the Ifpo/AUF scientific research programme, Heritage at War Around the Mediterranean (2015–2017), organised by the French Institute of the Near East (Department of Contemporary Studies) in collaboration with the Lebanese University (Institute of Fine Arts, Department of Urban Planning) at the Lebanese University, Beirut, 29–30 June 2017 (https://iismm.hypotheses.org/27517). I would like to express my great appreciation to Caecilia Pieri, the scientific manager of the research programme, for her diligent work and leadership in bringing the programme to a successful conclusion. I would also like to acknowledge the help provided by Enna-Zone Đonlić, my former student and a current researcher at Transparency International BiH, for the translation of the texts from the first edition of *Glasnik*, published in 1889, from Bosnian to English. In addition, I would like to acknowledge the help of our hardworking Haris Heljo, the creative content specialist at the Communications Office, International University of Sarajevo. Last but not least, I would like to thank another former student, Yunus Demirbaş, a professional photographer, for the images in this chapter.

2 The terms National Museum of Bosnia and Herzegovina and National Museum are used interchangeably in this chapter.

 https://doi.org/10.11647/OBP.0388.11

'Sniper Alley' during the 1992–1995 Bosnian War, with its internationally recognised collections housed in a quadrangle of four pavilions from the Austro-Hungarian period. It was founded on 1 February 1888 by BiH's Austro-Hungarian administration (1878–1918) as both a scientific and an academic institution.[3] It evolved during the Socialist Federal Republic of Yugoslavia (1963-1992) to become BiH's National Museum and its foremost institution for research and the collection of artefacts.[4] This chapter problematises the term 'National' in the English designation of the title of the museum—namely, the National Museum of Bosnia and Herzegovina—within the current political, socio-economic and legal context of BiH.

The museum consists of an archaeology department with prehistoric, ancient and medieval collections; an ethnology department with exhibits on the material, spiritual and social cultures of the peoples of BiH; and a natural sciences department with geological, zoological and botanical sections. In addition, the museum has a variety of significant collections, such as the charters of the Bosnian kings and the Sarajevo Haggadah (a Jewish illuminated codex manuscript from 1350 with an estimated value of $700 million).[5]

In the outdoor areas of the museum, in the front and in the botanical garden, some of the best examples from across the country of *stećci* (singular: *stećak*)—the massive tombstones surviving from medieval Bosnia—are displayed. The museum's Botanical Garden also features around 1,700 species of plants.

---

3 Uredništvo 'Glasnika' [Editorial Board of Glasnik], 'Citaocima "Glasnika",' *Glasnik Zemaljskog Muzeja u Bosni i Hercegovini*, 1 (1889), 1–5 (p. 1).

4 Helen Walasek, 'Culture Wars in Bosnia,' *Apollo: The International Art Magazine*, 27 March 2017, https://www.apollo-magazine.com/culture-wars-bosnia/

5 Immediately following the arrival of Germany's 16th Motorized Infantry Division in Sarajevo on 15 April 1941, a well-informed German officer tried to confiscate the Sarajevo Haggadah, but it was saved by the director of the museum and hidden for the duration of the war in a mountain village. Noel Malcolm, *Bosnia: A Short History* (London: Pan Books, 2002), p. 175.

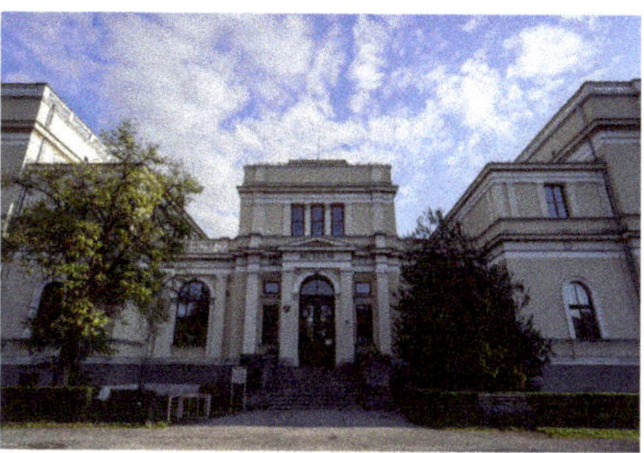

Fig. 11.1 Entrance of the National Museum of Bosnia and Herzegovina. Photograph by Yunus Demirbaş, 2021, CC BY-NC-ND.

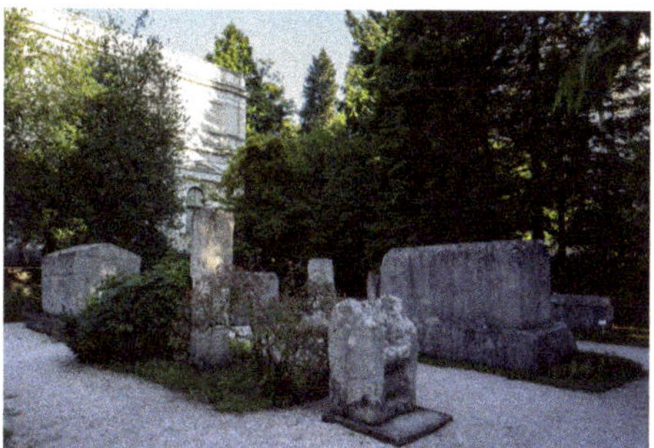

Fig. 11.2 *Stećci* in the Botanical Garden, National Museum. Photograph by Yunus Demirbaş, 2021, CC BY-NC-ND.

The mission and vision of the National Museum

The museum has a research library that was established in 1884, with a collection of around 25,000 volumes including journals, monographs, books, reprints and manuscripts in the fields covered by the National Museum—namely, archaeology, history, ethnology, folklore, geology, botany and zoology. It also has a research journal that has been published in both Latin and Cyrillic since 1889, titled *Glasnik Zemaljskog Muzeja u Bosni i Hercegovini* [Herald of the National Museum of Bosnia and Herzegovina][6].

Glasnik has presented close to four million artefacts, which attest to the rich culture and history of Bosnia and Herzegovina. In the first

6 *Glasnik Zemaljskog Muzeja u Bosni i Hercegovini* will be referred to as *Glasnik* in the rest of this article.

issue, published in March 1889, the mission of the journal was stated as follows: '[W]e want to have a public herald [to] knowingly study and describe each profession [...] in the museum. [W]e want this Herald to be instructive [and] we are guided in this by the principle of cultural community and common good'.[7]

In the same issue, both the National Museum and *Glasnik* are presented as sharing a dual mission:

> The task of our museum is not only to act purely scientifically; it also has a cultural and educational task: to awaken the sons of the country, [...] to think about their duty and to study and get to know their fatherland; and as they get to know it, to start to love and appreciate it [...] The dual aim of the museum´s '*Glasnik*' corresponds to the true dual task of the museum: material-scientific and moral-cultural[8].

The mission of the founders of the National Museum—those who made up the Museum Society, which was established before the museum and took an active role in the collection of artefacts from all around BiH—states that 'worthy followers [...] collect every remnant made by the creative head and crafted by the hardworking hands of our people in all parts of Bosnia and Herzegovina [to judge] the life and deeds of our grandfathers. [...] these valuable successors united and founded a museum society'.[9] The frequent usage of the terms 'we', 'our' and 'us', highlighted in the texts quoted above, refers to the presence of a collective imagination of a Bosnian and Herzegovinian nation by the end of the nineteenth century. This point is revisited in the discussions below.

The opening of the National Museum

As of 1886, all the artefacts in the museum, initially collected by the Museum Society with the permission of the provincial government, were housed in the ground-floor rooms of the Renaissance-style Government Palace built on Musala Street in accordance with the project of the architect Joseph Vancas. As the collections grew, two apartments

7 'Citaocima "Glasnika",' *Glasnik Zemaljskog Muzeja u Bosni i Hercegovini*, pp. 2–3.
8 Ibid., p. 3.
9 Ibid., p. 1.

were rented in the new building of the Official Pension Fund, and the collections were officially opened to the public as a state institution called *Zemaljski muzej za Bosnu i Hercegovinu*.[10] Soon, the premises of private residential buildings and businesses were acquired to provide further space for the expanding collections. Eventually, the construction of a museum building with modern facilities was offered as a permanent solution to the space problem by the then Joint Minister of Finance, Benjamin Kallay. The first location proposed was within the vicinity of the Main Post Office in Sarajevo, but this proposal was rejected by Kallay because of the estimated high costs, and by K. Hörmann, the director of the museum at the time, because of space limitations that could affect possible future expansion. All these discussions caused a delay in the construction of a museum building.[11]

Discussions regarding the construction of a building to house the museum collection emerged again in 1905. A pavilion concept was considered the most favourable in terms of the cost-effectiveness of construction; it also allowed the enlargement of the space if needed without disrupting the existing architectural and urban design. At a conference held in Ilidža on 26 October 1906, the final decision was made to construct the new buildings according to this pavilion concept, which included plans for the outdoor botanical garden. The buildings were designed to house prehistory, antiquity and natural history collections, as well as an ethnography department and library.[12] At the beginning of 1908, Karel Pařik (1857–1942), a Czech-born architect and construction consultant of the Fourth Construction Department of the Regional Government established in 1890, prepared the preliminary design of the museum complex.[13]

---

10 The building of the Official Pension Fund was constructed according to the project of architect Karel Pařík on the Cathedral Square near the Cathedral of the Heart of Jesus (*danas Gazi-Husrevbegova palata*-Ask Adi) in 1888. Jela Božić, 'Izgradnja i arhitektura Zemaljskog muzeja u Sarajevu', in *Spomenica Stogodišnjice Rada Zemaljskog Muzeja Bosne i Hercegovine 1888-1988*, ed. by Almaz Dautbegović (Sarajevo: Zemaljski muzej Bosne i Hercegovine, 1988), pp. 413–21 (p. 413).

11 Ibid.

12 Ibid., pp. 414–15.

13 Karel Pařík was one of the first-generation architects of the Austro-Hungarian period whose works left their imprint on Sarajevo. Among the constructions he designed in Sarajevo are the Shariah Judicial School (today's Faculty of Islamic Sciences) built in neo-Moorish style in 1887-89, the Evangelistic Church (today's Academy of Visual Arts) in 1899, the National Theatre in 1899, the Officers'

Although the preparatory work for the construction of the National Museum began as early as 1908, it was not completed until 1913. The museum was also part of a new plan for the area of Marijin Dvor, where it is located. Consisting of four pavilions in the style of the late neo-Renaissance, with connecting terraces and a botanical garden in the middle, the building is considered one of Pařik's most important works. It was one of the few purpose-built museums in Europe, where museums were most often former palaces. In addition, it was the first construction in the region designed to meet the needs of a museum, and one of the first such in the Austro-Hungarian Empire.

Surviving the long twentieth century

It is both ironic and tragic that the heir apparent to the Austro-Hungarian Empire, Archduke Franz Ferdinand, was on his way to open the new buildings of the National Museum on the morning of 28 June 1914, when Gavrilo Princip shot and mortally wounded him and his wife Sophie. This assassination initiated the chain of events that led to the outbreak of World War I and the eventual downfall of the Austro-Hungarian Empire.[14] The buildings and collections of the National Museum of Bosnia and Herzegovina survived three wars: They remained undamaged during World War I and World War II, but they were subject to wartime devastation between 1992 and 1995.[15] Thanks to the dedication and efforts of the museum staff, its permanent exhibitions and collections were preserved in good condition.

Ćiro Truhelka, a Croatian archaeologist who studied Bosnia extensively, became one of the first curators of the National Museum.

Pavillion erected in the Filipović's Camp (a military complex) in collaboration with Ludwig Huber in 1901, the Ashkenazi Synagogue in 1902, Villa Mandić (today's Olympic Museum) and Heinrich Reiter's Villa (1903), the Ulema Medžlis (1912), and the Church of St. Joseph (1940). In addition, he was also the architect of successively erected primary schools in Bosnia and Herzegovina in 1890, 1893 and 1905, in collaboration with Karl Panek. Tatjana Neidhart, *Sarajevo through Time* (Sarajevo: Bosanska Riječ, 2007), pp. 61–234.

14 Marian Wenzel, *Bosanski Stil Na Steccima i Metalu/Bosnian Style on Tombstones and Metal* (Sarajevo: Sarajevo Publishing, 1999), p. 180.

15 For a detailed description and explanation of the wartime damage to the museum, see Rizo Sijarić and Peter Cannon-Brookes, 'World of Museums: Update on the Zemaljski Muzej, Sarajevo', *Museum Management and Curatorship*, 12:2 (1993), 195–206.

Several of his archaeological finds connected Bosnia to its long-forgotten Catholic past, including the discovery of the alleged remains of the fifteenth-century king, King Stjepan Tomašević.[16] Truhelka published an anonymous pamphlet titled *Hrvatska Bosna: Mi i 'Oni tamo'* [Croatian Bosnia: Us and 'Them over There'] in 1907. In this pamphlet, he discussed the racial characteristics of the people of the region. He concluded that Muslims and Croats had broader chests, a higher incidence of blue eyes and fairer hair than the Orthodox Serbs, who represented a 'swarthy, physically weaker developed type'.[17]

Truhelka's interest in Bosnia and his analyses were part and parcel of Croat intellectuals' general renewed interest in Bosnia because of its inclusion in the Dual Monarchy. The founder of the Croatian Party of Rights, Ante Starčević, reinforced this trend by defining Bosnian Muslims as Croats.[18] Such incidences signalled the arrival of 'the pseudoscientific racial politics of Central Europe' in the Balkans.[19] Ever since, as a cultural institution, the museum has not been immune to such discussions in and outside BiH.

During the 1992–1995 Bosnian War, the National Museum endured its share of what Ivan Lovrenović called 'the hatred of memory'—the destruction of a certain culture or civilisation by deliberately targeting its historical, cultural, literary and artistic productions, whether printed, handcrafted, manufactured or constructed.[20] A much-cited story, based on a news report from September 1992 by BBC journalist Kate Adie, asserts that the National Museum in Sarajevo was intentionally targeted by Bosnian Serb artillery. Adie asked a Bosnian Serb artillery commander on the heights above Sarajevo why the Holiday Inn, where she and other foreign correspondents were known to stay, was continually shelled. The officer apologised and explained that they were aiming at the roof

16 Cathie Carmichael, *A Concise History of Bosnia* (Cambridge: Cambridge University Press, 2015), p. 46.

17 Nevenko Bartulin, *The Racial Idea in the Independent State of Croatia: Origins and Theory* (Leiden: Brill, 2014), pp. 52–55.

18 Mario S. Spalatin, 'The Croatian Nationalism of Ante Starčević, 1845-1871', *Journal of Croatian Studies*, 16 (1975), 19–146 (p. 94–100).

19 Carmichael, *A Concise History of Bosnia*, p. 46.

20 Ivan Lovrenović, 'The Hatred of Memory: In Sarajevo, Burned Books and Murdered Pictures', *The New York Times*, 28 May 1994, p. 19, https://www.nytimes.com/1994/05/28/opinion/the-hatred-of-memory.html

of the National Museum opposite the hotel and had missed.[21] As also demonstrated clearly and in considerable detail in Helen Walasek's work titled *Bosnia and the Destruction of Cultural Heritage*, 'the catastrophic attacks on cultural heritage of Bosnia-Herzegovina were almost entirely intentional and systematic'.[22]

During the siege of Sarajevo, the National Museum was struck by hundreds of shells and small arms fire from the positions of the Bosnian Serb Army directly behind it. These deliberate attacks shattered the glass roofs of the museum's main exhibition halls, and three years of rain and snow substantially damaged the structure of the building. The director of the museum at the time, Dr. Rizo Sijarić, was killed by a shell blast on the morning of 10 December 1993 while walking across a Sarajevo park to visit the director of the Institute for Protection of Monuments, who had been helping him to obtain plastic sheeting from humanitarian aid agencies to cover the holes in the museum's walls and windows.[23] By the end of the war, the museum's dedicated staff (of all ethnicities) was reduced to thirty-one from a pre-war total of ninety-five; its elegant turn-of-the-century neoclassical buildings were badly damaged and leaking and its collections were at risk.[24]

The museum continued to function despite the significant challenges stemming from the Dayton Peace Agreement (DPA), signed on 14 December 1995, which marked the legal conclusion of the Bosnian War. The DPA divided BiH into two entities: 1) the Federation of Bosnia and Herzegovina, which is subdivided into ten cantons with either Bosniak (Bosnian Muslim) or Croat (Bosnian Catholic) majority populations; and 2) the Republika Srpska, a unitary authority dominated by a Serb (Bosnian Orthodox) majority. The treaty's endorsement of Bosnia's three 'constitutive peoples'—namely, Bosniaks, Serbs and Croats—worked towards the reinforcement of ethno-national/ethno-religious identities and the entrenchment of powerful ethnocracies that came to dominate

21 Helen Walasek with contributions by Richard Carlton, Amra Hadžimuhamedović, Valery Perry and Tina Wik, *Bosnia and the Destruction of Cultural Heritage* (New York: Routledge, 2016), p. 65.

22 Ibid., p. 20.

23 Christopher Wood, Peter Wakefield, Peter Addyman, Peter Cannon-Brookes, and Marian Wenzel, 'World of Museums', *Museum Management and Curatorship*, 13:1 (1994), 67–80 (p.79).

24 *Bosnia and the Destruction of Cultural Heritage*, p. 67.

the post-war realm. Broad political powers were devolved to the entities, and new institutions were formed at the entity level. Meanwhile, central state structures remained fragile and constantly undermined by the activities of (typically) Serb and Croat ethno-nationalist politicians. Many former state institutions—including cultural institutions, such as the National Museum—struggled for legal recognition and consequently a place in central state budgets and funding streams.[25] This was mainly due to the lack of a state-level ministry of culture. The Ministry of Civil Affairs was responsible for international interaction regarding cultural activities. This left the support for state-level cultural institutions representing BiH at the mercy of the minister, and thus, dependent on the political interests of the post-holder—that is, the 'national' group and the political party this person represented.[26]

The post of Minister of Civil Affairs was held by Sredoje Nović (a Bosnian Serb and a close political ally of Milorad Dodik, the President of the Republika Srpska) from 2007 until 2015. In his speech dated 22 December 2011, Nović recalled that it is the Constitution of BiH that stipulates that the field of culture is under the jurisdiction of the entities and cantons, and hence, there is no institution in the field of culture at the level of the state of BiH. He added that the Ministry of Civil Affairs had been co-financing those institutions for years, and because the budget for 2011 was adopted, his ministry could only provide heating for the National Museum.[27]

In this context, the National Museum closed its doors to the public on 4 October 2012, for the first time in its 124-year history, because of the continued lack of funding stemming from its legal status. The status and funding of the National Museum was still not settled, and its staff had not been paid for more than a year. The museum's director at the time, Adnan Busuladžić, announced that the museum—the largest employer of field archaeologists in the country—would remain closed to the public until the politicians clarified its funding situation. Wooden planks reading 'closed' and '*zatvoreno*' (closed) were nailed over the

25 Ibid., p. 13.

26 Walasek, 'Culture Wars in Bosnia'.

27 'Nović, Kultura je po Ustavu BiH u nadležnosti entiteta', *Klix.ba Magazin Kultura*, 22 December, 2011, https://www.klix.ba/magazin/kultura/novic-kultura-je-po-ustavu-bih-u-nadleznosti-entiteta/111222109

main entrance. Enver Imamović, the wartime director of the museum, considered its closing a shame, as it had remained open even during the war.[28]

The reopening of the National Museum

Despite public accusations of mismanagement, incompetence and negligence widely broadcast in the media, the museum's management and staff looked after the building and its exhibits for almost four years, between 4 October 2012 and 15 September 2016. Meanwhile, among the campaigns drawing attention to the situation and the importance of the museum, the civil society initiative of the Bosnian cultural non-governmental organisation (NGO) Akcija Sarajevo called *Ja sam Muzej* (I am the Museum) was the most effective in capturing the attention of the public.[29] The main goal of the initiative, as stated on their website, was 'to remind the public in Bosnia and Herzegovina and internationally of the fact that the biggest and most important institution in Bosnia and Herzegovina has been closed for almost three years, and to influence those in charge to resolve this problem as soon as possible'.[30]

Ja sam Muzej consisted of portraits and stories of the museum's workers, literary works about the museum by notable writers and essayists from BiH and the region and calls for the museum to engage relevant social actors, public figures and citizens to share the message of the urgent need to address the National Museum's status. *Ja sam Muzej* revived the spirit of the Museum Society, which had been initiated even before the founding of the museum, but this time, with an emphasis on 'I' rather than 'We'.[31] At the Europa Nostra Awards 2016, employees and activists of the National Museum won the EU Prize for Cultural Heritage, the largest European award in the field of heritage. They received the award for their commitment to working for years to maintain the museum without any salary or contributions and despite the difficult political situation in BiH, as noted in an article published

28 Elvira M. Jukic, 'Bosnia's National Museum Shuts Down', *Balkan Insight*, 5 October 2012, https://balkaninsight.com/2012/10/05/nailed-wooden-planks-close-bosnian-national-museum/

29 Walasek, 'Culture Wars in Bosnia'.

30 #jasammuzej, 'About us', http://jasam.zemaljskimuzej.ba/about-us

31 Ibid.

on 8 April 2016 by the English-language Bosnian news portal *Sarajevo Times*.[32] The then acting director of the museum, Mirsad Sijarić, claimed that the award had been granted to them 'for doing the very work for which the politicians and the media had condemned them'.[33]

Despite the effectiveness of the *Ja sam Muzej* campaign in renewing public interest, it was the appearance of two new actors in the political arena that raised hopes for the reopening of the museum in early 2015—the then incoming US Ambassador Maureen Cormack and the Minister of Civil Affairs, Adil Osmanović, appointed by the recently elected Bosniak-led government. Minister Osmanović, insisting on the significance of the National Museum for BiH, took the initiative to resolve the problems of all state-level institutions facing issues similar to those of the National Museum.[34] On 15 September 2015, the National Museum re-opened its doors to balloon-waving schoolchildren in the presence of Ambassador Cormack, who announced a donation of more than 500,000 euros from the US Ambassadors Fund for Cultural Preservation (AFCP).

Earlier the same day, a memorandum of understanding had been signed in the *Parliamentary* Assembly of *Bosnia and Herzegovina* ensuring financial support for all seven state-level cultural institutions until 2018. The support for the memorandum came only from Bosniak majority cantons and municipalities in the Federation, not any of the Croat majority cantons or the Republika Srpska. It did not take long for politicians and cultural institutions from Republika Srpska to start speaking out in opposition to the memorandum. Nevertheless, Osmanović continued to defend the seven institutions as indisputable

32 'Employees and Activists of the National Museum won the Europa Nostra Award', *Sarajevo Times*, 8 April 2016, https://www.sarajevotimes.com/employees-and-activists-of-the-national-museum-won-the-europa-nostra-award/

33 Walasek, 'Culture Wars in Bosnia'.

34 There are six other state-level cultural institutions sharing the same issues as the National Museum:
The National Art Gallery (*Umjetnička Galerija BiH*)
The Historical Museum (*Historijski Muzej*)
The Cinematheque of Bosnia and Herzegovina (*Kinoteka BiH*)
The National Museum of Literature and Theatrical Arts (*Muzej Književnosti i Pozorišne Umjetnosti BiH*)
The National and University Library of BiH (*Nacionalna i Univerzitetska Biblioteka BiH*)
The Library for Blind and Visually Impaired People (*Biblioteka za Slijepa i Slabovidna Lica*)

legal state-level institutions inherited from the former Republic of Bosnia and Herzegovina that preserved the cultural heritage of all the peoples of BiH. He reminded his opponents that the constitution, in theory, incurs an obligation to maintain the state-level institutions that had operated up until the signing of the DPA.[35] Nevertheless, the legal status of the National Museum and the source of its operating funding remain uncertain.

Politics of the identity of the National Museum

Having outlined the tragic struggle to preserve the memory and treasures of BiH over the decades, this chapter will proceed to problematise the term 'national' in the English designation of the title of the museum. It is important to recall at this point that the term 'national' is present in neither the original Austro-Hungarian designation, *Lándesmuseum*, nor the Bosnian version, *Zemaljski Muzej*, which can both be translated as Country Museum in English. In the English designation, the term 'country' is replaced with the term 'national'. What does the term 'national' refer to in relation to the three constitutive nations of Bosniaks, Croats and Serbs?

The last population census—namely, the Census of Population, Households and Dwellings in Bosnia and Herzegovina 2013—took place between 1 and 15 October 2013, twenty-two years after the previous one.[36] The Census was prepared, organised and conducted in accordance with the 'Law on Census of Population, Households and Dwellings in Bosnia and Herzegovina in 2013' by the Institutes for Statistics of the Federation of Bosnia and Herzegovina and Republika Srpska, in cooperation with administrative bodies and organisations of BiH determined by the law and units of local self-government. The data collected by the Census were to be used for statistical purposes only according to Article 16 of the Law. In accordance with Article 13, the Census forms were printed in the languages of the constitutive peoples—Bosnian, Croatian and Serbian—and the answers written in the forms were to use Latin or Cyrillic scripts. Article 12 allowed for optional declaration of ethnic/national and

35 Walasek, 'Culture Wars in Bosnia'.
36 Referred to as the Census hereinafter.

religious affiliations: Persons covered by the Census 'are not obliged to provide data on their ethnic/national and religious affiliations and the questionnaire shall have an informative note about it'.[37]

The Census revived discussions about identity. Question 24 in the Household and Dwelling Questionnaire (P-1) is about the ethnic/national declaration of the respondent, and the options provided are 'Bosniak', 'Croat', 'Serb' and 'Undeclared' (as allowed by Article 12). The Bosniak, Croat and Serb categories represent the constitutive people recognised by the current Constitution of Bosnia and Herzegovina, which is actually the DPA, as mentioned above. The options provided for question 25, which is about the declaration of religion, are 'Islamic', 'Catholic', 'Orthodox Christian', 'Agnostic', 'Atheist' and 'Undeclared'. The categories provided for question 26, which is about the mother tongue of the respondent, are 'Bosnian', 'Croatian' and 'Serbian'—the languages of the constitutive people.[38]

The answers provided for the three questions mentioned above had to be entered using the options given. In cases where enumerators (parties going household by household and filling in the forms) could not obtain an answer, they were obliged to enter 'Unknown'. All the answers that did not align with the options offered on the form were listed under the 'Other' category.[39] In such a framework, the plurality of ethnicities in BiH is not recognised. Any discussion about Bosnia´s pluralist society is inclined towards an explanation of the peaceful coexistence of the three constitutive people, without any reference to the seventeen recognised national minorities in BiH.[40]

---

37 This work utilised the unofficial English translation of the 'Law on Census of Population, Households and Dwellings in Bosnia and Herzegovina in 2013', https://popis.gov.ba/popis2013/LEGISLATION/ZakonOPopisu_EN.pdf

38 For samples of the Personal Questionnaire (Form P-1) and Questionnaire on Household and Dwelling (Form P-2) in Bosnian and English, see the Annex of *Popis Stanovništva, Domaćinstava i Stanova u Bosni i Hercegovini, 2013. Rezultati Popisa/ Census of Population, Household and Dwellings in Bosnia and Herzegovina, 2013. Final Results* (Sarajevo: Agency for Statistics of Bosnia and Herzegovina, June 2016), https://www.popis.gov.ba/popis2013/doc/RezultatiPopisa_BS.pdf

39 Ibid., pp. 12–13.

40 The Law on the Protection of Rights of Members of National Minorities adopted by the Parliamentary Assembly of Bosnia and Herzegovina in 2003 states that BiH is to protect the status, equality and rights of 17 national minorities, namely: Albanians, Montenegrins, Czechs, Italians, Jews, Hungarians, Macedonians, Germans, Poles, Roma, Romanians, Russians, Ruthenians, Slovaks, Slovenians, Turks, and Ukrainians. OSCE, 'National Minorities in BiH',

In the Bosnian and Herzegovinian context, national identity is defined based on ethnic identity, which is actually based on religious affiliation, as Bosniaks, Serbs and Croats are all mainly descendants of South Slavs. Historically, the great majority of Serbs were Eastern Orthodox by religion, Croats were Roman Catholic and Bosniaks were descended from local converts to Islam (variously Orthodox, Catholic and followers of the local schismatic Bosnian Church) after BiH became part of the Ottoman Empire following the conquest of Mehmed the Conqueror in 1463. The sensitivity towards the protection of the rights of the constitutive peoples within the legal, political, economic and cultural frameworks works against not only the minority groups in BiH but also a collective understanding of the peoples of BiH as a nation, defined by Benedict Anderson as 'an imagined political community'.[41] Instead, it allows for variations on three 'imagined political communities' based on constitutive peoples. The meaning of the term 'national' in the current English title of the museum, within the context of the current tripartite system in BiH, is being left to varying imaginations.

The National Museum has been one of the major beneficiaries of aid and development since the end of the last war; as stated by Torsten Kälvemark in his evaluation of the activities of the Cultural Heritage without Borders foundation between 2001 and 2007, it 'has been regarded and treated as a major monument and a symbol of the common cultural heritage of the country'.[42] There are varying interpretations in the academic literature regarding the investments by the international community for the renovation of the National Museum and the maintenance of its collections. Some scholars consider the investments

---

https://www.osce.org/files/f/documents/7/b/110231.pdf

41 Benedict Anderson, *Imagined Communities: Reflections on the Origin and Spread of Nationalism*, revised ed. (London: Verso, 2006), p. 6.

42 Torsten Kälvemark, *Cultural Heritage for Peace and Reconciliation: An Evaluation of Cultural Heritage without Borders* (*CHwB*), p. 31, http://chwb.org/bih/wp-content/uploads/sites/5/2016/05/Cultural-Heritage-for-Peace-and-Reconciliation.pdf. The foundation Cultural Heritage without Borders (CHwB) is an independant Swedish non-governmental organisation founded in 1995. It was established 'to work in the spirit of the 1954 Hague Conventions for the protection of cultural property in the event of armed conflicts, natural catastrophes, neglect, poverty or political and social conflicts.' It has been primarily active in the former Yugoslavia with building restoration, museum development and experience. Cultural Heritage without Borders, 'Who we are / History', http://chwb.org/bih/who-we-are/history/

as attempts to present BiH as a multi-cultural/multi-ethnic/multi-confessional country on a path similar to that of many Western European countries.[43] Others, as argued by Tonka Kostadinova in her article titled 'The Politics of Memory and the Post-Conflict Reconstruction of Cultural Heritage: The Case of Bosnia and Herzegovina', interpret them as attempts to create the image of a monolithic Bosnian society that has remained unchanged across time and to highlight representations of common history at the expense of less symbolically charged sites.[44]

Conclusion

Despite the varying imaginations corresponding to the term 'national' as it is used in the English designation of the title of the museum, and despite varying interpretations of the museum's mission, the international community, with its investments, and civil society, with its initiatives, continue to recall and promote a possible collective imagination in today's BiH. This collective imagination was very much present at the time of the National Museum's establishment. By the end of the nineteenth century, the collective imagination was denoted by the terms 'we', 'our' and 'us' in the mission and vision set forth in the first issue of the museum's journal, *Glasnik*.

Today, the collective imagination is left mainly to the investments and initiatives of civil society. In this regard, *Ja sam Muzej* (I am the Museum) provides a successful metaphor in terms of recalling and raising awareness of the collective within the individual. In his work titled *Learning from Bosnia: Approaching Tradition*, Rusmir Mahmutćehajić, president of the International Forum Bosnia and former vice-president of the government of BiH, underlines the significance of understanding

43 Vanja Lozic. 'National Museums in Bosnia-Herzegovina and Slovenia: A Story of Making "Us"', *Building National Museums in Europe 1750–2010. Conference Proceedings from EuNaMus, European National Museums: Identity Politics, the Uses of the Past and the European Citizen, Bologna 28–30 April 2011*, ed. by Aronsson, Peter and Gabriella Elgenius, EuNaMus Report No 1 (Linköping: Linköping University Electronic Press, 2011) http://www.ep.liu.se/ecp_home/index.en.aspx?issue=064, p. 78.

44 Tonka Kostadinova, 'The Politicis of Memory and the Post-Conflict Reconstruction of Cultural Heritage: The Case of Bosnia and Herzegovina', Cas Working Paper Series, Issue 6, Advanced Academia Programme 2012-2014 (Sofia: Centre for Advanced Study Sofia, 2014).

'I in we and we in I' to fully appreciate the Bosnian reality. Adam B. Seligman also articulates this point in his foreword to Mahmutćehajić's work:

> The Bosnian reality as it was experienced before the war ("neither Serbian nor Croatian nor Muslim, but rather as inclusively Serbian and Croatian and Muslim") is a social reality as well as an ideational truth that we have to learn to abide by if we are not to enter into that chasm of barbarism that seems to open before us.[45]

Despite discussions in literature regarding whether it provides a full or a partial representation of the cultural heritage of all the peoples of BiH, the National Museum continues to offer a unifying Bosnian alternative to the tripartite division that ended the war. Nevertheless, its preservation and maintenance are still characterised by the temporary patchwork resolutions of local and international political actors.

Bibliography

Anderson, Benedict, *Imagined Communities: Reflections on the Origin and Spread of Nationalism*, revised ed. (London: Verso, 2006).

Bartulin, Nevenko, *The Racial Idea in the Independent State of Croatia: Origins and Theory* (Leiden: Brill, 2014), https://doi.org/10.1163/9789004262829.

Božić, Jela, 'Izgradnja i arhitektura Zemaljskog muzeja u Sarajevu' in *Spomenica Stogodišnjice Rada Zemaljskog Muzeja Bosne i Hercegovine 1888-1988*, ed. by Almaz Dautbegović (Sarajevo: Zemaljski muzej Bosne i Hercegovine, 1988), pp. 413–21.

Carmichael, Cathie, *A Concise History of Bosnia* (Cambridge: Cambridge University Press, 2015), https://doi.org/10.1017/cbo9781139060134.

Cultural Heritage without Borders, 'Who we are / History', http://chwb.org/bih/who-we-are/history/.

'Employees and Activists of the National Museum won the Europa Nostra Award', *Sarajevo Times*, 8 April 2016, https://www.sarajevotimes.com/employees-and-activists-of-the-national-museum-won-the-europa-nostra-award/.

#jasammuzej, 'About us', http://jasam.zemaljskimuzej.ba/about-us.

45 Rusmir Mahmutćehajić, *Learning from Bosnia: Approaching Tradition*, The Abrahamic Dialogues Series (New York: Fordham University Press, 2005), p. xxii.

Jukic, Elvira M., 'Bosnia's National Museum Shuts Down', *Balkan Insight*, 5 October 2012, https://balkaninsight.com/2012/10/05/nailed-wooden-planks-close-bosnian-national-museum/.

Kälvemark, Torsten, *Cultural Heritage for Peace and Reconciliation: An Evaluation of Cultural Heritage without Borders* (*CHwB*), http://chwb.org/bih/wp-content/uploads/sites/5/2016/05/Cultural-Heritage-for-Peace-and-Reconciliation.pdf.

Kostadinova, Tonka, 'The Politicis of Memory and the Post-Conflict Reconstruction of Cultural Heritage: The Case of Bosnia and Herzegovina', *Cas Working Paper Series, Issue 6, Advanced Academia Programme 2012-2014* (Sofia: Centre for Advanced Study Sofia, 2014).

'Law on Census of Population, Households and Dwellings in Bosnia and Herzegovina in 2013', https://popis.gov.ba/popis2013/LEGISLATION/ZakonOPopisu_EN.pdf.

Lovrenović, Ivan, 'The Hatred of Memory: In Sarajevo, Burned Books and Murdered Pictures', *The New York Times*, 28 May 1994, p. 19, https://www.nytimes.com/1994/05/28/opinion/the-hatred-of-memory.html.

Lozic, Vanja, 'National Museums in Bosnia-Herzegovina and Slovenia: A Story of Making "Us"', *Building National Museums in Europe 1750–2010. Conference Proceedings from EuNaMus, European National Museums: Identity Politics, the Uses of the Past and the European Citizen, Bologna 28–30 April 2011*, ed. by Aronsson, Peter and Gabriella Elgenius, EuNaMus Report No 1 (Linköping: Linköping University Electronic Press: 2011), http://www.ep.liu.se/ecp_home/index.en.aspx?issue=064.

Mahmutćehajić, Rusmir, *Learning from Bosnia: Approaching Tradition*, The Abrahamic Dialogues Series (New York: Fordham University Press, 2005).

Malcolm, Noel, *Bosnia: A Short History* (London: Pan Books, 2002).

Neidhart, Tatjana, *Sarajevo through Time* (Sarajevo: Bosanska Riječ, 2007).

'Nović: Kultura je po Ustavu BiH u nadležnosti entiteta', *Klix.ba Magazin Kultura*, 22 December, 2011, https://www.klix.ba/magazin/kultura/novic-kultura-je-po-ustavu-bih-u-nadleznosti-entiteta/111222109.

OSCE, 'National Minorities in BiH', https://www.osce.org/files/f/documents/7/b/110231.pdf.

Popis Stanovništva, *Domaćinstava i Stanova u Bosni i Hercegovini, 2013. Rezultati Popisa/ Census of Population, Household and Dwellings in Bosnia and Herzegovina, 2013. Final Results* (Sarajevo: Agency for Statistics of Bosnia and Herzegovina, June 2016), https://www.popis.gov.ba/popis2013/doc/RezultatiPopisa_BS.pdf.

Sijarić, R. and P. Cannon-Brookes, 'World of Museums: Update on the Zemaljski Muzej, Sarajevo', *Museum Management and Curatorship*, 12:2 (1993), 195–206.

Spalatin, 'Mario S., The Croatian Nationalism of Ante Starčević, 1845-1871', *Journal of Croatian Studies*, 16 (1975), 19–146.

Uredništvo 'Glasnika' [Editorial Board of Glasnik], 'Citaocima "Glasnika"', *Glasnik Zemaljskog Muzeja u Bosni i Hercegovini*, 1 (1889), 1–5.

Walasek, Helen, 'Culture Wars in Bosnia,' *Apollo: The International Art Magazine*, 27 March 2017, https://www.apollo-magazine.com/culture-wars-bosnia/.

Walasek, H. with contributions by R. Carlton, A. Hadžimuhamedović, V. Perry and T. Wik, *Bosnia and the Destruction of Cultural Heritage* (New York: Routledge, 2016), https://doi.org/10.4324/9781315569789.

Wenzel, Marian, *Bosanski Stil Na Steccima i Metalu/Bosnian Style on Tombstones and Metal* (Sarajevo: Sarajevo Publishing, 1999).

Wood, C. and P. Wakefield, P. Addyman, P. Cannon-Brookes, and M. Wenzel, 'World of Museums', Museum Management and Curatorship, 13:1 (1994), 67–80, https://doi.org/10.1080/09647779409515389.

Conclusion
Heritage in the Age of Globalisation

Lilia Makhloufi

This book, *Tangible and Intangible Heritage in the Age of Globalisation*, has highlighted different case studies analysed by researchers and practitioners from various backgrounds and countries. Among the contributors were architects, urban planners, landscape architects, historians, sociologists, archaeologists as well as heritage marketing, museum and cultural tourism professionals. They analysed local heritage over time and examined socio-cultural challenges and opportunities. This interdisciplinary book dealt with topics related to four key levels—namely, built heritage, cultural heritage, living heritage and heritage sites.

The first half of the book addressed the difficulties of safeguarding built heritage on the one hand and of protecting the cultural heritage on the other. Architects, archaeologists and cultural tourism and museum professionals focused on the preservation of traditional buildings, housing and equipment and, in particular, their social and spatial practices. They highlighted the importance of built heritage with respect to its historical richness, architectural layouts and construction materials as well as crucially, its role in people's lives. Moreover, the contributors examined the protection of the cultural identities of communities and the specificities of their collective memory. They analysed the conditions of the past with a particular emphasis on their intangible components, with the aim of informing the present and future.

 https://doi.org/10.11647/OBP.0388.12

The second half of the book addressed the complications of protecting and maintaining living heritage on the one hand and of safeguarding and renovating heritage sites on the other. Architects, historians and heritage management professionals discussed the preservation of historic sites and their shapes and contents in particular. More specifically, they analysed selected sites according to socio-cultural values and memorial aspects, with an emphasis on the historical, environmental and political contexts of heritage sites and the cultural identities of their local communities.

Thus, the approach of the book did not treat architectural and urban spaces as independent from their social and cultural contexts. The contributors examined the traditional cities, traditional buildings and traditional construction materials that make up tangible heritage, while simultaneously considering the human elements that endow these sites with their intangible heritage value. This invisible value is embodied in culture, religion and communal identities as well as societal values, ways of life, local customs and social practices.

The book sought to elucidate past architectural, urban and cultural heritage in light of the present and to introduce new approaches to the safeguarding and management of heritage in the era of globalisation, as well as preventive conservation and development opportunities. Case studies were presented on heritage in the Middle East (Egypt, Iran, Oman and Syria), North Africa (Algeria, Morocco and Tunisia), Eastern Europe (Bosnia and Herzegovina), South America (Chile) and Eastern Asia (Japan)—all with the objective of protecting the collective memories and cultural identities of communities.

Urban life in the twenty-first century cannot be interpreted without accounting for globalisation, as this process offers extensive opportunities for truly worldwide development. For the International Monetary Fund, 'Globalisation' is a historical process resulting from human innovation and technological progress. It refers to the increasing integration of economies around the world, particularly through trade and financial flows. The term sometimes also refers to the movement of people (labour) and knowledge (technology) across international borders.[1]

1 International Monetary Fund, 'La mondialisation: faut-il s'en réjouir ou la redouter ?', *Études thématiques du FMI* (Imf.org, 12 April 2000), https://www.imf.org/external/np/exr/ib/2000/fra/041200f.htm

According to Kofi A. Annan, globalisation is made possible by the progressive dismantling of commercial barriers and the mobility of capital, as well as by technological progress and the steadily decreasing costs of transportation, communications and data processing. Advantages of globalisation are manifested in sustained economic growth, elevated standards of living, increased innovation and faster diffusion of technologies and management techniques, as well as new economic perspectives for individuals and countries.[2]

Globalisation has broadened access to capital and technology, lowered the price of imports and enlarged export markets. However, markets do not necessarily ensure that the benefits of increased efficiency will be shared by all.[3] This is important to consider because, like it or not, even today, identities are constructed in an essentially territorialised dimension.

Indeed, there are also larger cultural, political and environmental dimensions of globalisation.[4] Populations that occupy a singular place and construct a singular world are fully integrated into a vast system.[5] Today, despite the processes of globalisation, the 'local' still produces culture, and as such, culture remains a privileged means of affirming local identity. The architectural and urban heritage in old cities is characterised by its tangible aspects (urban networks, urban spaces and buildings). In the meantime, it acquires another intangible dimension relating to cultural and human heritage (identities, cultures, religions, values, social life, local feasts, festivals, lifestyles and spatialized practices). Therefore, heritage constitutes an inexhaustible source from which one can draw lessons concerning architectural and urban production.

The tangible and intangible parameters of heritage are composed according to society, cultural identity, daily practices, lifestyle and the physical and natural environment.

---

2 Kofi A. Annan, 'Mondialisation et gouvernance', *Rapport du millénaire du Secrétaire général des Nations Unis* (Un.org, 2000), https://www.un.org/french/millenaire/sg/report/chap2.html

3 International Monetary Fund, 2000.

4 Ibid.

5 Jonathan Friedman, 'Des racines et (dé)routes', *L'Homme*, 156 (2000), 187–206 (p. 200).

This book set out to analyse heritage in the context of globalisation from an interdisciplinary perspective. However, the approach of this book was not limited to the past and did not praise a particular type of architecture. Instead, it emphasised interdisciplinary approaches to the challenges faced in historic cities and aging structures. Here, contributors examined the specificities of local heritage in both past and contemporary contexts with the aim of drawing attention to human cultures and needs.

Thus, in redefining local heritage as an interdisciplinary and intercultural concept, the book assessed the conditions of the past in order to adapt them to the needs of the present and future. The contributors emphasised the existence of different cultural aspects and ways of life in various countries to ensure the maintenance of local identity and respect for the cultural needs of the local population.

In placing the 'local' at the centre of each study, to include both its tangible and intangible specificities, this book has made an important contribution to the fields of architecture and urban studies, tempting the refutation of the ideology of globalisation. The resounding message of this research, which must continue to be reinforced by scholars and practitioners alike, is that in the course of balancing the preservation of cultural identities and financial aspirations, architectures must be tailored to precise places by constructing multiple faces, as an alternative to the totalitarian features of the so-called global city.[6]

6 Lilia Makhloufi, 'Globalization facing identity: A human housing at stake—Case of Bab Ezzouar in Algiers,' proceeding Book of ICONARCH II, *International Congress of Architecture, Innovative Approaches in Architecture and Planning* (Konya: Selçuk University Faculty of Architecture, 2014), pp. 133–144 (pp. 140–41).

Index

About the Team

Alessandra Tosi was the managing editor for this book.

Monica Hanson-Green performed the copy-editing.

Lucy Barnes proofread this manuscript and indexed it.

The authors created the Alt-text.

Jeevanjot Kaur Nagpal designed the cover. The cover was produced in InDesign using the Fontin font.

Cameron Craig typeset the book in InDesign and produced the paperback and hardback editions. The text fonts is Tex Gyre Pagella and the heading font is Californian FB.

Cameron also produced the PDF, and HTML editions. The conversion was performed with open-source software and other tools freely available on our GitHub page at https://github.com/OpenBookPublishers.

Jeremy Bowman produced the EPUB edition.

This book need not end here...

Share

All our books — including the one you have just read — are free to access online so that students, researchers and members of the public who can't afford a printed edition will have access to the same ideas. This title will be accessed online by hundreds of readers each month across the globe: why not share the link so that someone you know is one of them?

This book and additional content is available at:
https://doi.org/10.11647/OBP.0388

Donate

Open Book Publishers is an award-winning, scholar-led, not-for-profit press making knowledge freely available one book at a time. We don't charge authors to publish with us: instead, our work is supported by our library members and by donations from people who believe that research shouldn't be locked behind paywalls.

Why not join them in freeing knowledge by supporting us:
https://www.openbookpublishers.com/support-us

You may also be interested in:

Cultural Heritage Ethics
Between Theory and Practice
Sandis Constantine (ed.)

https://doi.org/10.11647/obp.0047

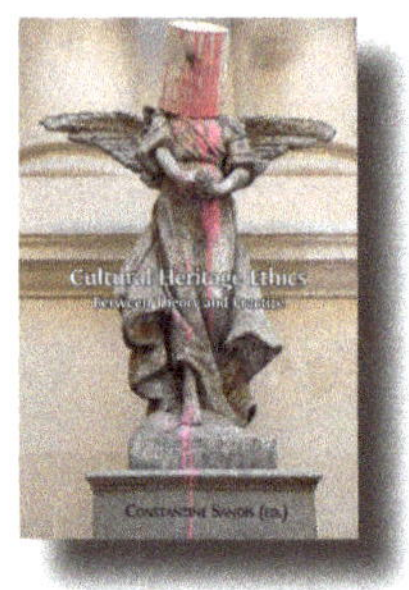

Living Earth Community
Multiple Ways of Being and Knowing
Sam Mickey, Mary Evelyn Tucker, and John Grim (eds)

https://doi.org/10.11647/obp.0186

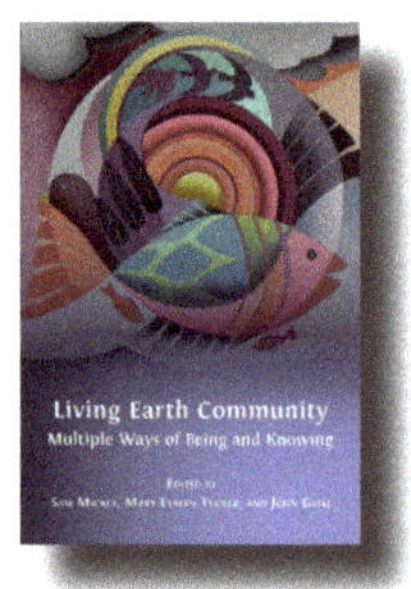

From Dust to Digital
Ten Years of the Endangered Archives Programme
Maja Kominko (ed.)

https://doi.org/10.11647/obp.0052

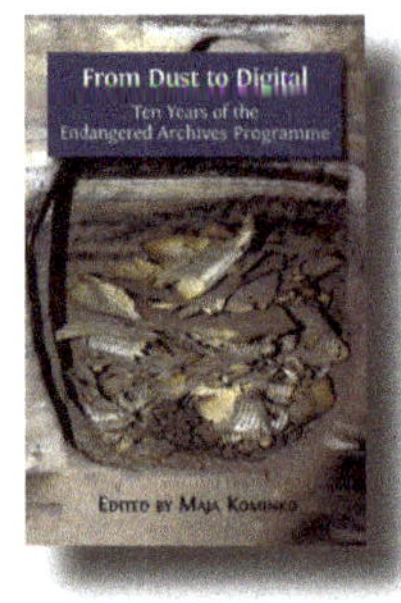

www.ingramcontent.com/pod-product-compliance
Lightning Source LLC
LaVergne TN
LVHW052351100826
845147LV00013B/811